The Theatre of Thomas Kilroy
No Absolutes

The Theatre of Thomas Kilroy
No Absolutes

JOSÉ LANTERS

First published in 2018 by
Cork University Press
Youngline Industrial Estate
Pouladuff Road, Togher
Cork
T12 HT6V
Ireland

British Library Cataloguing in Publication Data
A CIP record for this book is available from the British Library.

ISBN: 978-1-78205-270-8

Printed in Poland by Hussar books
Print origination & design by Carrigboy Typesetting Services

www.corkuniversitypress.com

Contents

Acknowledgements

The seeds for this book were planted in 2004, when Thomas Kilroy came to Milwaukee to address the Midwest Regional ACIS conference I had organised with my colleagues in the University of Wisconsin-Milwaukee Center for Celtic Studies. Tom talked about 'A National Theatre' and took part in a roundtable discussion that also included Joe Dowling. Mary Ann Ryan, then a doctoral candidate in the UWM English department, presented a conference paper on Kilroy's *The O'Neill*; having the play's author in the audience caused her equal measures of delight and trepidation. It struck me then how comparatively little critical work had been done on Kilroy, given his reputation as one of the major playwrights of his generation. That realisation eventually led to this project. Tom gave courteously and generously of his time on that first occasion I met him, as he did, too, in the exchanges I had with him during the years I worked on the present study of his plays. For his unfailingly prompt responses to emails, his readiness to answer questions, and his willingness to share unpublished materials, I simply cannot thank him enough. I only hope I have done his work some justice.

I would not have been able to carry out the research for this project without the generous support of the University of Wisconsin-Milwaukee. The English department provided travel grants, as did the graduate school. A substantial Research Committee Award in 2011 allowed me to spend a week with the Kilroy Papers in the James Hardiman Library at the National University of Ireland, Galway, while a Moore Institute Visiting Fellowship at NUIG the following year gave me the time and opportunity to finish reading through the forty boxes of notes, scripts, correspondence and background materials. Archivists Vera Orschel, Kieran Hoare and Barry Houlihan were extraordinarily accommodating and helpful; Barry subsequently also assisted me in accessing the newly available Abbey Theatre Digital Archive at NUIG.

I am grateful to my many Irish Studies friends in ACIS, IASIL and beyond, for responding to the conference papers in which I presented my work in progress, sitting down for conversations, offering corrections, insight and suggestions, and sending emails, copies and scans of useful information. To everyone who helped in some capacity during the time it took me to write this book, and especially to Csilla Bertha, Mark Corcoran, Gerald Dawe, Joan Dean, Dawn Duncan, Adrian Frazier, Nicky Grene, Charlotte Headrick, Donald Morse, Cormac O'Brien, Tony Roche, Mary Ann Ryan, Mary Trotter, Shelley Troupe: thank you. My fellow past presidents of ACIS and loyal friends Brian Ó Conchubhair and Eamonn Wall read through the entire manuscript when it was much longer and in need of editing. Their generous comments and suggestions were instrumental in my thinking about what to cut and how to reorganise the chapters; for that and many other kindnesses I am forever in their debt. I thank Maria O'Donovan, Mike Collins and the board of Cork University Press for their encouragement and their belief in the project. The anonymous reviewers who read the text provided extremely helpful feedback. Any remaining flaws in the book are entirely my responsibility. My colleagues affiliated with the UWM Center for Celtic Studies have been and continue to be a source of inspiration and support on so many levels: Bettina Arnold, Bairbre Ní Chiardha, Alison Donnelly, John Gleeson, Andrew Kincaid, Tim McMahon – I am fortunate to know you all and work with you. To my husband, Keith Busby, who was writing his own 'Irish' book while I was writing mine, I owe more than I can express here. We always have things to talk about.

I am grateful to the photographers and copyright-owners who gave me permission to include images of productions of Kilroy's plays and who sent me photos or put me in touch with other individuals who might: Cormac Deane (Field Day), Ros Kavanagh, Tom Lawlor, Kevin McFeely, Donal Shiels (Verdant Productions) and Joe Vaněk. I also acknowledge the friendly support and assistance of Joe Dowling and Elizabeth Deacon at the Guthrie Theater in Minneapolis, MN.

All quotations from the work of Thomas Kilroy are used by kind permission of the author and the Gallery Press, Loughcrew, Oldcastle, County Meath, Ireland (www.gallerypress.com). Materials from the Kilroy Papers are cited courtesy of the archivist at the James Hardiman Library of the National University of Ireland, Galway. The National Library of Ireland granted permission to quote from the Brian Friel Papers. Cormac Deane permitted the use of materials from the Field Day Archive. Permissions were granted to cite from the following: copyright © John Arden, 1965, *Armstrong's Last Goodnight*, Bloomsbury Methuen Drama, an imprint of Bloomsbury Publishing Plc; and copyright © Thomas Kilroy, 1991, *The Madame MacAdam Travelling Theatre*, Bloomsbury Methuen Drama, an imprint of Bloomsbury Publishing Plc. Permission to quote from *Signatories* (Dublin: UCD Press, 2016) was granted by UCD Press. All reasonable efforts have been made to contact copyright-holders prior to publication. The author and the publisher will, if notified, be happy to amend the acknowledgements in any future edition.

Introduction

A consistent motif in the ten stage plays by Thomas Kilroy considered in the following chapters is the rejection of absolutism and certainty in favour of provisionality and doubt. This quality of contingency in his work finds reflection in the themes that have dominated his oeuvre from the 1960s onwards, as well as in the theatrical practices he has favoured throughout his career. His resistance to firm categories and boundaries forms a reaction against remnants of rigidity and inflexible thinking that remain stubbornly embedded in many facets of Irish culture, including in the theatre. Kilroy has consistently challenged his audiences by confronting them with dramatic forms not usually seen in Ireland, and subject matter often perceived as disturbing, even shocking. His plays have tackled numerous taboos within Irish culture: homophobia and misogyny, marital unhappiness, child abuse, mental illness, the perils of nationalist extremism (of any variety), and the disturbing features of religious fanaticism. Frequently pushing at the boundaries of what he has called 'the limiting effects of stage space', Kilroy admits to experimenting at times with 'material which doesn't sit easily within a stage play'.[1] Yet, to quote Brian Friel's assessment of his friend's stagecraft, it is these very experimental qualities that 'subject the theatre itself to an onstage scrutiny that renovates both the medium and our response to it'.[2] By stretching and foregrounding the imaginative possibilities of the stage while addressing sometimes traumatic episodes in the lives of his characters and the history of the nation, Kilroy's work alerts audiences to the complexities of the human psyche and of the realities surrounding them, while also suggesting new avenues for understanding, configuring, or transcending them.

The generation of playwrights that emerged in Ireland in the 1960s – Brian Friel, Tom Murphy, Hugh Leonard and Thomas Kilroy prominently among them – had to contend with a powerful theatrical legacy shaped by the likes of J.M. Synge and Seán O'Casey but which had, by the 1940s and '50s, become increasingly pedestrian under the influence of a narrow-minded nationalism and Catholicism. The younger generation could only approach that tradition with a degree of iconoclasm. As a student in the 1950s, Kilroy had been involved in drama at University College Dublin (UCD) but it was in England, where he worked during the summer months, that he was confronted with forms of new writing for the stage, often at London's Royal Court Theatre, that were much more stimulating than anything he had seen in Ireland. In Dublin in the second half of the 1950s, the productions Kilroy saw that excited him – at the Gate Theatre, sometimes at the Abbey, but also in small venues like Alan Simpson and Carolyn Swift's Pike Theatre (where he worked for a time in the box office) – were of mainly European and American plays by writers such as Jean Anouilh, Jean-Paul Sartre and Tennessee Williams. But what was 'freeing and exciting and interesting' about young playwrights like Joe Orton, John Osborne, Arnold Wesker and John Arden was that 'they were reading English culture in such a close way', whereas the Irish playwrights of the day, by and large, 'read Irish culture without any angle'.[3] Kilroy's excitement about such productions led him to ask Bill Gaskill, who had joined the Royal Court in 1957 and would later succeed George Devine as its artistic director, for a job: 'I wanted to act, I wanted to direct, I wanted to do everything . . . '.[4]

In 1959, Kilroy made his interest and belief in the importance of all aspects of theatre production evident by writing an article, published in the journal *Studies*, that amounted to a manifesto of sorts. In 'Groundwork for an Irish Theatre' he set out his ideas for what the modern Irish theatre should be, drawing on the innovative approaches he had encountered outside Ireland. Kilroy argues that theatre-making should be a communal effort, and that the constituent members of that community – writer, actor, director, designer – should be 'very responsive to the demands of the society about it'.[5] To achieve this most effectively, he advocated the creation of a theatre workshop along the lines of Joan Littlewood's Theatre Workshop at the Theatre Royal, Stratford East, which had successfully produced Brendan Behan's *The Quare Fellow* (1956) and *The Hostage* (1958), and the experimental playwright's workshop established by Devine at the Royal Court, to produce a theatre that would be part of the intellectual life of the country. Such a communal approach, he argued, would not only 'keep playwrights alive to the experiments and advances of modern stage-craft', but would also encourage serious dramatists to 'fulfil the role of commentator on current values, practising espionage for everyman'.[6] Kilroy's passionate call for innovative practices and greater engagement was met with scepticism and some hostility by Gabriel Fallon in a subsequent issue of *Studies*, and generally fell on deaf ears within the Irish theatre establishment. While the Irish theatre workshop consequently failed to materialise, Kilroy's own modus operandi over the years has generally followed that model. 'I am inclined to first decide on a director and even a number of actors that will play the parts before I write a play,' he told Jonathan Mullin in 1998. 'Then I also involve the director in the writing stage.'[7] Regarding the written script as only one pliable element in a collaborative effort, Kilroy invariably relies on contributions from others to hammer his ideas into the most effective shape for the stage.

Kilroy regards the director as 'someone who will help you to imagine the final text' of a play.[8] Over the course of his career, he has had especially close working relationships with English directors Max Stafford-Clark and Patrick Mason. The former worked extensively with him on revising the script of *Tea and Sex and Shakespeare* in 1976, and suggested the Irish 'Big House' setting for Kilroy's 1981 version of Anton Chekhov's *The Seagull*, which Stafford-Clark directed. With Mason, Kilroy created *Talbot's Box* in 1977 and *The Secret Fall of Constance Wilde* in 1997; for the Abbey Theatre production of the latter, designer Joe Vaňek was instrumental in developing and creating the overall aesthetic concept that Kilroy had broadly envisioned when he wrote the script. In devising *Henry* (2005), his free adaptation of Luigi Pirandello's *Enrico IV*, Kilroy worked closely with Andrew S. Paul, the director of the Pittsburgh Irish and Classical Theatre (PICT), and wrote the part of Henry with actor Stephen Rea in mind, just as, in 1986, he had imagined Rea as the two protagonists of *Double Cross*; the actor's remarkable performance as both Brendan Bracken and William Joyce in that play gained him universal plaudits. Rea's artistic input was an integral part of the planning process for *Henry*, which also closely involved scenic designer Frank Conway and video artist Ciara Moore. When the play was already in rehearsal, however, serious differences of opinion about the interpretation of the lead role arose between Paul and Rea, which caused the latter to withdraw from the production. In practical terms, actors are often the most elusive components in the collaborative process. For example, Kilroy had hoped to engage Diana Rigg or Helen Mirren for the part of the Anglo-Irish sculptor Nell Jeffrey in *The Shape of Metal*, but that proved impossible. He first sent the script of *My Scandalous Life* (2001), a one-act monologue spoken by Lord Alfred Douglas towards the end of his life, to the English actor Michael York, who turned it down but thought it would be 'a superb play for radio'.[9] Fiona Shaw was interested in the part but too nervous about taking on 'any more cross-dressed projects'[10] in the wake of her 1995 performance as the male lead in Shakespeare's *Richard II*.

In 'Groundwork', Kilroy contended that contemporary Irish playwrights were inclined 'to shirk the painful, sometimes tragic problems of a modern Ireland which is undergoing considerable social and ideological stress'.[11] From his earliest plays onwards, Kilroy has made a point of using the stage both to confront unprobed questions at the heart of Irish society, and to bring his protagonists face to face with their darkest subconscious secrets. This imperative to 'open the box', whether that box stands for the psyche or a repressive society, is in many ways a response to what James M. Smith has dubbed post-Independence Ireland's 'architecture of containment'.[12] The phrase describes the social and physical infrastructure by which the state, in collusion with the Catholic Church, attempted to regulate undesirable thought and behaviour and constrain individuals who were deemed guilty of such transgressions. After the creation of the Free State, postcolonial efforts to decontaminate Irish society from corrupting foreign influences gave rise to a notorious censorship culture, while Éamon de Valera's 1937 Constitution consolidated a narrow delineation of Irishness that privileged the Catholic Church, emphasised the nuclear family as an indispensable moral institution within the state, and defined the domestic role of women (for practical purposes conflated with 'mothers') as essential for achieving the common good.

Kilroy's plays address how individuals are affected by the normalisation of such categorical moral and social parameters, whose imposition created a fundamentally fragmented society. De Valera's fetishisation of a pastoral image of Ireland fostered a cultural rift between rural and urban populations. The emphasis on a puritanical Catholic morality pitted different expressions of Christianity against each other and alienated women from men, while the centrality and sanctity of the family within both a secular (legal) and religious (moral) context completely sidelined sexual minorities and others whose behaviour fell outside the established boundaries. For much of the twentieth century, unwed mothers and unruly minors faced the likelihood of confinement in Magdalen laundries and industrial schools, while individuals not conforming to heteronormative codes of conduct risked imprisonment and had their existence virtually erased from public discourse. When, in his 'Groundwork' article, Kilroy called for a theatre that would express the younger generation's 're-evaluation of old beliefs' and 'their vision of modern Ireland',[13] he was also implying the need for greater debate, openness, and inclusiveness in society at large.

'Plays that don't deal with modernity are totally irrelevant,' Kilroy told a journalist in 1969.[14] His own work reflects 'the modern' both in its choice of themes and his techniques. Kilroy's fascination with the psychology of his characters, for example, also extends to an interest in the use of modes such as expressionism and surrealism to explore and give shape to that interiority. His concern with the fragmented state of Irish society finds a reflection in his resistance to a cohesive narrative style and his frequent choice of episodic techniques. Christopher Murray has argued that, because Kilroy uses his art to seek 'an adequate language to imagine a habitable world elsewhere', his oeuvre should be considered as modernist rather than postmodernist, but he concedes that Kilroy's penchant for intertextuality and his dexterous use of 'theatrical collage' move his work in the direction of the latter.[15]

With regard to such distinctions, Kilroy's own remarks about the relationship between the writer and society are illuminating. In a lecture presented at an Irish literature conference in 1979, he expressed some dismay at the way in which, in the Anglo-American tradition of criticism, modern literature 'has been converted into documentation, decoration' detached from a firm grounding in the real world, leading to 'a cult of estrangement' and a focus on the personality of the writer.[16] He confessed to being somewhat heartened by Fredric Jameson's presentation, in *Marxism and Form* (1971), of an alternative European tradition that eclectically combines philosophy, history and sociology in one model. For him, this alternative tradition has three crucial implications. It restores ideas 'to a proper place in the working of the imagination'; it radically questions 'the mystique of autonomy of the individual artist and of the individual art-work', placing them rather within history and society and thereby reacting against 'the extreme egoism of the modernist'; and it considers art to be 'inextricably bound up with all other forms of human expression', both lofty and low, by which means 'the sovereignty of any one form of human expression becomes suspect, a version of the totalitarian impulse in the human character'.[17] Kilroy's assessment of this critical approach comes close to describing the main characteristics of his own theatrical art: his engagement with important historical and contemporary issues; his consistent resistance to all kinds of absolutism; his refusal to separate the intellect from feelings and the imagination; his insistence on collaboration; and his openness to an eclectic variety of styles and forms of expression. All these traits place him on the side of postmodernism, at least insofar as that term suggests the 'rejection of totalized explanations' and the 'fragmentation of truth', the 'acceptance that all that is solid *has* melted into air', and the awareness 'that reality and morality are not givens but imperfect human constructs'.[18] That latter realisation, in particular, is central to Kilroy's philosophy and distinguishes his work from the mainstream of Irish writing for the stage since the mid-twentieth century.

While the range of Kilroy's themes is relatively well-defined, his choice of forms is more eclectically diverse. His method is to allow each play to find the particular shape it requires, and in that search process he looks for inspiration in the dramatic styles and techniques of others. Kilroy would be the first to acknowledge that he is a magpie, and that at the heart of his theatrical enterprise there is 'a sort of cultural plunder, a busy burial, a furtive seeding and reseeding'.[19] Peter Brook's breathtaking staging in 1964 of Peter Weiss' *Marat/Sade*, for example, had a lasting impact on his work; it was still in his head when he came to write *Talbot's Box* (1977) over a decade later, and formed part of his deliberations with Patrick Mason in their search for 'a naked imagery on stage' for that play.[20] Its influence is also still strongly evident in *Blake* (2011). In 1967, the innovative staging in Paris of *The Temptation of St Anthony* by Jean-Louis Barrault and Maurice Béjart introduced Kilroy to the notion of 'total' theatre, a concept that is particularly prominent in *Talbot's Box*. Several of Kilroy's plays – notably *The O'Neill* (1969) and *The Madame MacAdam Travelling Theatre* (1991) – take their inspiration from Bertolt Brecht; Samuel Beckett is an important echo in *The Shape of Metal*; *Talbot's Box* takes some of its cues from Jerzy Grotowski; and *The Secret Fall of Constance Wilde* borrows from Japanese Kabuki and Bunraku theatre. A strand of theatrical inventiveness and meta-theatrical self-consciousness in Kilroy's work owes a debt to similar playful elements in Shakespeare's late romances; another, more visceral streak echoes the brutal elements of Jacobean revenge tragedy. Some of the most specific influences on individual plays go back to contemporary English playwrights: Arden's innovative approach to the history play in *Armstrong's Last Goodnight* served as one of the models for *The O'Neill*, while David Rudkin's *Afore Night Come* may have given Kilroy the idea for the central premise of *The Death and Resurrection of Mr Roche* (1968). More than any other playwright of his generation, Kilroy tends to marry Irish subject matter to forms of expression inspired by (predominantly) modern European and contemporary British dramatic models, a practice that uniquely positions him as a conduit between different theatre traditions.

Kilroy has frequently made the point that 'the history of European theatre . . . is a history of adaptation' – a history of 'variation, imitation and recycling of other material' – and speculates that the reason why 'playwrights have always been inspired by the plays of other playwrights' is that performance is 'itself an imitative art'.[21] His inherent fascination with the work of a wide range of other playwrights has led him to write versions of classic European plays by Chekhov, Ibsen and Pirandello. Such commissioned adaptations require the playwright to adopt a workmanlike approach; however, Kilroy will only agree to adapt a play if he feels an affinity with its subject matter and is granted a degree of freedom to express his own angle of vision.

With Pirandello, Kilroy shares an interest in the artifice of theatre, as well as the psychology of sexuality and madness. His playful but straightforward version of *Six Characters in Search of an Author* (1996) contemporises the play's language, shifts some of the emphases, and tightens the structure. In *Henry* his approach is bolder; Kilroy's version, in which a Hollywood actor believes himself to be the eleventh-century Emperor Henry IV, gives greater significance to the themes of fantasy, escapism and performativity, and strengthens the connection between Henry's madness, his subconscious incestuous desire, and his sense of guilt. Both Pirandello adaptations make use of video material, in acknowledgement of the Italian playwright's interest in the medium of film. Kilroy's versions of Chekhov's *The Seagull* and Ibsen's *Ghosts* (1989) have the added interest that they both employ an Irish setting. In consultation with Stafford-Clark, Kilroy relocated *The Seagull* to an Anglo-Irish Big House to solve some of the problems the director saw as inherent in existing English versions of the Russian drama, particularly his sense that they invariably made the characters sound as if they were living in the English home counties rather than on a country estate. Kilroy transposed the action of *Ghosts* to an Irish provincial town in the mid-1980s. He retained Ibsen's focus on loveless marriage but changed the son's affliction, syphilis, to HIV-AIDS; this allowed him to include echoes of the 1986 Irish divorce referendum and the developing international AIDS crisis. One 'ghost' stalking Kilroy's characters is Article 41 of the Irish Constitution, which relates to 'The Family' and particularly affects the position of women.[22] While Kilroy's mediation in the four aforementioned adaptations between historical and contemporary material is worthy of consideration, the alterations he made to his source texts were not first and foremost intended as major, original interventions into a contemporary or historical cultural debate. Each of the four plays retains its original title and in each, the source text is preeminent. As adaptations, therefore, they are not given further consideration in the pages below.

In this regard, *Christ, Deliver Us!* (2010) is markedly different. While inspired by Frank Wedekind's notorious 1891 play *Spring Awakening*, it reverses the balance between borrowed and original material, as the new title also indicates. Kilroy makes the plight of young people in a morally repressive culture entirely his own by focusing their travails through the lens of 1950s Ireland and consistently drawing on recent and ongoing revelations of clerical and institutional abuse, as well as the harrowing details of the Kerry babies case, the death of Ann Lovett, and the X case, all of which involved young women and crisis pregnancies. The play's reception in Ireland also indicates the extent to which it was considered as

Kilroy's engagement with these traumatic events of recent Irish history more than his interpretation of Wedekind. For these reasons, *Christ, Deliver Us!* is considered in this study as an original play by Kilroy.

From his classical studies in secondary school, Kilroy always remembered 'the way in which Greek theatre . . . carried the barbaric, the monstrous in such high, aesthetic definition', and the intriguing double meaning of the word *deina*, which meant both 'the sublime and the monstrous', a duality that lay 'at the very core of tragedy'.[23] For much of his career, Kilroy has been drawn to figures 'who have put themselves beyond the pale with a demented belief in their own exceptionalism'.[24] Such characters in his work include Matt Talbot in *Talbot's Box*, the fascist broadcaster William Joyce in *Double Cross*, the self-absorbed sculptor Nell Jeffrey in *The Shape of Metal*, and the visionary poet William Blake in *Blake*. How a person who behaves 'monstrously' in his or her private life can also create sublime beauty in art is a conundrum that has preoccupied Kilroy a great deal. It is a relevant and, indeed, topical question that arises in the opinion pages of newspapers and magazines every time a contemporary artist is accused of abusive behaviour. 'Can we appreciate art even if it was created by someone who behaved deplorably?', Clyde Haberman asked in *The New York Times* after revelations surfaced about Kevin Spacey's conduct;[25] 'What Do We Do with the Art of Monstrous Men?', asked the header of Claire Dederer's essay in the *Paris Review*, which references the questionable behaviour of artists ranging from Caravaggio and Pablo Picasso to Roman Polanski and Woody Allen.[26] Kilroy has asked such questions for decades, but also believes that the depiction of various kinds of 'monstrosity' on stage is itself intensely exciting, in that it plunges us 'into an abyss, beyond control, perhaps beyond understanding. We experience features of human life that, perhaps, we would have preferred to have left undisclosed' – not least because 'the revelation, or the possibility, of kinship' frightens us.[27] He suggests that great acting can nevertheless discover 'a glimmer of humanity which animates the darkness' at the heart of such monstrous figures, since 'even in extremes there may be an inkling of the ordinary'.[28]

Based on the reoccurrence of certain motifs in Kilroy's oeuvre, the present study divides his ten plays into three groups, which are characterised in broadly thematic terms: nationalism and identity

(*The O'Neill*, *Double Cross* and *The Madame MacAdam Travelling Theatre*); gender and sexuality (*The Death and Resurrection of Mr Roche*, *Tea and Sex and Shakespeare*, *The Secret Fall of Constance Wilde* and *Christ, Deliver Us!*); and art and mysticism (*Talbot's Box*, *The Shape of Metal* and *Blake*). That division should be regarded as conditional, however, since plays often speak to each other across these somewhat arbitrarily imposed boundaries, which should therefore be understood as permeable and flexible. For example, a work's primary concern with nationalism or its predominant focus on the figure of the artist does not preclude a thematic engagement with gender, and vice versa. Some themes are pervasive: an interest in madness, for example, runs like a thread through Kilroy's entire oeuvre. It was already an important element in his first completed play, a radio drama called *The Door* (1967), in which an elderly man enlists a priest and a handiman to persuade his mentally ill brother Johnny, who has locked himself into his late mother's room, to be moved to an institution; when the door is finally broken open, Johnny is wearing his mother's clothes.[29] In one form or another, mental illness plays a part in *Double Cross*, *The Madame MacAdam Travelling Theatre*, *Tea and Sex and Shakespeare*, *The Shape of Metal* and *Blake*. The analysis of the plays in the present study is deepened and enriched by the backgrounds, contexts and connections provided by the notes, drafts, letters and research materials contained in Kilroy's archive, which was acquired in 2009 by the National University of Ireland, Galway (NUIG). These yield a wealth of insight into the process by which each individual work was developed and constructed, as well as the personal, professional and theatrical contexts from which the plays emerged and in which they were produced.

The O'Neill, Kilroy's first completed script, depicts Hugh O'Neill, the last great Gaelic chieftain, as a man divided in his personal and political loyalties. The drama's subject matter was inspired by Kilroy's reading of Seán O'Faolain's biography of O'Neill, while its form was modelled on modern versions of the history play first conceived by dramatists such as Brecht and Arden. *The O'Neill* is centrally concerned with questions of identity and ideology. Born into the traditional culture of the Irish clan system but raised by an English family in the ways of the colonisers, O'Neill attempts to negotiate a tenable position for himself between these two affiliations, but finds his efforts consistently thwarted by the rigid attitudes he encounters on both sides of the cultural divide. Eventually, pressured by his anti-English clansmen and half-persuaded by the fiery arguments of his fanatical Jesuit advisor, who envisages Ireland as part of a yet to be established united Catholic Europe, the embattled chieftain agrees to lead a military campaign against the English presence in Ireland, with disastrous consequences for the future of his followers. When *The O'Neill* was first performed in 1969, the sixteenth-century historical subject matter resonated with the tensions and divisions just then erupting into violence in Northern Ireland, and with the Irish Republic's aspirations to join the European Economic Community.

Both *Double Cross* and *The Madame MacAdam Travelling Theatre* were produced by the Derry-based Field Day Theatre Company, founded in 1980 by Brian Friel and Stephen Rea. Set during the Second World War, the plays explore the connection between fear, self-hatred, absolutism and extreme nationalism, but from two very different dramatic perspectives. *Double Cross* portrays two Irishmen who masqueraded as Englishmen but chose opposite alliances during the war. The play's first half revolves around Brendan Bracken, Churchill's Minister of Information; in the second half, the stage is taken by Nazi broadcaster William Joyce, better known as Lord Haw-Haw. Both characters are played by the same actor to bring home the similarity of their underlying motivations; each man's fanatical devotion to his chosen ideological cause masks a deep-seated insecurity and self-loathing. By making both men claim to have the best interests of the British Empire at heart, Kilroy implies that all forms of extreme nationalism – whether expressed as imperialism, fascism, republicanism or unionism – share at their root a fundamental fear of Otherness. Such fear, Kilroy argues, frequently leads to 'pathological politics' and 'forms of tyranny' even within ostensibly democratic frameworks.[30] Whereas the ideological extremists in *Double Cross* find human weakness and ambivalence intolerable, the thematic emphasis in *The Madame MacAdam Travelling Theatre* is placed precisely on the need for individuals, if they are to grow and progress, to accept their own fallibility as well as that of others, and to embrace life's inevitable challenges. A self-consciously theatrical comedy, the play depicts a British touring company stranded in the Irish Free State during the

'Emergency', and focuses on performance and costuming in life and on the stage to convey that, while pretence and deception are the tools of tyrants (petty or otherwise), make-believe in art has a power that is, at its best, positively transformative.

Kilroy first explored the notion that a profound sense of insecurity propels the strong and powerful to bully the weak and marginalised in *The Death and Resurrection of Mr Roche*. As the action of that play progresses, a gay man is first verbally and then physically molested before being apparently killed by a group of men of his acquaintance. In this work, Kilroy endeavours to make visible the cracks in the facade of the ostensibly homogeneous Irish nation. Touching on divisions in terms of regional and ethnic origin as well as class, *Mr Roche* exposes above all the harmful consequences for individuals of the repressive state and church-enforced moral regime of mid-twentieth-century Ireland, when Catholic guilt, fear and ignorance thwarted the development of healthy relations between men and women, and homosexuality was taboo. As the play implies, under these conditions, in an environment of limited economic opportunity, violent expressions of misogyny and homophobia become ways for frustrated men to assert their masculinity.

Sex and masculinity are explored from a different angle in *Tea and Sex and Shakespeare*, described by Kilroy at the time of its first production as a 'marriage play' and a work about the isolation of the creative artist. Its protagonist is Brien, a struggling writer in the throes of a mental breakdown, whose writer's block has a correlation in his stalled communication with his wife about the couple's childlessness. To express Brien's tormented, almost delusional state of mind, Kilroy adopts a surrealistic approach in which the protagonist's insecurities are acted out by the occupants of the boarding house where he lives with his wife, who improbably keeps popping her head out of the wardrobe to berate her husband about his many shortcomings. The play introduces several important thematic strands that Kilroy revisits in later works: the fine line between sanity and madness; the self-absorption that is necessary for the artist to create his art but also alienates him from his family; the absent child as symbol of loss and guilt; and the need to acknowledge the complex nature of human sexuality.

The complexity of the latter forms the premise of *The Secret Fall of Constance Wilde*, which probes the psychosexual relationship between Constance, her husband Oscar, and his lover Alfred Douglas, from the perspective that all three were traumatised, albeit each in their own way, by the abusive deeds of their fathers. This, then, is another play that focuses on marriage and family, since protecting the innocence of the Wildes' two young sons lies at the core of the main characters' arguments about the demands of art, morality and society, and forms the main cause of the widening rift between the children's parents as the action progresses. In examining these questions, *The Secret Fall* makes indirect reference to reports about child abuse that were prevalent in the media around the time Kilroy was working on the play. Fifteen years later, he deals with such ongoing revelations much more directly in *Christ, Deliver Us!* Set in 1950s Ireland, the drama confronts again, as did *Mr Roche*, the culture of sexual repression that confused ignorance with purity and infused the nation's young people with fear and self-loathing. This time, however, the focus is on the dark legacy of that inflexible moral tyranny: the maltreatment of children in orphanages and industrial schools, and of young women and girls in Magdalen laundries.

Kilroy's fascination with what motivates fanatics to embrace their extremist views led him to the early twentieth-century spiritual icon Matt Talbot, who was venerated in Catholic circles as Ireland's working-class 'saint'. *Talbot's Box* explores the tension between its protagonist's punishing regime of mortifying the flesh, which Kilroy abhorred, and the ascetic's genuine spirituality, which elevated him to a place beyond common understanding. Another iteration of the extremist is the artist-as-monster. In *The Shape of Metal*, Nell Jeffrey is such a figure: a sculptor nearing the end of her career, she is forced, in the course of the play's action, to face her own limitations both as an artist and as a parent. Always an absolutist, Nell comes eventually, however imperfectly, to accept her culpability in the disappearance, decades earlier, of her daughter Grace, whose mental illness she had refused to acknowledge. Kilroy uses Nell's recollections of encounters with Beckett and Giacometti, whose art is forever 'in progress' and hence embodies the notion of achievement in failure, as a foil for her deep-seated need to achieve artistic perfection and finality. In *Blake*, the last in a series of works dealing with the obsessive visionary artist, Kilroy imagines that the eighteenth-century English poet and artist William Blake is confined by his own relatives to a lunatic asylum, in a misguided effort to make him see 'reason'. The theme broadly expresses Kilroy's wariness of official attempts to constrain forms of irregular behaviour and expression; it echoes the historical reality of such confining practices both in eighteenth-century Europe and mid-twentieth-century Ireland. In *Blake*, the asylum serves as a metaphor for Blake's psyche, much as Brien's room does in *Tea and Sex and Shakespeare*, since the poet can only overcome his writer's block and marital difficulties through a confrontation with his own deeply repressed fears and desires. The play turns the stage into a space where Blake's relationship with his wife, his politics, his mental state, and his artistic vision are seamlessly integrated with each other and with many of the themes that have preoccupied Kilroy throughout his career as a dramatist.

Over the past half century, Kilroy has established himself as Ireland's leading intellectual playwright, a label he has acquired in part because his approach to theatre makes him less easy to categorise within an Irish dramatic paradigm. In an article published in 1976, Kilroy contended that there is in Ireland 'a curious intellectual resistance . . . to the life of intelligence', which 'reflects a rooted prejudice within the country as a whole' perpetuated by an education system 'marked by fear, restrictiveness and a lack of confidence in the human mind'.[31] Ten years later, Fintan O'Toole concurred that in the Irish theatre, plays that endeavour 'to interpret the world for us, to add to our understanding of politics and history, have generally been either ignored or travestied'.[32] Yet Kilroy suggests that there is such an embrace of ideas and intellectual probing within the Anglo-Irish theatrical tradition: the 'plays of ideas' by writers ranging from Farquhar to Beckett combine a penchant for abstraction and 'cool, dispassionate observation' with a high awareness of the formal possibilities of the stage.[33] To the extent that these qualities of creative distancing and stage artifice are also, for Kilroy, 'very much a statement of my own personal aesthetic',[34] he does not contest the assessment that he is a 'difficult writer'. Indeed, he argues, if some people consider his drama demanding, he himself, too, finds the work he does 'extremely difficult', especially because the issues he wrestles with – social, political and personal – are not always 'fully overcome'.[35] The difficulty of his work can be overstated, however. Kilroy himself finds the distinction between the intellect and the emotions spurious, and suggests that he has

'... ideas with feeling, feelings with ideas. They are inextricable.'[36] Absolute divisions are odious in Kilroy's dramatic oeuvre and his theatrical practice, both of which embody the principle that any kind of human endeavour, including artistic expression, can only ever be a process of exploration.

PART I

Nationalism and Identity

1

Divided Loyalties: *The O'Neill*

In 1959, when he was in his mid-twenties, Kilroy expressed his dissatisfaction with the state of theatre in Ireland in an article published in *Studies*. The established playwrights, he argued, tended to shirk the problems of 'a modern Ireland which is undergoing considerable social and ideological stress', rather than serving as commentators on current values and 'practising espionage for everyman'.[1] He urged that the construction of the new Abbey Theatre should also be a moment of opportunity for a new generation to express its 'vision of modern Ireland'.[2] In a subsequent issue of the same journal, Kilroy was taken to task for his youthful impatience and iconoclastic enthusiasm by Gabriel Fallon – actor, theatre critic and, in 1959, newly appointed director on the Abbey board – in an essay that refused to engage seriously with any of Kilroy's criticisms. Fallon concluded that the quickest way for the young man to release Ireland's dramaturgy from what Kilroy had called its 'rut of sophisticated triviality' would be to write plays himself and 'become in the shortest possible space of time a startlingly good dramatist'.[3] Many years later, Kilroy – himself now an Abbey board member – would recall this advice and quip: 'I think he was surprised when I did so.'[4]

Kilroy had started writing during his student days at UCD and did not really need the incentive of the gauntlet thrown down by Fallon. Indeed, it was around this time that he embarked on a script that would, eventually, emerge as *The Death and Resurrection of Mr Roche*. While holding a day job as headmaster of Stratford College, the Jewish school in Dublin, he wrestled with the plot for a number of years, but the play would not come together. In 1963 or '64 he therefore turned away from it and began a different script, inspired by his reading of Seán O'Faolain's fictionalised biography of the last great Gaelic chieftain, Hugh O'Neill. Published in 1942, *The Great O'Neill* provides a fascinating account of a man raised, and torn, between two cultures, the traditional way of life of the Irish clans and the early modern customs of British courtiers and politicians. In his preface, O'Faolain suggests that a 'talented dramatist might write an informative, entertaining, ironical play on the theme of the living man helplessly watching his translation into a star'.[5] The phrase has often been quoted in relation to Brian Friel's *Making History* (1988), which deals with precisely this subject matter, but it was Kilroy who, a quarter century earlier, first took up O'Faolain's idea of using O'Neill as the protagonist in an 'ironical play'.

The first play Kilroy ever attempted to write, but never finished, dealt with a historical character, Charles Stewart Parnell; Kilroy recalls it must have been prompted by 'some historical play' he had seen in the English theatre at the time.[6] In light of the motifs that have dominated his oeuvre throughout his career, it is not hard, in hindsight, to see why Kilroy would have found Parnell so fascinating. In the various aspects of the man's life and persona Kilroy discovered many of the major themes that have continued to preoccupy him throughout his writing life: his charismatic and complex personality, the transgressive nature of his extra-marital relationship with Katharine O'Shea, his Anglo-Irish Protestant background within a predominantly Catholic culture, as well as his fight for Irish Home Rule within a British parliamentary context, and the tensions between the needs of his private life and the demands of his political career in the public arena. The protagonist of *The O'Neill*, Kilroy's first play to be produced, is a similarly multi-faceted figure whose ambitions to negotiate between two different cultures, religions and political systems lead to a demise that, in its tragic scope, equals the fall of Parnell.

Kilroy was intrigued by the conflicting nature of Hugh O'Neill's loyalties and, taking some licence with historical situations whose precise details are lost to the sands of time, organised his play to reflect that doubleness on every level; he would subsequently use a similar principle in other works, most markedly in the structure of *Double Cross*, his 1986 drama about the perils of nationalism set during the Second World War, and the relationship between its two protagonists. In 1969, not all reviewers grasped what he was trying to accomplish. Seamus O'Neill of the *Irish Press* perceived the marked split between Irish and English cultural ways in *The O'Neill* as a flaw, and generally felt the work 'suffered unnecessarily from historical errors', which he attributed to Kilroy's lack of familiarity with his subject.[7] Kilroy's concern, however, was less with creating accurate historical detail than, as Anne Fogarty puts it, with asking 'vexed questions about the truth claims of history', depicting O'Neill as 'a symbolic interface and mediator between past and present and between competing versions of history'.[8] Fogarty suggests that the modern history play operates with a 'double time register' where the past reverberates in the present, so that 'the problems facing the sixteenth-century Ulster chieftain are shown to have a peculiar relevance to Ireland in the 1960s'.[9] With hindsight, Kilroy himself felt that, in dealing with 'the treatment of the Irishman in relation to the English', he had not satisfactorily resolved 'the problems of historical drama'.[10] In subsequent plays containing historical characters – Matt Talbot in *Talbot's Box*, William Joyce and Brendan Bracken in *Double Cross*, Constance Wilde in *The Secret Fall of Constance Wilde*, William Blake in *Blake* – Kilroy's approach to his material would be bolder and his creative interventions more assured.

Kilroy himself has stressed that *The O'Neill* is 'an ironical work in the sense that it is about a rebel who actually is drawn to, even loves, the culture of the enemy'.[11] O'Faolain's book had 'unlocked' in Kilroy an interest in 'the Anglicization of Ireland and of the Irish character and temper' which he saw 'as much more than merely linguistic but as a profound mind shift'.[12] This cultural and psychological split within Irishness appealed to him on a very personal level: Kilroy has always maintained that he feels 'in some profound way alienated from [his] own culture', and that, from an early age, he resisted and rebelled against 'the shaping forces of that culture which were predominantly Catholic'. His sensibility found itself more in sympathy with Anglo-Protestant forms of cultural expression; from childhood on, Kilroy's 'instinctive nature was drawn towards a kind of privacy, a sense of personal judgment and a heavy reliance on rationalism',[13] a mindset that has had significant implications for the kind of theatre he has sought to create from the very outset of his career.

Kilroy's depiction of the character and actions of O'Neill broadly follows the picture painted by O'Faolain. Born in 1550 into a Gaelic aristocratic family torn by feuding, O'Neill was taken, at age nine, to be fostered by a noble English family as a favour granted by Queen Elizabeth – though not in England, as O'Faolain asserts, but by the Hovenden family in the Irish Pale. Back in Dungannon in the 1570s, O'Neill was happy to cooperate with the English insofar as 'he would work with anybody who could advance him', concerned as he was then, O'Faolain argues, 'only with feathering his own nest'.[14] Advance he did, and by 1590 he 'was speaking already for all Ulster, and claiming openly the rights and needs of Gaelic law and tradition, while admitting that in time they must yield place to the New System'.[15] In that year he asked Henry Bagenal, marshal of the English army in Ireland, for his sister Mabel's hand in marriage; when Henry refused, the pair eloped. Although O'Neill showed himself loyal to the English crown by aiding Bagenal in putting down a rebellion against the English in 1593, Henry showed little gratitude. Fearing that his brother-in-law would have him arrested and killed, O'Neill submitted a list of grievances to Elizabeth, but this did not stop the conflict between them from escalating.

Historian Hiram Morgan suggests that O'Faolain 'overdramatised and overpersonalised' O'Neill's negotiations with the commissioners of the queen,[16] whereas in actuality O'Neill 'feigned inability to control a confederacy of Gaelic lords who were in fact applying political and military pressure on his behalf'.[17] O'Faolain depicts the more mature O'Neill as a man guided by caution and prudence who, in the end, allowed himself to be led into war against the English by his instinct rather than his intelligence. The ostensible motivation for the war against the colonists was a desire for religious liberty. Morgan argues that a Catholic conspiracy 'must be relegated to the background' of the conflict between the various factions in Ulster,[18] but O'Faolain suggests that O'Neill saw the religious cause as a means to a greater end, in that it served to unite and inspire his men against the English. In 1598 the resolve of the Irish led them to engage Bagenal's forces in battle at the Yellow Ford. After the fight, in which his brother-in-law was mortally wounded, O'Neill sought to consolidate his victory by demanding, 'in effect, what later centuries called Home Rule'.[19]

The 'coagulant' of religion served O'Neill well at the Yellow Ford, but the sense of unstoppable momentum that took possession of his men after the victory would turn them against O'Neill's inclination to be cautious and patient: 'they would have rounded on him had he thought of compromise',[20] and so in 1601 when the Irish confronted the English at Kinsale before O'Neill thought it was prudent, they ended up losing the battle. O'Faolain sums up O'Neill as a modern man who had attempted both to perpetuate the Gaelic clan system and to recognise the English colonisation, 'only demanding that room be made, now, for all to live side by side',[21] but who lacked the conviction and the persuasive political skills to make that happen. By the mid-seventeenth century, Ulster had turned into 'the great citadel of English influence in Ireland'; by the time O'Faolain wrote his biography, it had become 'the last outpost of empire on the edge of Europe';[22] in the mid-1960s, when Kilroy was writing *The O'Neill*, that outpost was fast turning into a powder keg.

Kilroy wrote *The O'Neill* specifically to submit to Hilton Edwards, whose initial response, in June 1964, was encouraging: 'I liked the play in so far as it holds the attention, is fresh in its approach, with . . . a contemporary parallel . . . I like its freedom of form.' But there were cautious notes, too, since the cast was 'larger than we can cope with in the Dublin theatre under present economic conditions'. He was also not enamoured of the play's negative and somewhat ambiguous ending, and suggested Kilroy work on tightening and revising the script before resubmitting it.[23] During the eighteen months that followed, Kilroy (in addition to being appointed Junior Lecturer in English at UCD) completed *The Death and Resurrection of Mr Roche* and revised *The O'Neill*, substituting a 'hopeful note' for the despairing one at the end, which was therefore, as he later put it, 'certainly ironical'.[24] He sent both plays to the Abbey, then still resident at the Queen's Theatre. In May 1966, Ernest Blythe reported that a decision had not yet been reached on *The O'Neill*, given 'the rather wide differences of opinion in regard to it here'. Although Blythe himself found the play 'very interesting' and 'far better than any previous play about O'Neill', he also felt that 'a satisfactory production of it would almost require the resources of our new theatre', scheduled to open later that year, which would allow for the use of 'different stage levels' and which would have more elaborate and effective lighting.[25]

In November 1966, after some back and forth, the Abbey's artistic advisor, Tomás Mac Anna, informed Kilroy that he was putting *The O'Neill* down for production in the Peacock, which was scheduled to open 'about the end of March' (in actuality, it opened at the end of July). This venue, he promised, would provide 'unlimited opportunity for experiment and a fresh approach'. The script of *Mr Roche*, meanwhile, had also been sent on to the directors, and while Mac Anna himself 'found this most interesting reading' on 'a theme very much up to date',[26] he informed Kilroy in February 1967 that Blythe had turned down the play.[27] When he wrote again in early December of that year it was to say that he would only guarantee *The O'Neill* 'a reading from our company', while the new Peacock also turned out to have its limits: to cast the play properly there 'would be impossible'.[28] But evidently it was not, for in March 1968 *The O'Neill* was accepted by the Abbey board and scheduled for production. Still, the play had to wait two more years, until 30 May 1969, before it finally saw its premiere. By then, Alan Simpson had taken over from Mac Anna as artistic advisor, and Kilroy's *The Death and Resurrection of Mr Roche* had been staged at the Olympia Theatre as part of the 1968 Dublin Theatre Festival, where it was very well received. Kilroy believes that, without the success of *Mr Roche* – his first play to be staged – 'it would have been virtually impossible to get a professional production of *The O'Neill* at the time'.[29]

The O'Neill uses a number of techniques borrowed from epic theatre, but does so in a fairly understated way. Kilroy admired 'the way Brecht embedded realism inside highly stylized staging, the frontal immediacy of the productions, the direct, startling way in which they engaged audiences',[30] but Desmond Rushe, in his review of the play's 1969 production, notes that the 'semi-documentary formula' of the opening scene 'is soon discarded':[31] Kilroy breaks the illusion of reality by interrupting the storyline only at the beginning of the play, where he has to convey a certain amount of information and create a moment for the action to revert back to an earlier point in time. He does so by having the English Sir Robert Cecil cut short the reading of O'Neill's demands 'given out at the Yellow Ford in the heat of this great victory over the English' by exclaiming, 'Stop! Stop! This can't go on. Utopia! Utopia!'[32] The interruption allows Lord Mountjoy to express his confusion regarding 'O'Neill and his Irish wars' and to ask if 'we might possibly begin at the beginning again' (p. 12), at which point Cecil's role subtly shifts to that of a stage director:

> CECIL: (*Grudgingly*) Very well. (*Aloud to the assembly*) Let us begin at the beginning once more, please. Everybody now. (*There is a disgruntled murmur from all present*)
> O'NEILL: Must I go back over all that, again?
> CECIL: I'm afraid so. We must go back once more before we can go on. (p. 12)

More than twenty-five years later, Kilroy was to use almost exactly the same phrasing in the opening scenes of *The Secret Fall of Constance Wilde* and maintain the technique much more consistently throughout that play; in *The O'Neill*, the opening argument between O'Neill and Cecil mainly serves an expository function and sets up the main conflicts of the play – the Earl of Tyrone's divided loyalties, the issues of religion and of Europe, of colonisation and modernisation – before Mountjoy sets the play in motion again: 'Let us begin, please.' Cecil chooses to restart by calling up 'first the three spies' (p. 14). Several reviewers understood the recurring vignette of the three Irishmen 'brooding like tatty vultures' and 'changing sides at the drop of a banner' to suggest that 'we are and always have been our own worst enemies'.[33] After these opening gambits, *The O'Neill*, by and large, unfolds episodically to its foregone conclusion: 'Everything leads logically and inevitably to the bitterness of Kinsale.'[34]

In finding a form for his history play, Kilroy took much the same route as John Arden did in *Armstrong's Last Goodnight* (first performed in Glasgow in 1964). Subtitled *An Exercise in Diplomacy*, and described by Arden as being 'founded upon history' but not 'an accurate chronicle',[35] it also dramatises historical material in a way that sets up parallels with the present. The play takes place some years after the Scottish defeat at Flodden Field in 1513, when King James V of Scotland is determined to impose his authority on the unruly traditional lairds of the Border region, whose freebooting activities are endangering the fragile peace between his realm and the England of Henry VIII. The events of the play lead up to the hanging of one of these Border reivers, John Armstrong of Gilnockie. Like *The O'Neill*, *Armstrong's Last Goodnight* has a large cast and opens with a diplomatic discussion – here between English and Scots Commissioners – about the terms of the peace process within 'the present disturbed state of Christendom'.[36] Although Arden's and

Kilroy's plays follow very different trajectories after the opening deliberations, both works depict personal, political, religious and sexual power struggles. Both convey the ruthlessness that accompanies the exertion of British imperial power in the interest of 'the Security of the Borders', as the Second English Commissioner puts it at the start of *Armstrong's Last Goodnight*,[37] and 'the security of the kingdom', as Lord Mountjoy has it at the conclusion of *The O'Neill* (p. 72). Arden was influenced by Conor Cruise O'Brien's *To Katanga and Back*, which prompted him to 'suggest here and there a basic similarity of moral . . . problems' between the historical situation of his play and the modern imperialist enterprise in Congo.[38] For Kilroy, the modern parallels were most immediate with the burgeoning conflict in Northern Ireland and the Irish Republic's entry into the European Economic Community.

The two acts of *The O'Neill* mirror each other in their almost identical opening scenes, set on the battlefield after Hugh's 1598 victory at the Yellow Ford over Marshal Bagenal of Newry, as the great Gaelic chief is about to let the English know 'what Ireland demands', notably freedom of religion and full rights for the O'Neill and O'Donnell clans to their ancestral lands and privileges (p. 11, p. 48). Each act, however, unfolds in a different direction: while the first is retrospective and examines the events leading up to the Battle of the Yellow Ford, the second takes us forward from that victorious moment to the defeat of the Irish three years later at Kinsale, culminating in O'Neill's formal surrender to the representatives of Elizabeth I. Whereas Act I begins with '[a] simple representation of a battle-field' after hostilities have ceased, with O'Neill standing in the centre surrounded by his 'illegitimate' brother Art, his brother Cormac, and his men (p. 11), the opening description of the second act adds battle noises, 'the black smoke of pillage' and corpses 'hang[ing] from poles roundabout', while the men surrounding O'Neill look 'drained of all energy, only supported by the fierce exultation of butchery and success' (p. 48).[39] The retrospective action of Act I ends as Hugh prepares his men for war against Bagenal, spurred on by the rhetoric of Master Mountfort, O'Neill's English Jesuit advisor, who urges the clans to take up arms for the faith and 'the restoration of Catholic Ireland as it was before this present darkness'. The clansmen are not persuaded by the idea of a holy war and more intent on simply burning 'everything English between here and Dublin' (p. 43), but O'Neill is opportunistically willing to go along with the cause because 'whether we like it or not', religion 'may be just what we need now' (p. 47). At the end of Act II, after the Battle of Kinsale, the English are equally aware of the power of religious symbolism when they stage the scene of O'Neill's submission to the Crown in Mellifont Abbey, intended by Mountjoy, Lord Deputy of Ireland, as an emblem signifying the 'stamping out of the old religion and the stamping out of the old tribal system, in one' (p. 69). In light of the ethnic and sectarian divisions coming to a head in Northern Ireland at the time of the play's first performance, O'Neill's statement after his surrender to the English, that 'Ulster is at peace again' (p. 73), strikes an ominously ironic note.

Kilroy explores the way in which O'Neill is torn three ways – between his responsibility to the Gaelic clan system, his respect for English culture, and his aspirations for a united Catholic Europe – by presenting him, in Act I, through his relationships with three women in his life, each of whom has an emblematic function: the English settler Mabel Bagenal, the Irishwoman Róisín, and (*in absentia*) Queen Elizabeth I. As Fogarty has pointed out, the centrality granted in *The O'Neill* to Hugh's brief marriage to Mabel Bagenal is 'a glaring and elaborate departure from historical facticity',[40] but so is the role created by Kilroy for Róisín, O'Neill's fiery 'courtesan', who mockingly refers to herself at one point as 'a kept woman of the O'Neills' (p. 30). Her closest equivalent in O'Faolain's biography is 'O'Donnell's Ineen Duv', one of the 'neighbouring amazons' who would have turned up their noses at O'Neill's 'mesalliance' with Mabel.[41]

The courtesan's name evokes Róisín Dubh or 'Dark Rosaleen', the personification of Ireland in distress after the Flight of the Earls in 1607, made famous by James Clarence Mangan's eponymous poem; as such the name reverberates for contemporary audiences with the premonition of O'Neill's eventual fate. Mangan explained in a note that his poem represents an allegorical address by Hugh O'Donnell to Ireland expressing his resolve 'to raise her again to the glorious position she held as a nation, before the irruption of the Saxon and Norman spoilers':

The priests are on the ocean green,
They march along the deep.
There's wine from the royal Pope
Upon the ocean green;
And Spanish ale shall give you hope,
My Dark Rosaleen!
My own Rosaleen![42]

The Earls were never able to return to Ulster, of course, and their confiscated lands were taken over by British settlers in the plantation of 1609. By pitting the Irish Róisín against the English coloniser Mabel, Kilroy endows both women with an emblematic status. Queen Elizabeth completes (and complicates) the triangle, since she is Hugh's personal benefactress as well as the head of the English monarchy, in which capacity Hugh respects her, and of the Protestant Church of England, in which role he opposes her. O'Neill may scoff at his men when they can think only in terms of the link between 'Mother Church and Mother Ireland' (p. 45), but he allows himself to go along with Master Mountfort's gendered rhetoric against the Queen, according to which 'Satan now reigns in the guise of a female' – a 'Jezebel' (p. 45). In the Jesuit's words, it is 'the tyrant Elizabeth' who caused 'the blood of martyrs' to be spilled in Ireland; Elizabeth is then also, by ironic implication, the 'raging enemy' who 'seeks to lay hands on the fair limbs of our virgin land' (p. 46). Kilroy employs Mountfort's tortured misogynistic metaphors of women as either bloodthirsty demons or helpless victims, along with Mabel's complex hybridity and Róisín Dubh's not-so-virginal combativeness, to expose the logical and rhetorical fallacies of extremist nationalism and sectarianism.

O'Neill hates the colonists (Mabel prefers 'loyalists'), but falls in love with Mabel in spite of himself, or perhaps because she is, like himself, positioned between two cultures. Whereas Hugh admires the English penchant for order and civilisation, Mabel finds the ways of the garrison town dull; and while he deplores some of the traditional Irish customs, she (though not speaking from experience) finds them romantic. From one perspective Mabel can be considered Irish because, as O'Neill proposes, '[h]istory will not be able to tell the difference between us'; from another vantage point, she 'will never be Irish' because she does not carry the weight of history on her back (p. 23). The contemporary parallel with the ambivalent position within Irishness of Northern Irish loyalists is evident, and it is the almost Arnoldian split in O'Neill's personality (between calculating Englishman and impetuous Celt) that allows him to present both points of view; indeed, that duality is what often leads him to play devil's advocate. His love for Mabel is as double as his cultural affiliations: at times cool and platonic, at times savage and animalistic. She, too, however, mixes her cultural metaphors when she asks Hugh to elope with her so they can be married, albeit in the presence of a bishop. The clergyman, of course, would have to be Anglican; elopements, on the other hand, form the core of a number of (tragic) romances of pre-Christian Irish mythology, most notably the tales of Deirdre in the Ulster Cycle and Gráinne in the Fenian Cycle. The plot of each of these tales hinges on a love triangle. A beautiful young woman is destined to marry the old king; she then sets eyes on a youthful, dashing hero and does not rest until she has made him run away with her. Deirdre falls in love with Naoise, whose black hair, white skin and red cheeks are first conjured up in her mind by the wintry scene of her foster father skinning a calf: 'and the blood of the calf lay upon the snow, and she saw a black raven which came down to drink it'.[43] Gráinne immediately falls in love with Diarmuid when she spies him from her lofty bower scoring the winning points in a hurling match at Tara. After each couple has eloped, the jealous old king – Conchobar in Deirdre's case, Fionn in Gráinne's – pursues the lovers and finally kills his younger rival, taking back the woman for what can then only be a bitter relationship. In the end, Gráinne reaches a reluctant truce with Fionn; Deirdre remains defiant and eventually kills herself rather than accept Conchobar's cruelty.

O'Faolain speculates about the attraction between O'Neill and Mabel: 'He was now at the height of his physical powers, and when he put on his courtier's costume, his crimson jazerant gold-studded jacket, and his lined cloak, or if she saw him in glinting mail, with his scarlet spade beard and his broad shoulders, on horseback, it is no wonder that she was fascinated.'[44] Kilroy presents the tableau of O'Neill on horseback – an image of his heroic leadership – through Mabel's eyes, and changes the details of O'Faolain's fanciful description to evoke the fateful meeting between the lovers in both the Deirdre and Gráinne legends. In *The O'Neill*, the conflicting parts of Hugh's persona are vividly portrayed in the colours that strike Mabel when she first sets eyes on him:

> I saw you first from my window in Newry riding through the frosty streets one November. The stones themselves were white with frost and everything rang with a sound in the air. You were on a roan mare and your beard was a flame under your face. You wore a scarlet jacket with slashed sleeves of yellow silk. There was a green cloak on your back but it was thrown over to give you freedom. (p. 24)

These are not the colours of O'Faolain's description of O'Neill, nor are they those of Naoise in the Deirdre legend; instead, they are the red and the green of O'Neill's divided English and Irish loyalties. The green cloak, thrown over to expose the red and give him freedom, suggests his unwillingness to be held back by the traditionalism of his Gaelic clan background, while the slashed yellow sleeves (perhaps recalling the 'gold' of the Irish tricolour) may point ahead to the Ulster of the centuries after its plantation in the wake of the Flight of the Earls.[45] In Kilroy's configuration, moreover, O'Neill is simultaneously the old king of the legends and the irresistible hero: when Mabel tells him she loved him from the moment she first saw him, he refers to himself as an 'old man', to which she replies, 'I happen to like older men . . . One is made to feel secure' (pp. 23–24). The conflation within Hugh of the old and young mythical rivals for the love of the woman suggests that O'Neill is his own antagonist, as indeed he is for much of the play: in his inability to choose sides between the Irish and the English, between tradition and modernity, he is left doubting himself to the point of allowing others to make decisions for him. When Mountfort and Art, who see things 'simply' (p. 64), begin to press their case for war against the English, the 'green cloak' begins to slip and enfold O'Neill again, and he lacks the conviction to hold it back.

Hugh is confronted, time and again, with the difficulty of negotiating a position between two worlds. Even his own court poet expresses disapproval at his patron's lack of commitment to his Irish heritage by citing 'something topical':

> Man who apes the English ways,
> Who cut short your curling hair,
> You are unlike the son of Donncadh.
> Him I praise.
> He would hate to have at his ankle a jewelled spur, stocking of the English.
> Little he cares for gold-bordered cloaks.
> The son of Donncadh, I praise. (pp. 28–29)

The lines, from the seventeenth-century poet Laoiseach Mac an Bhaird's 'Courtier and Rebel', suggest the impossibility of divided loyalties: 'Give praise to one and you have to take something from someone else' (p. 29). Immediately following this scene, Róisín offers her lover a compromise based on her understanding that it is not she but Mabel who is the object of O'Neill's affection: 'Let you come back here with me and in the darkness – I'll let you see her face and not my face' (p. 30). The impossible illusion of rivals Mabel and Róisín united in one body diminishes both women. Mabel urges Hugh, to no avail, to give himself to one cause only because he is 'one thing to one man and something else to another' (p. 34). 'Am I still The O'Neill?', Hugh wonders; 'What in God's name am I at all?' (p. 31).

O'Faolain reports that the historical Hugh 'used a dual title – "The O'Neill" with the Irish, and "Earl of Tyrone" with the English', and that this caused a problem for Catholic theologians, 'seeing that as "Tyrone" he was indubitably a traitor and could not be supported by the orthodox, but as "O'Neill" he was no traitor and not only could be supported but should be, according to every moral law'.[46] Hugh asserts himself in the face of his English wife's warning that his clan's 'savagery' and 'fear of everything that isn't Irish' will drag him down (p. 42) by calling on his heritage: 'You can never know what it is to be O'Neill. . . . Take away my name and I am a nobody' (p. 42). Yet in an earlier scene he had berated his own clansmen for overstating their importance: 'Who are the O'Neills, I ask you? An obscure declining family in the northwest corner of Europe trying to stand upright after centuries of sleep' (p. 20). At the close of Kilroy's play, when 'Hugh, Earl of Tyrone' has been forced to surrender 'all lands, titles, arms, and dependencies' to the Crown (p. 73), his name becomes his last resort: 'I'll go back to my kinsmen,' he tells

Mountjoy; 'I am still O'Neill, am I not? My name has not been taken away from me. I may not have two spears to support me but even in poverty I am still their Prince. (*Whisper*) O'Neill' (pp. 73–74). As John Jordan points out, Hugh's curtain line echoes Webster's 'I am Duchess of Malfi still', but one might well ask, to quote another Elizabethan playwright, what, at this point, is 'in a name': to future generations it will resonate with tragedy, loss, and the decline of an entire way of life.[47]

Echoes of the tensions and divisions in the (Northern) Ireland of his own day are evident in Kilroy's treatment of O'Neill's dilemma. While he was working on the script, Kilroy noted that Hugh's defeat by the English 'marked the end of the ancient, aristocratic Gaelic civilization'. His note does not mention Northern Ireland; rather, it makes a more global point by suggesting that Kinsale 'was the first of the modern wars of colonization whose pattern was followed in the Spanish Conquest of the Americas, the white destruction of American Indian culture and later wars of invasion in Africa and Asia'.[48] Talking to Aodhan Madden in 1969, shortly after *The O'Neill* had finished its run at the Peacock, Kilroy maintained that he had 'tried to dramatise the question facing every thinking Irishman today', namely 'the Irish personality in conflict with the all-pervading American pop culture'. Madden comments that Kilroy 'feels very strongly on this subject and made quite an argument out of it in the historical situation of the last of the great Gaelic chiefs, Hugh O'Neill. "We're selling this country out," he says. ["]Our soil, our soul. For what? Transistors?"'[49] A reading of the play as a comment on American cultural and economic imperialism has not found critical currency, but Kilroy was not the only playwright voicing such concerns in the late 1960s; around the same time, Brian Friel argued that 'Ireland is becoming a shabby imitation of a third-rate American state . . . We are rapidly losing our identity as a people and because of this that special quality an Irish writer should have will be lost.'[50] Yet while Kilroy was lamenting a degree of cultural erosion, he was not suggesting that the country should turn back to a traditional way of life: 'This country is undergoing a social revolution. So for someone my age, the pace of development has been so great, there's the enormous difficulty of relating one's background to this revolution. Plays that don't deal with modernity are totally irrelevant.'[51]

Writing in the 1990s, Christopher Murray called *The O'Neill* 'altogether prophetic in an uncanny way. Staged in May 1969 it preceded the outbreak in August 1969 of the violence in Belfast',[52] although that violence did not, of course, emerge out of nowhere. Regardless of whether Kilroy consciously planned the various parallels between historical and contemporaneous events that have subsequently been detected by commentators on the play, it is clear that he managed to engage with a number of topical issues and debates. In a 2002 interview, he agreed that '[o]f course it was intentional to write an historical play which would glance off issues of immense importance in contemporary Ulster. Issues like nationalism, rebellion, the foundation of a state.'[53] Talking to the *Derry Journal* in 2007, however, he suggested that 'Ireland's move into Europe' had been on his mind when he wrote the play: 'it seemed to me to be a very good example out of history to explore early ideas of Ireland and Europe, which is what O'Neill represented'.[54] British colonisation and Irish Europeanisation were each, in their own time, sources of profound cultural anxiety. After throwing off British rule, the Irish spent the first decades of independence trying to define, assert, and in some cases (re-)invent their Irishness; that debate about identity received a renewed impetus when Seán Lemass announced on 1 August 1961 that Ireland intended to apply for membership of the European Economic Community.

Terence Brown's analysis in *Ireland: A Social and Cultural History* of the effects on Irish culture and society of the decision to open the country 'to the forces of the international marketplace' helps throw light on the similarity between the effects of colonisation and those of internationalisation (both often presented by their supporters as modernising efforts), and on the relevance for the 1960s and '70s of O'Neill's predicament in Kilroy's play. Much of the national debate in those decades concerned 'considerations of national identity in circumstances where many of the traditional essentialist definitions – language, tradition, culture, and distinctive ideology – are widely felt to fly in the face of social reality, no longer commanding anything much more than sentimental respect'.[55] Brown brings this argument around to the issue of Northern Ireland by reminding us that it was Lemass 'who managed in the 1960s to wed a commitment to economic renewal to the aspiration for unity'.[56] In Kilroy's play, the irony of O'Neill's position is that he uses the idea of European unity as a rallying cry for the Gaelic clans to move against the colonising English. The fact that the Spanish help on which he was counting is not, in the end, forthcoming, due to a breakdown in communications, adds a poignant note. Murray notes that the focus of O'Neill on European unity serves as a parallel to 'Ireland's joining the Economic Community, which didn't happen until . . . 1973', and suggests that, especially in the wake of the 1992 Maastricht Treaty, *The O'Neill* provides a comment both on the 'necessity' of such a move 'and on its cost'.[57]

The several ways in which issues facing the protagonist of *The O'Neill* resonate with what was happening in Northern Ireland in the 1960s are perhaps more evident in hindsight than they were to audiences at the time. The demands read out in the play's opening scene by the Irish on behalf of the victorious Prince of Ulster evoke a complex set of historical friction points as well as contemporary ironies:

> One: That the Catholic, Apostolic and Roman religion be openly preached and taught throughout Ireland as it was in times past.
> Two: That there be erected a university . . . wherein all sciences shall be taught according to the manner of the Roman Catholic Church.
> Three: That O'Neill and O'Donnell with all their partakers may peaceably enjoy all lands and privileges that did appertain to their predecessors two hundred years ago. (p. 11)

In the late 1960s, O'Neill's claims would have resonated differently with audiences in Northern Ireland and in the Republic. Vis-à-vis O'Neill's third demand – the restoration of the lands and privileges – audiences would, on some level, have been aware that, after Kinsale, the clans' ancestral lands were confiscated, the Earls were forced to flee, and from 1609 onwards Ulster was being planted by, predominantly, Scottish Presbyterian settlers, laying the foundation for the divisions within the troubled province that became Northern Ireland. In the two centuries that followed Kinsale, the battle for freedom of religion in Ireland was hard-fought and protracted and not settled, by and large, until Daniel O'Connell secured Catholic Emancipation in 1829; the establishment of a Catholic university, however, remained a vexed question that eventually resulted, in 1908, in the creation of the National University of Ireland which was, at least in theory, non-denominational. Mountfort's aspiration in *The O'Neill*, to create 'unity of state and faith, where Pope and Prince may encompass our total existence', so that the 'fixed poles of our universe' would be 'Church and State' (p. 44), came to pass with a vengeance in the Free State; by the 1960s, Catholicism was firmly embedded in most institutions of the Irish Republic. When he was growing up, Kilroy personally experienced the dominant presence of the church in everyday life as oppressive, since it 'presented itself . . . as something associated with fear and guilt',[58] and therefore as something to resist. O'Neill's words to his fanatical priest, who advocates a Christian state, reflect Kilroy's reservations: 'It'd be worth beating the English just to see how far you'd go, Father Mountfort, and whether I'd be able to stop you' (pp. 64–65). In contrast with their status in the Republic, Catholics in Northern Ireland in the 1960s suffered real discrimination, and the question of a Catholic university – raised in O'Neill's second claim – was still alive and well. When a second university was being planned for the province, there was an expectation that it would be established in Derry, which unlike Belfast had a majority Catholic population. In 1965, however, the government Lockwood Committee, which included no Catholic members, decided the new campus should be located in Coleraine, in the Protestant heartland.

Kilroy's O'Neill sees himself as having been born 'for small fights and the trickery of peace-making' (p. 64), half-hearted qualities which neither his own men nor the English are ultimately prepared to take seriously. Unlike his Jesuit advisor, he lacks the conviction to give his words the power they need to be transformative, of himself as well as others. His moderate vision is to 'salvage the best of our past among the leaders of a new, united Christian Europe' (p. 63) while, on the extreme wing, Mountfort envisages 'A new Holy Roman Empire' (p. 65). O'Neill's main criticism of his own people is that he cannot depend on them because they 'are split. They are seldom one on anything' (p. 44). Kilroy's subsequent plays, too, have consistently been preoccupied with what he has called the Irish 'failure to achieve a wholeness of community',[59] or with what, in specific relation to Northern Ireland, he has referred to as 'the social sickness which is deeply rooted in the country' and which comes out of a 'fear of ideas'.[60] O'Neill's criticism of his men is precisely that they are unwilling to reflect on their shortcomings, and unable to project themselves imaginatively into a viable future:

> CORMAC: Don't be hard on the men, Hugh. They will follow you anywhere.
> O'NEILL: Ah, Cormac, they have to do more. They have to see themselves transfigured. But how can I make them believe in this miracle when I can hardly believe in it myself?
> ART: Words! Words! There is a battle to be won.
> O'NEILL: And there is a battle to be lost, too. . . . And if we lose it there is nothing left. A darkness will descend upon Ireland. . . . [The people] will go backward, having nothing but what is in the past. And they may take centuries to find a future.
> ART: That's enough. We'll fight the English first. Then we can talk words. (p. 63)

In the end, it is the Jesuit's fiery rhetoric that spurs the Irish into a losing battle.

For most of the 1960s, the Northern Irish prime minister was Terence O'Neill (Baron O'Neill of the Maine). The echo in his name and title of his Elizabethan namesake may be serendipitous, but there are also broad parallels between the career trajectories of the two men that Kilroy may have noted. Like Hugh O'Neill, and like Seán Lemass in the Republic, Terence O'Neill was committed to modernisation, in which he faced opposition from traditionalists within his own Ulster Unionist Party. Like Hugh, Terence was a man trying to walk a tightrope between the different cultures and traditions of Northern Ireland, unwilling to firmly favour one side over the other. As he pursued a policy of minimal appeasement, his eventual aim was to end sectarianism and forge working relationships between Catholics and Protestants. This put him in a difficult political position: 'On the one hand, placating the civil rights movement was likely to mean consolidation of the opposition to him. One the other, failing to do so would probably lead . . . to British intervention and a complete dissolution of local autonomy.'[61] Amidst rising sectarian tensions, O'Neill's ideas became increasingly unpopular, and the erosion of his authority within his party forced

Frank Grimes, Joseph O'Connor, and John Kavanagh in *The O'Neill*, Peacock Theatre, 1969. Directed by Vincent Dowling. Photograph: Fergus Bourke. Courtesy Abbey Theatre.

him to announce his resignation in April 1969, a month before the premiere of Kilroy's *The O'Neill* in Dublin.

Early on in *The O'Neill*, Sir Robert Cecil, speaking from the supercilious position of the coloniser, characterises the Irish as treacherous people who 'can be split by one hard word in anger, by the jingle of coins', particularly brothers who 'will slit each other's throats' out of sheer hatefulness and personal ambition. O'Neill evokes instead a sense of Irish 'brotherhood' (p. 14), but the divided nature of his own family is immediately evident in his disagreement with his brothers Art and Cormac about the future of the Gaelic way of life, and in the ongoing feud with his cousins, the 'breed of my father's murderer' who must be 'stamped out like vermin' (p. 19). The tragic reality of this familial and societal split is poignantly symbolised towards the end of the play, when the battle with the English has ended in defeat and the way back to Ulster is cut off by other Irish: 'Remember we burned the land on the way down. They'll be waiting for us on the way back. Every mile of the road' (p. 67).

During an earlier moment, Róisín had assuaged O'Neill's doubts about his identity by reciting his family lineage: 'You are Hugh, son of Ferdorcha, son of Con Bacach, son of Con, son of Henry, son of Owen – ' (p. 31). This, as Thierry Dubost points out, renders him a 'link in the male chain' and embeds him inexorably in 'the course of history'[62] until that chain is broken. Róisín's retrospective litany ends with Owen, the name of Hugh's ancestor but also that of his son. In a conversation with Mabel, Hugh had spoken of him as if he were dead – 'But I remember my son Owen, now . . . There was a boy! . . . There was a spark of greatness in him' – before explaining that the child had been taken away by his estranged wife Siobhán 'when she went back to her own people' (p. 26). After Kinsale, a headless corpse is put down at O'Neill's feet, which he initially fails to recognise as Owen. Once his son's identity is revealed, Hugh's desperate plea, 'Oh take him up, for God's sake, and find the head. If ye have to go into Kinsale, find the head . . . D'you hear? The head! The head!' (p. 68), expresses a wish for a wholeness that is now impossible to achieve. The death of the son signals a break in the family lineage and the thwarting of a viable future: the severed head not only presages the Flight of the Earls but signifies, on a national scale, internal Irish division and the eventual partition of the island. By contrast, the death of Queen Elizabeth at about the same time, the 'head' of the monarchy and of the Church of England, barely causes a ripple on the surface of the nation; as Cecil puts it, 'There is no need for concern. The state has been well provided for. All opposition has been effectively destroyed. We mourn the passing of a great queen, yes, but her imperial monument will outlive all of us' (p. 69).

When it finally made its way onto the Peacock stage in 1969, *The O'Neill* was critically very well received. Bernard Share suggested that the play deserved 'a production "upstairs" and a permanent place in the Abbey repertoire',[63] but *The O'Neill* did not make it to the main stage, and far from becoming an Abbey staple (unlikely, in any case, because of its cast of twenty-five), the play would not see another production until 2007,[64] the year that marked the 400th anniversary of the Flight of the Earls. While Letterkenny, the location of the performance, was replete with 'historical and geographical resonances' (O'Neill's ally Hugh O'Donnell was from Donegal), and the text still echoed 'contemporary debates over nationhood and identity', the nature of the community production at An Grianán theatre reflected the successful outcome of the Northern Irish peace process, which had rendered cross-border collaborations both possible and desirable. Directed by David Grant, former artistic director of the Lyric Theatre and head of drama at Queen's University Belfast, the production featured a cast of players drawn from several different groups in Donegal, while the part of O'Neill was played by Belfast actor Andrew Roddy. In Grant's production the English politicians were dressed in modern business suits 'to underline the continuity of exasperation that has characterized English attempts to govern the north of Ireland up until the Good Friday agreement'; their encounter with O'Neill dressed in period costume emphatically brought home the extent to which the chieftain and his culture were already doomed.[65] In its own small way, this spirit of cross-community cooperation in putting *The O'Neill* on the stage constituted an aspect of what Kilroy had imagined when, in his 1959 *Studies* essay, he envisioned a theatre *of* the community, as much as *for* it, that would absorb the topical issues around it and enable the re-evaluation of old beliefs.

2

Deformities of Nationalism: *Double Cross*

When *The O'Neill* premiered in 1969, Northern Ireland was about to erupt into violence. Two years later, Kilroy published a novel the themes of which were similarly intended to reverberate with the growing sectarian conflict. Set in a town called 'Kyle', a thinly disguised version of Kilroy's home town of Callan, *The Big Chapel* takes as its subject a notorious feud that took place there in the 1870s.[1] A parish priest named O'Keeffe (William Lannigan in the book) pig-headedly defied the equally unbending higher church authorities on the issue of papal infallibility; the ensuing stand-off sparked violent riots between supporters of either side in the dispute. The novel, Kilroy said, 'is about lunacy, about rigid orthodoxy of any kind in a community of persons trying to live together'.[2] Extreme ideology as madness is also central to Kilroy's play *Double Cross*. When the Derry-based Field Day Theatre Company produced the work in 1986, the 'Troubles' were at their peak, unionists and republicans were firmly entrenched in their positions, and political solutions to the conflict seemed remote. Against this backdrop, Kilroy set out to write about nationalism which, in its extreme form, becomes 'a dark burden, a source of trauma and debilitation'.[3] Taking place during the Second World War, euphemistically known in neutral Ireland as the 'Emergency', *Double Cross* creates a distance between the action of the play and the immediate present; as he had done in *The O'Neill*, Kilroy designed *Double Cross* to comment at best indirectly on the situation in Northern Ireland. Rather, the play's themes function within a broader paradigm that seeks to 'undermine the black and white division of all wars, to subvert the righteousness of all political causes'.[4] *Double Cross* dramatises 'the deformities of nationalism' by troubling the distinction between victor and victim, coloniser and colonised.[5] Kilroy makes such abstractions personal by filtering them through the psyches of two historical figures on opposite sides of the conflict: Brendan Bracken, Churchill's wartime Minister of Information, and William Joyce, the Nazi radio propagandist also known as 'Lord Haw-Haw'.

Brendan Bracken was born in Templemore, County Tipperary, in 1901 while William Joyce, born in 1906 in Brooklyn, NY, of an Irish father and an English mother, spent his childhood in Galway. Both moved to England around the time they came of age (and the Irish Free State came into existence) and began erasing their Irish pasts. Each man claimed to be thoroughly English and to have the best interests of the British Empire at heart. Both relied on performance, deception, and make-believe to fashion their own reality. Joyce, Kilroy suggests, came into his own in front of a microphone: 'His sense of himself before his listeners was histrionic, a performer who could transform political reality by simply saying, in brilliant fashion, that it was so transformed.'[6] His counterpart was also a performer: 'Larger than life and constantly overacting, having arrived mysteriously from nowhere, Bracken provided Evelyn Waugh with a model for his character Rex Mottram in *Brideshead Revisited*. "Everything about you is phoney," one interlocutor told Bracken, "even your hair which looks like a wig, isn't."'[7] After the war, the Nazi propagandist was hanged for treason; the member of the British wartime cabinet was elevated to the peerage. In Kilroy's depiction, both Bracken and Joyce were driven to deny their Irish origins – to 'eliminate . . . their ancestors'[8] – by the same self-hatred each projects onto his double in the play. Having thus emptied themselves out they substituted ultra-English personas, in a racist and fascist pursuit of some higher ideal of civilisation and human perfection. Kilroy argues that the 'seed-bed of fascism is a pathological insecurity related to national or racial identity', which seeks to appease itself in the extreme embrace of a sense of group superiority. 'In our troubled century,' he continues, 'no other obscenity has been as malignant as this one: the notion of absolute power or absolute truth or absolute anything else being the property of any one group of individuals. . . . If religion is one model of this pathology, nationalism is another.'[9] In Northern Ireland, of course, the entanglement of religion with nationalism on both sides of the political divide made for a particularly toxic mixture.

As in *The O'Neill*, Kilroy's mode in *Double Cross* is irony, which implies a double perspective; this doubling is evident in the play's title and structure – two parts, the 'Bracken Play' set in London and the 'Joyce Play' set in Berlin, that present their protagonists as each other's mirror images and opposites – as well as its requirement that both characters are played by the same actor. In the Field Day production, Kate O'Toole played Bracken's mistress Popsie and Joyce's wife Margaret, as well as the female Narrator and the Lady Journalist. Richard Howard displayed 'an extraordinary versatility' as he changed himself into the male Narrator, a Fire Warden, Lord Castlerosse, Lord Beaverbrook, and Margaret's lover Erich.[10] Stephen Rea, whom Kilroy already had in mind for the two main characters as he was writing *Double Cross*, performed both parts to universal acclaim. As O'Toole describes it, his transformation 'from the nervous, watchful arrogance of Bracken to the haunting, melancholic mania of Joyce' was masterful.[11] Rea himself wrote to Kilroy afterwards that he had never worked on anything that demanded so much, and gave him so much satisfaction.[12] While Bracken and Joyce never meet in the play, each is haunted by his opposite number via the other's voice on the radio or his image on a video screen placed on stage. By having the characters react to each other in this way Kilroy not only creates, as Carmen Szabó argues, 'an unusual dialogue between presence and absence, between stage and screen, between Self and Other', but also reinforces the extent to which the characters are, in fact, reflections of each other.[13] At the end of Part One, the on-stage transformation of Rea from Bracken into Joyce exposes and foregrounds, as Mary Trotter points out, 'the actor's craft of imitation'. When Bracken's overcoat is taken off to reveal Joyce's fascist black shirt and tie underneath, and Bracken's spectacles and red wig are removed to expose Joyce's scar, Rea's performance 'creates a semiotic three-way mirror' in which the three identities 'infinitely reflect and refract one another' and an audience comes immediately face to face with 'the theatricality of identity formation'.[14]

Double Cross had its beginnings in a radio play Kilroy proposed to BBC Northern Ireland in 1982. In a letter to drama producer Robert Cooper he described the centre of the piece as a drunken all-night vigil during the 1940 London Blitz involving Prime Minister Winston Churchill, his Parliamentary Private Secretary Brendan Bracken and Lord Beaverbrook, owner of the *Daily Express* and Minister of Aircraft Production. During the bombardment, Bracken undergoes a kind of inner journey into his Irish past, represented elsewhere in the radio drama via a series of letters exchanged during the 1920s between Bracken in London and his mother in Ireland. In addition to wanting to write about a man who invents his own personality, Kilroy saw this Irish–English angle of Bracken's story as an opportunity to address the notion that the British imperialist vision is frequently postulated by outsiders such as the figures in the play: Bracken hailed from Ireland, Churchill's mother was an American socialite, and Beaverbrook (Max Aitken) was born in his mother's native Canada. When the centre eventually crumbles, the Empire is likewise defended, 'in furious, enraged commitment' by those on the periphery.[15] The BBC ended up shelving the script of *That Man Bracken*, however, and by early 1985 Kilroy was being encouraged by Field Day directors Seamus Deane, Stephen Rea and Brian Friel to turn the radio drama into a full-length stage play that would give the Bracken piece a counterpart focusing on William Joyce, who had similarly denounced his Irish roots in favour of an English identity.

Field Day, as Marilynn Richtarik reminds us in her history of the company's early days, was founded 'with the intention of finding or creating a space between unionism and nationalism and proving by example the possibility of a shared culture in the North of Ireland'.[16] In addition to Friel, Deane and Rea, Field Day's board of directors included David Hammond, Tom Paulin and Seamus Heaney; Kilroy was to join them in 1988. By 1985, the company had produced six plays; between 1983 and 1988 it also published a series of pamphlets (fifteen in total, the first three written by Deane, Paulin and Heaney) in which noted intellectuals commented on questions of nation, language and identity. In the early 1980s, Field Day asked Kilroy to contribute a pamphlet to the series – for publication in 1984 alongside those by Richard Kearney (no. 5) and Declan Kiberd (no. 6) – which, however, he failed to deliver. This explains why the author of pamphlet no. 4 was, again, Seamus Deane. Richtarik suggests that Field Day's two separate endeavours created a 'fault line . . . between art and criticism' that led the company away from its original theatre mission: plays are suggestive but 'pamphlets assert and thus, in a divided society such as that of Northern Ireland, may appear more confrontational than challenging'.[17] As it turned out, in writing *Double Cross* Kilroy ended up giving Field Day a work that was in many ways closer to a pamphlet than a conventional history play; indeed, Colm Tóibín remarked in his review of the 1986 production that it was 'as though Kilroy wrote it with Seamus Deane looking over one shoulder and Tom Paulin looking over the other',[18] which was not that far removed from the reality. Deane recognised the play's subject matter as quintessential Field Day material, and later concluded that, in writing the play, Kilroy had written a Field Day pamphlet after all, 'but one that subverts FD as much as it does anything FD thinks it is there to subvert'.[19]

As the members of the Field Day board were debating the transformation of Kilroy's radio drama into a full-length stage play, Rea suggested that the expanded version might use a theatrical device to highlight Bracken's 'virtuosity and his being a no-man' that would hinge on his relationship with W.B. Yeats, an idea that attracted Deane because it would show 'two of the great colonial comedians going through their paces'. Deane also proposed that Kilroy, should he consider using the idea, might give it a parallel by pairing William Joyce with the Irish novelist Francis Stuart who, having moved to Berlin in January 1940, spent the war years broadcasting Nazi propaganda to Ireland, hoping that a victorious Germany might have some role in unifying his country.[20] Deane's idea is intriguing, but Kilroy opted instead to use Yeats in both halves of *Double Cross* to underline the similarities as well as the differences between his two main characters. Perhaps drawing on Walter Benjamin's definition of fascism as the '[i]rruption of aesthetics into politics, the desire to invent the world as an ordered, symmetrical work of art',[21] Kilroy noted that 'art and fascism intersect most disturbingly in our century', and that the fascist intolerance of human frailty that is so evident in the Joyce of *Double Cross* might also 'have its place in the art of major artists like Yeats'.[22] The notion that great art can be created by deeply flawed human beings is only hinted at here, but it forms a central theme in other plays by Kilroy, notably *The Shape of Metal* and *Blake*.

Brendan Bracken cultivated a friendship with Yeats. Each man's estimation of the other is captured by Kilroy in two quotations recorded in his working notes for the radio play *That Man Bracken.* The first is from Yeats, who felt that Bracken suffered 'unduly from the exaggerated importance of those around him' and was 'a bit of a snob'.[23] In *Double Cross*, Lord Castlerosse (the sixth Earl of Kenmare, gossip columnist for newspapers owned by his friend, Lord Beaverbrook) tells the (true) story of how Bracken once invited Yeats to 'Freddy Britton-Austin's house' (Frederick Britten Austin, First World War army captain and author of military stories), pretending it was his own: 'He even gave Yeats a book out of the library . . . '.[24] Kilroy's note also cites Bracken as believing that Yeats had spent his life 'in the pursuit of what might be called, for want of a better term, good breeding in literature'.[25] 'Good breeding' is, of course, what Kilroy's Bracken believes British imperialism is spreading around the world. Popsie's observation about her lover, that he keeps talking different Brendan Brackens into existence, is not that far removed from the idea of the Yeatsian 'anti-self' that Mary Trotter associates with William Joyce – 'a man trying through his art to make real his created identity, and his imaginings of and for the world'[26] – although Bracken claims 'to subscribe to the Wildean notion that one must make of one's life a work of art' by shaping the 'petty dismal material' one starts with into 'significance' (p. 35).

In the second part of *Double Cross* it is Margaret Joyce's lover Erich, the German Anglophile dressed in 'plus-four tweeds, Norfolk jacket, Fair Isle pullover, good brogues', who is romantically infatuated with Yeats' verse, while it is Joyce who disabuses him of the notion that the poet is English: 'Yeats is Irish. He is writing about Ireland. Different place, alas' (p. 66). 'Alas', because Ireland chose to remove itself from the Empire in which Joyce emphatically insists he was born. Joyce's mockery of Erich as a caricature of Englishness, a 'ridiculous buffoon' who imagines himself 'master of the English lyric' (p. 69), ironically rebounds on himself given that he is, as the play's Actor-Narrator puts it, 'American but also Irish. He wanted to be English but had to settle on being German' (p. 60), although in a further supreme irony an English court eventually declared him British so that he could be hanged for treason.

Bracken and Joyce both fabricated ultra-English identities for themselves while allying themselves with opposite sides in the war, but then, as Bracken remarks, 'all things are opposites of other things as my old chum Willy Yeats would say' (p. 34). In making Bracken aspire to the perfect British aristocratic manner, and Joyce to the eradication of imperfection in the human species, Kilroy wanted their conflict to reflect this opposition between 'effete sophistication and fascist brutalism . . . while retaining the threads . . . binding them together'.[27] Kilroy sees the fascist passion for purification as a 'bizarre relic of Puritanism in the modern world'.[28] Bracken's goal is to eliminate 'the forces of darkness which threaten our very civilization' (p. 30), among which he counts the 'foreign poison' of socialism (p. 40), the 'alien races, the riff-raff of Russia, the refuse of the dens of the East' (p. 41), as well as the 'Wogs and Frogs and Whatnots from every corner of Europe' who have dared to set up their domicile in England (p. 49). During his early teenage years in Galway, Joyce's motivation for wanting to serve the Black and Tans in rooting out the town's Sinn Féiners had been his desire to 'clean out the scum' (p. 64); for the older Joyce it is 'the Jew' who is 'the parasite of our British economy, the corrupter of our British heritage. He is our evil otherness, the fault in our nature which we must root out' (p. 56). His war is fought 'on behalf of the species' (p. 87), and he believes that an eventual cataclysmic conflagration will burn man 'out of his imperfection and into the shape of his dreams' (p. 65).

Kilroy proposes that there is 'a perfectly visible connection between British imperialism and fascism'. Such a suggestion cannot be made without risk, as the playwright discovered when some English members of his play's audience met it with 'an almost incoherent rage'.[29] In Ruth Sherry's words, '*Double Cross* invites speculation that it is a matter of chance who chose which side, who triumphed, who died . . . Kilroy indicates what lies in common between Churchill's Britain and Hitler's Germany'.[30] In the play, 'what lies in common' between wartime Britain and Germany is visualised in the cardboard cutout portraits suspended from a washing line over the scene in each act. Winston Churchill, King George V and Sir Oswald Mosley preside over the Bracken Play, while Goebbels, Hitler and Mosley, again, oversee the Joyce Play. Mosley, member of the aristocracy, British conservative MP turned Labour politician turned founder of the British Union of Fascists, is the pivot between Empire and Reich. In the 1930s, '[t]he cat could have jumped either way', as Castlerosse says in *Double Cross* (p. 39). Outside of Ireland, the outbreak of hostilities distilled the political muddle of the pre-war decade into clarity, resolving the ambiguities into a clear divide between British patriotism and German fascism, but Irish neutrality meant that citizens could not be seen to take sides in the conflict. Censorship and propaganda helped enforce the state of 'neutral-mindedness' in the Free State, a position also maintained by Raidió Éireann in its practice of compiling news digests about the conflict from both Allied and German sources. This, as Clair Wills explains, 'left the reader or listener with no way of telling what was true and what wasn't', the upshot being that Irish radio 'ceased to mean much at all' during the 'Emergency'.[31]

Irish people who did make a choice in favour of one side or the other were not necessarily more clear-sighted than their more ambivalent compatriots. Seán O'Casey, who spent the war in England, argued in 1940 that the brutal nature of English imperial rule in Ireland and elsewhere in the colonies made it hard to back Britain as a viable force of 'liberty and justice' against the Nazi regime. Instead, he put his faith in international socialism, only to be taken aback when Germany attacked the USSR: 'I thought Hitler would go Left,' he wrote to a friend.[32] Kilroy reveals that his father was among Lord Haw-Haw's sizeable radio audience in Ireland, delighting in the anti-British rhetoric while being fully aware of the broadcaster's nationality: 'Only an Irishman, indeed only a Galwayman, could preside over the sinking of so many flotillas of the British Navy. Only one of our own could so effectively mock Churchill's cigar!' But, as Kilroy goes on to point out, during the War of Independence, while William Joyce was passing information about the local republicans to the Black and Tans in Galway city, Kilroy's father had been an IRA commandant in the county. 'So much,' he concludes, 'for crossed lines.'[33] In *Double Cross*, the choices made by Bracken and Joyce are acts of denial and betrayal that masquerade as liberating moves. Kilroy argues that the characters' retreat into rhetoric and performance is a withdrawal from facing the full reality of the war: 'But that's not too far removed from the condition in which I grew up as a child.'[34]

An 'audaciously intellectual play',[35] *Double Cross* is less a history play than a drama of ideas. Kilroy allows himself considerable licence with factual detail and chronology, and makes this approach to his historical subject matter overtly clear early on via the narrative commentary of the 'Actor' and 'Actress':

ACTRESS: Ladies and gentlemen! We cannot vouch for the accuracy of anything that is going to follow –
ACTOR: Even of what is verifiable in the history books –
ACTRESS: It has been put together to make a point. (pp. 26–27)

In *Double Cross*, much of that point – that, whatever side they are on, fascists and racists are driven by a quest for impossible purity – is made by drawing attention to the intersection of identity and language, a notion central to Field Day's projects from its very beginning, and evident in the premise of the company's first play produced in 1980, Brian Friel's *Translations*. Both Bracken and Joyce are involved in propaganda. Bracken's favourite means of communication is the telephone, where he can use his voice to flatter, threaten and cajole. English 'civilisation' for him equals the English language in a racially essentialised way; in his infatuation with Empire he envisions a future world divided into those who speak English and those who do not, and he imagines the latter as having 'slanted eyes and indifferent pigmentation' (p. 26). Ironically, it is his own voice that eventually betrays him when, during a heavy bombardment, he breaks down and retreats into the world of his childhood, lapsing into a strong Tipperary accent. Joyce uses his English voice to broadcast the odious Nazi ideology to listeners in Britain, but his wife Margaret notes that there was always a gap 'between what he said and what he really felt' (p. 75). When his carefully fabricated persona begins to unravel and he hits her she insists that he recover himself by living up to his own words – 'Violence controlled and directed is power' (p. 74) – but to no avail. An ironic gap opens up between Joyce's words and his behaviour. In his last, 'incoherent' broadcast he rants drunkenly against '[t]he American Jew-lover Churchill and his cronies, effete degenerates like Bracken, monied gangsters like Beaverbrook' who, by opposing the Nazis, had denied England her place in the foundry 'of human progress' that was creating the 'new Adam' of the idealised future (p. 79).

Although Joyce's personal allegiance to Hitler appears somewhat perfunctory, a photograph of the Führer hangs above the mantelpiece in his sitting room. The same space is occupied in 'The Bracken Play' by George Romney's portrait of Edmund Burke, which the historical Bracken owned and to whose subject he sometimes claimed to be related. Bracken is heavily invested in his ideological hero, an Irishman like himself who made his political career in England; Seamus Deane calls the eighteenth-century conservative thinker 'the greatest of all Irish political theorists', although his convictions doomed him to 'considerable neglect' in the country of his birth. 'The English, however, took him to their hearts and used him as the most far-seeing and the most readable imperialist thinker. For Burke consistently thought of Ireland as a central part of the Empire and devoted considerable effort to keeping her within it.'[36] Bracken's admiration for Burke, then, is unsurprising given his own loyalty to what his character in *Double Cross* calls 'our great Empire' (p. 40). As Terry Eagleton puts it, Burke 'drew a veil over his Irish past' – as does Bracken – and became 'his own best instance' of the kind of 'thoroughly hegemonized colonial' that would keep British imperial rule stable and intact.[37]

In *Double Cross*, Bracken goes to great and inventive lengths to inscribe himself and his family onto the British establishment and the various parts of the Empire. At one point he has himself introduced as 'the son of a distinguished officer in the Indian Army', with homes in England, Scotland and Northern Ireland (p. 40), while subsequent fabrications include a father who was a 'Bishop on the Cape' (p. 25) or 'an admiral' (p. 50), and a brother who is 'high-up in the Admiralty, in charge of vast tea plantations in Ceylon while . . . conducting a lucrative business in the City' (p. 47), as well as being an RAF hero (p. 50). When Kilroy's Bracken is elevated to the peerage, the titles he considers are Viscount Bracken 'of Pretoria' (in South Africa) and 'of Hobart' (in Australia), before settling on 'of Christchurch' – which evokes New Zealand but is, in fact, part of his former constituency in Southampton (p. 62). In that noble capacity he swears to serve his country and king 'against the forces of darkness which threaten our very civilization' (p. 30). As Bracken, Stephen Rea captured this absence of a fixed identity by speaking in a 'pained' voice that was 'a mockery of the authority and certainty of the English accent' but also at times veered towards South African; when the mask slips and his Irish vowel sounds reappear, the tragedy of his loss of self is forcefully brought home.[38]

The Bracken of *Double Cross*, for whom civilisation is 'the British inheritance' (p. 44), resorts to a quotation from Burke to define what that means: 'To be bred in a place of estimation, to see nothing low or sordid from one's infancy – to be habituated in the pursuit of honour and duty' (p. 44). This is Bracken's dream of the cultivation that is spread around the world by the British imperial influence. But the words he uses to make his case are a selective (mis)representation of their source, for here Burke is not speaking of 'the British inheritance' in a broader sense but of England's 'true natural aristocracy', within an argument that seeks to defend the concept of government fixed in King, Lords and Commons, as expressed in the Constitution, from new notions of government by 'the people' based on the French post-revolutionary model he so despised. According to Burke, the qualities bred into English aristocrats by the circumstances described in the phrase quoted by Bracken enable them 'to take a large view of the widespread and infinitely diversified combinations of men and affairs in a large society', and guide them to 'a guarded and regulated conduct' vis-à-vis their fellow citizens, possessing as they do 'the virtues of diligence, order, constancy, and regularity'. Such traits of moderation and restraint define the natural aristocracy 'without which there is no nation',[39] prepared as such leaders are to enlighten and protect 'the weaker, the less knowing, and the less provided with the goods of fortune'.[40] As Eagleton remarks, 'Burke is shrewd enough to perceive that governing classes survive only by engaging the affections of their inferiors, and that a loveless sovereignty is politically bankrupt'.[41]

Bracken not only selectively takes Burke's words out of context, but also violates his notion that good government, at home and overseas, cannot be based on contempt for the people by launching into a tirade against Gandhi who, in Beaverbrook's words, 'wants to dismantle the Empire': 'I despise him, begging bowl in one hand, dagger concealed in the other. Determined to prove the superiority of the primitive. I would happily trample him into the ground. What do these people know of law? Of grace? Cultivated living? They would overrun us, mark you. With their foul smells. Their obscene rituals. Animalism' (pp. 44–45). Burke, of course, argues that it is precisely such immoderate attitudes in rulers that foster rebellious thoughts in their subjects. A just and mild regime prevents the colonies from demanding Home Rule, a pursuit Bracken so deplores in the country of his birth that he no longer wishes to be associated with it. There are many layers of irony here, not the least of which is that Bracken dehumanises Gandhi by reducing him to an animal in the same way

Joyce does the 'Jew-pig' (p. 25), and denounces his peasant poverty for being a threat to the values of British civilisation much as Joyce despises the plutocrat with his 'fur coats at the opera' for threatening 'our British heritage' (p. 56).

Bracken relishes the rumour that he is the illegitimate son of Sir Winston Churchill and contends that he replaced Churchill's real son Randolph in his father's affections: 'Winston was, always will be, a father to me' (p. 25). Bracken's claim that both his real father and his brother Peter have 'the face of a condemned people' (p. 45, p. 89) goes to the heart of his self-hatred and explains why his origin must be 'totally suppressed' (p. 44) but always emerges again to haunt him when he is psychologically most vulnerable. When Bracken is not inventing his father and brother as members of the British establishment, he portrays them as villains and traitors. In actuality, Peter did indeed pester his brother Brendan for money and once stole the portrait of Burke from his London home to enforce his demands for a loan, and Bracken once declared his brother had been killed in action in the war, but Kilroy turns the brother into Bracken's shadow double or enemy within, who stands for all that he has suppressed, especially his Irish background. Bracken imagines Peter lurking beneath a lamp post outside his house from where he 'may never go away'. Popsie remarks that her lover appears to dread the moment his brother will appear on his doorstep to confront him with 'a bundle of possessions, the swaddling clothes of a lost child' (p. 47), reclaiming him for Ireland.

As for his actual father, Bracken refuses to acknowledge the 'Tipperary stonemason who was also a dynamite terrorist', as Joyce refers to him (p. 23), except in moments of extreme fear and crisis, most poignantly in the Oedipal scene during the Blitz when, terrified by the bombing, he 'remembers' his father belittling him in front of his brother: 'Come here, Peter, me son.... You'll stand up for Ireland, won't you, boy ... not like ... Brendan-Brendy, the little scut, Mammy's pet' (p. 51). This largely imagined father figure is close to the 'tyrannical shadow' or 'dark father' from whom, Bracken argues, revolutionaries everywhere try to distance themselves, to experience that brief sense of freedom before 'the space is filled again' (p. 34). For a man who believes in the Empire and deplores Ireland's separation from it, his confession to Beaverbrook is ironic in this regard: 'As a child, I was unfree. Every day of my childhood

I would say: Tomorrow, tomorrow I'm going to be free' (p. 43). Yet on other occasions Bracken admits that he is an 'orphan' and never knew his father, while simultaneously giving the impression that he has a deep longing for a father figure to 'fill in the space' left by the ogre constructed in his memory. 'Like every orphan' he claims to be travelling towards a closed door that will eventually reveal someone he will 'instantly recognise' (p. 35). Perhaps the face appearing in the doorway will resemble that of Winston Churchill, who to Bracken has been 'Like a father . . . Like a father' (p. 52); or perhaps the figure will, like his real father, have 'the face of a condemned people' (p. 45). The British Empire or revolutionary Ireland: which father will walk through that door to claim his true son?

At the end of *Double Cross*, Bracken appears to Joyce on the video screen in his prison cell '*as if behind bars or a grille of iron*', an image that can suggest the two men are on opposite sides of the partition, or each in his own cage. Bracken is seeking his brother, and although Joyce claims that '[y]our brother isn't here', he admits that there are many faces in the 'places of detention' that have the look 'of a condemned people' – his own presumably among them – and that Bracken should 'come back again, tomorrow' (p. 89). It is only fitting that both self-deniers should fail to recognise this brother figure in each other, and in themselves: both are prisoners of their inability to accept life as it really is, and in that sense, too, they are each other's doubles, and brothers beneath the skin. When Kilroy did some 'reshaping and rewriting' of the play in 2015 for a planned revival, this aspect of the work struck him especially: 'I came to realize that this is a play about a kind of fraternal relationship, a relationship born out of similarity but also out of enmity. The execution of Joyce became a fraternal killing in the rewriting. I became aware that there was, indeed, an ancient mythic shadow behind this play, that of the biblical Cain and Abel.'[42]

In his introduction to the Gallery Press edition of *Double Cross*, Kilroy states: 'I have always been fascinated by the fact that the act of deception is common to theatricality and criminality.'[43] The concept of role playing lies at the heart of *Double Cross*, as Deane wrote to Kilroy when his friend was still working on the script: 'Performance makes a man present to others rather than to himself; it is therefore opposed to self-consciousness; it gives action to privilege and disdains thought or contemplation. In its dandy form it is comic; in

Richard Howard and Stephen Rea in *Double Cross*, Field Day Theatre Company, 1986. Directed by Jim Sheridan. Photo copyright Field Day.

its revenge form it is violent; somewhere between these two you have William Joyce and Brendan Bracken.'[44] Given that Kilroy believed the root cause of his main characters' personality distortions – their performance of identity – was psychosexual, the scenes between the men and the women in their lives serve to crystallise the gap that exists between the absolutist ideal they strive for and the inevitable messiness of the lives they lead. Bracken's 'dream, an image' (p. 33) of English lawfulness, grace and cultivated living is given comic substance by Popsie's performance as a boy scout – her other costumes include a 'Highland tartan' and 'Florence Nightingale' – to embody and eroticise her lover's fantasy of British regimented pluck, servitude and fair play. Popsie realises that such a performance is of greater benefit to the audience than the actor: 'Perhaps one needs to distance oneself from roguery in order to enjoy it' (p. 34). Through their sexual relations, Bracken also reaches a level of awareness that his ideological quest is as hollow as his fabricated persona. Recognising, deep down, the impossibility of achieving his dream of perfection, he prefers a 'prolonged dalliance in the outer chambers' to 'proceeding to the inner sanctum' (p. 32). The 'composition' must be cherished as a stand-in for '[w]hat might otherwise be beyond our reach'; in fact, the entire purpose of art, and indeed of sex, might be '[t]he contrivance of what is really inaccessible' (pp. 32–33). An aesthetic distance must be maintained for the illusion of an absolute ideal to be sustained.

Joyce, who insists that, within their marriage, he and his wife Margaret should be free and above 'vulgar little middle-class inhibitions and restrictions' (p. 69), has a similar epiphany when he states that 'Freedom is just beyond what is, it is the perfection of our desires and therefore cannot be achieved in the present dimension' (p. 88). Indeed, his discovery of his wife's affair with Erich, the German she has been teaching English, exposes his own imperfection as it unleashes a prolonged tirade in which his attitude swings back and forth between needy insecurity and violent bullying. Even when facing the noose for treason, however, Joyce still deludes himself into thinking that he will be 'purged of all impurity' in death to defy 'the Jew-boy' beyond the grave (p. 25). His counterpart Bracken's last act in Part One is to write a letter to his mother (one of the liberties the play takes with the facts, since Bracken's mother died in 1928) in which he projects his own absolutist ideas about English civilisation onto her when he berates her for not putting behind her the memories of the horrible abuse she suffered at the hands of his father: 'one must utterly reject that which diminishes one, all that betrays one's higher instincts. One's sense of what it is to be civilized is what is important to one. There is nothing else' (p. 55).

Since for Bracken to be civilised is to be English, he attacks Joyce by stressing his own Britishness while playing up his opposite number's Irishness, calling him a '[v]ulgar little shit from Connemara' and a 'Paddy' (p. 22). Joyce, who in his racist radio rhetoric refers to 'the Jew' as 'the parasite of our British economy, the corrupter of our British heritage' (p. 56), projects these qualities onto Bracken when he calls him a 'poseur and parasite' (p. 22) and an 'effete degenerate' (p. 79), all while claiming to have 'more Norman blood' in his veins than the 'titled duds' in England who want him dead (p. 85). It is, of course, as Gerald Dawe argues, the claims to Englishness and the 'rhetoric of self-hate' that link Bracken with Joyce.[45] A casually racist attitude towards other peoples within the Empire was almost de rigueur among the English. This is evident even in Rebecca West's account of the trial of William Joyce, which she calls 'an Irish drama', when she describes the defendant as an example of 'the small, nippy, jig-dancing type of Irish peasant' who has 'the real Donnybrook air'.[46] The words, Kilroy comments, 'drip with that racism reserved for the next-door neighbour who having once been an exploited tenant now refuses to change address and go away'.[47] In *Double Cross*, Lord Castlerosse, who claims to be 'Irish' himself in the sense that he is 'Earl of Kenmare' and has 'a bit of a family seat in County Kerry' (p. 38), refers to Bracken as a 'flamboyant Celt' and 'a red-haired golliwog' (p. 37). Even Popsie's reference to Ireland as 'the land of the shamrock' (p. 35) betrays a belittling attitude towards the country. Oddly, then, in their anguish about national origins, Bracken and Joyce 'cast a strange murky but also chastening light upon the glum or complacent composure of Beaverbrook, Erich, Popsie, Castlerosse – all those who actually know their own places'.[48]

In *Double Cross*, Rebecca West is the model for the Actress in her guise as a 'lady journalist', although Kilroy stated in a note to the typescript of the play that he did not want 'to press the identification'.[49] Much of the language and imagery used by the Lady Journalist towards the end of the play is derived from West's account of Joyce's trial in her book *The Meaning of Treason* and serves the function of recapitulating what the play has shown of Joyce's persona and motivations. West mentions Joyce's 'Irish peasant background' on more than one occasion;[50] in *Double Cross* the Journalist rather absurdly considers Joyce's undernourishment to be 'the product of generations of peasant breeding' (p. 83) rather than the deprivations of the recent war. West makes much of the fact that there were 'strong traces of Irish origin in the followers of Joyce who watched the trial',[51] described as 'a group of wild and unhappy young men in Hitler raincoats with a look of Irishry about them'.[52] Although Joyce himself claimed to be of pure British descent, West suggests that the families of these 'wild Irishmen' had 'the same roots as the Joyces, who had been supporters of the British occupation of Ireland and who had had to leave the country for safety's sake when Home Rule was granted'.[53] In West's view, such 'native Irish . . . often felt a love of England which struck English people as excessive and theatrical',[54] all the more so because the love was for 'an obsolete England'[55] that no longer existed; therefore they showed no gratitude when Joyce betrayed 'his real motherland', Ireland, for it.[56]

In the Journalist's monologue that closes *Double Cross*, the focus is on Joyce's followers:

> What I remember was the group of young fascists, the acolytes, the loyal ones, the young men in the gallery, those pale, blue faces, their dark, shining eyes, that look of inspired poverty, inspired promise. They were weeping. Those lilting Celtic voices in grief at the death of their christus. They put on their old raincoats, like vestments, and talked raucously of patriotism. It was as if they had taken the idea of England to some terrible logical meaning of their own which England itself could never tolerate. And before they left in the rain for some secret meeting, some illicit upper-room, the tears poured down those long, emaciated, Celtic faces. They wept for Joyce. They wept for England. (p. 90)

The note of fascism as religion is palpable here, and presented in more concisely lyrical terms than West's observation that in modern times, politics has taken the place of religion, and that political leaders who 'bring to earth . . . the God for whom their ancestors had always hungered' inevitably surround themselves with a hard core of loyal followers 'to terrorize those more critical'.[57] In *Double Cross*, the Journalist's description of Joyce's followers conveys a messianic element in the young fascists' infatuation with their leader, while the words 'acolytes', 'christus', and 'vestments' evoke an overtly Christian context that could be Catholic or Protestant. The faces are 'Celtic' rather than 'Irish' to include a broader spectrum of followers, including Scottish – Joyce's best friend was a Scotsman named Angus MacNab – or, indeed, Ulster Scots. Kilroy's anger at the sectarian nature of 'the whole North business' seems relevant here. In an interview with Ciaran Carty shortly before *Double Cross* opened in London at the end of the 1986 Field Day tour, he argued that the 'pathological hatred' of the Northern Irish conflict resulted from 'the collision of two completely absolutist Christian creeds', and expressed scepticism at the possibility of rational political discourse 'while you have this incredible primitive religion inborn on the two sides'.[58] Within the context of a Field Day production, then, the 'patriotism' of which Joyce's acolytes speak, and the idea of England they construct 'which England itself could never tolerate', is surely meant to resonate with the most extreme forms of both sectarian nationalisms on the island of Ireland.

After the play's opening run in Derry's Guildhall, Field Day took *Double Cross* on tour through Northern Ireland and the Republic and on to England. As Trotter suggests, 'the *face* of the company changed with its *interface* with each new community. *Double Cross* . . . looked very different in performance at the Guild Hall in Derry, at the small Hawk's Well Theatre in Sligo, and at the Royal Court in London.' In each new context, the play 'challenged the community . . . to examine personal and communal connections to the idea of Ireland'.[59] For that reason, reactions to the play were very different in the two parts of the island, and from town to town. Brian Friel attended the performance in Coleraine and sensed the audience stiffening at 'every reference to Englishness/loyalty/treason' and so on.[60] Helen Dady observed that, while Dubliners might be amused at a set 'featuring an enormous Union Jack' and the inclusion of 'a phrase such as "No man can decide for himself what it is to be loyal to the Crown – it is decided for him"', these same expressions were received 'with tense attentiveness in Portadown, Northern Ireland, scene of such loyalist unrest in recent weeks'. London audiences, on the other hand, 'may not draw such parallels with contemporary politics'.[61] Nevertheless, John Cunningham's review in *The Guardian* noted that the dangers of an exaggerated notion of nationalism and patriotism are something 'Little Englanders need to think about' as well as 'Little Irelanders – North and South'.[62] In his review in the Irish *Evening Press*, Timothy O'Grady provocatively remarked on the powerful significance of the opening performance of *Double Cross* in Derry's Guildhall, 'where just outside British troops patrol the road, and further out, unionists, in their Irish way, attempt to convince the English that they are as British as themselves'.[63] Reviewing the published text of the play in 1987 for *Fortnight*, Ruth Sherry suggested it might be 'an oblique contribution to the rather incoherent debate on neutrality recently conducted in the Republic'.[64] Several years later, commenting on the newly published Gallery Press edition of *Double Cross*, a reviewer noted the topicality of the play's theme 'in view of the passions aroused by Conor Cruise O'Brien's journey from anti-partitionist propagandist in the old Department of External Affairs to pro-British advocate in Bob McCartney's UK Unionist Party'.[65] When the Abbey Theatre announced the revival of *Double Cross* for the autumn of 2018, co-produced with the Lyric Theatre, Belfast, its website noted that the play's focus on the propaganda battle between Bracken and Joyce 'takes on a new relevance in an era of heightened nationalism and "fake news"'.[66]

Overall, *Double Cross* was well received, although it was generally criticised for being an undramatic, even static play. Commenting on a draft of the script in a letter to Kilroy, Deane had compared it to a 'lecture with slides', albeit an absorbing one,[67] and this quality in the finished play remained an issue for some reviewers. When *Double Cross* opened, Kilroy's agent Peggy Ramsay declared it extremely interesting and 'frightfully well staged and performed' but was not sure 'that it was a play as we know it'.[68] Kilroy himself felt he was continuing an experimental theatrical strand he had begun with *Talbot's Box* in 1977, which meant doing away with a naturalistic plot and trying to create a dramatic environment that would allow an intellectual response to the action on stage; some reviews indeed called the play 'technically exciting', but while David Nowlan found it 'intellectually absorbing' he also warned that it 'failed dangerously to engage the emotions', especially in the first half.[69] Kilroy thought the problem stemmed from the origin of the first part in 'radio writing'; additionally, because he had investigated Bracken so thoroughly in that context, he had become more interested in the Joyce material while writing the stage play.[70] He was still tweaking Part One by the time the play was transitioning to the Royal Court in London, after its tour of Northern Ireland and the Republic. Around that time, the BBC finally broadcast the radio play *That Man Bracken*, in which Alan Rickman, who had also appeared in Kilroy's 1981 version of Chekhov's *The Seagull*, gave 'an exceptional, and outsize performance' in the title role.[71]

With *Double Cross*, Kilroy intended to write a play about nationalism as a 'dark burden, a source of trauma and debilitation'. Using the Second World War setting as a platform for making a broader point about extremism and absolutism of any kind, he showed the dangerous absurdity of, on the one hand, basing one's identity exclusively on a mystical sense of place, and, on the other, dedicating one's life to the systematic betrayal of the same notion.[72] This is serious and demanding theatrical fare; in contrast, Kilroy conceived his next play, produced by Field Day in 1991, as a comedy, in much the same way Brian Friel had counterbalanced his 1980 Field Day play *Translations* with the more lighthearted *The Communication Cord* two years later. While Kilroy had dedicated *Double Cross* to Field Day director Seamus Deane, the dedication in *The Madame MacAdam Travelling Theatre*, 'for Julie', is to his wife, Julia Carlson. These inscriptions indicate crucial ways in which the two plays differ: while *Double Cross* explores the negative implications of such concepts as identity and nationalism, fascism and empire, the later play, while sharing many of the earlier work's themes, is ultimately about the healing power of individual human relations. Kilroy suggests that life itself in all its weakness and frailty is intolerable to the fascist. Brendan Bracken and William Joyce share this inability to accept life's insecurities and messy contradictions; the main characters of *The Madame MacAdam Travelling Theatre* eventually come to recognise the importance of embracing whatever life throws at them, unconditionally and in all its ambiguity.

3

Mum's the Word: *The Madame MacAdam Travelling Theatre*

In *Double Cross*, Kilroy wrote about the dark side of nationalism within the contexts of both the British Empire and the Third Reich. From the perspective adopted in that play, Irish neutrality during the Second World War might be viewed as the evasion of a choice between two negative extremes; however, Kilroy's second Field Day play, *The Madame MacAdam Travelling Theatre*, depicts the insularity of the 'Emergency' rather as an occasion for nationalist paranoia. The Emergency Powers Act of 1939 suspended the operations of the Irish Parliament and handed the government broad powers to take any action necessary to safeguard Irish neutrality. The government's main concern in that regard was not only that Germany might attempt to invade Ireland, but also that Britain might seize back and occupy the Treaty Ports they had surrendered to the Free State only the year before. Unlike some recent historians who argue that neutrality was less 'a policy forged in isolation' than a strategy designed, against a full awareness of the changing international order, to 'put Ireland first',[1] Kilroy depicts neutral Ireland as a small-minded country in the grip of self-righteousness and xenophobia. Speaking the day before the play's opening in Derry on 9 September 1991, he explained that its subject matter came out of his interest in 'the psychology of fascism, insane militarism growing out of repression, fear of the foreign', themes that also informed *Double Cross*.[2]

More lighthearted than its predecessor, *The Madame MacAdam Travelling Theatre* overtly advocates the rejection of dead certainty and rigidity in favour of life-affirming conditionality and doubt. The play's eponymous heroine heads a small fit-up theatre troupe which, while touring Northern Ireland during the early war years, has strayed across the border and now finds itself stranded, due to the wartime petrol shortage, in a small provincial town. 'Someone mentioned the Free State,' Madame explains in her opening monologue. 'The name beckoned. So here we are!'[3] But no sooner have the actors entered the town than 'Bun' Bourke, baker by day and leader of the Local Defence Force (LDF) by night, spots the potential threat of a foreign invasion. During the war years, the auxiliary forces of the LDF took over many duties of the regular army; through the figure of Bourke, Kilroy suggests that a little power in the hands of a paranoid man in uniform can be a dangerous thing. The Squad Leader is feeling the pressure 'with the whole fuckin' country under possible attack' from the 'Jerries', the 'Tommies', the 'Yanks', and the 'fuckin' Japs' (p. 3); the fact that a young child has gone missing in the town only adds to his combative zeal. Although the actors' van has the theatre company name emblazoned on it in bright letters, Bourke orders his squad to surround the vehicle and take prisoners if necessary. What from a global perspective looks like a comically misguided, overambitious move turns, on the small, enclosed stage of neutral Ireland, into a menacing act that threatens to restrict the freedom of innocent individuals and violate their personal dignity. As such, the LDF leader's actions and mindset come to represent the broader culture of repression and containment prevalent in mid-century Ireland that forms such an important thematic strand in Kilroy's oeuvre.

The Madame MacAdam Travelling Theatre was commissioned for the Royal Court Theatre by its artistic director, Max Stafford-Clark, who also intended to direct the play. In January 1990, having read the first complete draft of the script then called 'Mrs MacAdams' Travelling Show', he characterised the writing as 'strong, witty and engaging', but felt that the work's 'important subject' needed a 'harder edge': while the play hinted at 'serious and grave moments', they needed 'some digging out'.[4] Between early March and late May Kilroy sent the script, now bearing its final title, to various literary friends for feedback. John McGahern declared he was delighted with the work, which he felt might prove itself 'a hit', 'but that is a dangerous invocation'.[5] Seamus Deane thought the 'marvellous piece' was unmistakably 'Kilrovian'.[6] Christopher Fitz-Simon, too, was '*greatly* taken' by *Madame MacAdam*, finding its expression and technique 'wonderfully economical' and its equation between actors in costume and fascists in uniform 'illuminating, and great fun'. The theatricality of the piece especially appealed to him, and he predicted that the opening of the troupe's 'mobile booth' would be 'stunning on the stage!'[7] His letter, however, reminded Kilroy that he had, years before, promised the Abbey Theatre (under Joe Dowling's artistic directorship) a play on an identical subject.[8] To redress this oversight, Kilroy gave the Abbey first refusal in any co-production of the play.

By mid-November, Stafford-Clark had agreed that *Madame MacAdam* be presented as a co-production with the Abbey, but neither it nor the Royal Court had yet offered a contract. Around this time, the company that had produced *Double Cross* also expressed an interest in the work: 'A play about a touring theatre company roving around Ireland sounds ideal for Field Day and would, I'm sure, be popular on a Field Day tour.'[9] Stafford-Clark would not finalise details of the production until Garry Hynes had taken up her position as the Abbey's artistic director in January 1991. By the third week of that month, after two days reading through the play with actors, he expressed the view that, while he still admired the 'breadth and ambition' of the piece, he also felt that Kilroy's 'determination to entertain' had led him away from 'the intellectual debate' so characteristic of his work: 'In fact the comedic situation makes the play seem lightweight.'[10] The following day, the Royal Court's literary manager, Mel Kenyon, also opined that, while the play 'could provide a strong analogy and comment on what is happening at this very moment', it would have to be 'more dangerous in the tactics it employs'.[11] Distressed by Stafford-Clark's assessment in particular, Kilroy decided, in the absence of a firm commitment to the play from the Royal Court, to give *Madame MacAdam* to Field Day. An arrangement was eventually reached that would see the play move to London in December 1991, after Field Day had finished touring it in Ireland.

Before this agreement was reached, and while Kilroy was still revising *Madame MacAdam* for Stafford-Clark, Jim Nolan, the artistic director of Waterford's Red Kettle Theatre Company, which had successfully staged a revival of *Talbot's Box* in 1988, requested that he be allowed to produce the first Irish revival of *Madame MacAdam* – the script of which he had read and admired – after its planned staging in Dublin and London. When Kilroy decided to offer the play to Field Day, the search for a director led, perhaps not surprisingly, to Nolan. The Field Day production opened at the Guildhall in Derry, followed by a punishing ten-week touring schedule that included stops in Galway, Tullamore, Claremorris, Cavan, Sligo, Armagh, Enniskillen, Omagh, Andersonstown, Downpatrick, Coleraine, Newry, Dublin (for the Theatre Festival), Belfast, Callan, Cork, Ennis and Limerick.

The Madame MacAdam Travelling Theatre is a self-consciously theatrical comedy, both in theme and execution, focusing on costuming and performance as a means of illumination, empowerment and deception, both on and off the stage. Kilroy has described the play as being 'about Theatre, its limits, its magic and what happens when the "theatrical" meets "real" life'.[12] Drawing on techniques of epic theatre, the work employs an episodic structure and uses distancing devices such as direct address to the audience. Each scene is introduced with a brief synopsis, which could be projected onto a screen or shown on placards; in the Field Day production the words were spoken by the recorded voice of Stephen Rea (who had no other part in the play) accompanied by ragtime piano.[13] Against the sounds of an overhead bomber and the sputtering engine noise of the troupe's dying van, the text displayed at the beginning of the play's opening scene provides context, presents the main character, and introduces the two main plot strands:

> *Music. Projection:* The World at War! Enter Madame MacAdam. The lost child. And the doctoring of a dog.

In her opening speech, Madame reiterates that the plot will contain 'the usual fare. A love story. A lost child. Villainy at large' (p. 1).

Madame MacAdam takes its inspiration in part from theatrical companies like Anew McMaster's renowned fit-up company, which toured the Irish provinces from 1925 until 1959, and from the Shakespearean plays that featured so prominently in its repertoire. In Kilroy's play, the rural Free State is a place of magic and transformation far removed from civilisation; neutral Ireland takes on the quality of the slightly otherworldly locations of Shakespeare's comedies and romances such as *The Tempest*, *Twelfth Night* and *A Winter's Tale*, elements of which also inform the plot.

The play's focus on performance and costuming is expressed in the juxtaposition of Madame's thespians with the authority figures in the town. Bourke the baker has as much invested in role playing as the actors and, early on in the play, berates his LDF corporal for addressing him as the wrong character: 'Listen, you fuckin' eedjit. Don't call me Bun. D'ya hear! In this uniform I'm not Bun Bourke. I'm Squad Leader Bourke' (p. 2). It is also the uniform that turns the local Garda Sergeant – an 'overly affectionate version' of Kilroy's own father[14] – into an authority figure, but he is less comfortable with that role, and more aware of the licence it affords to abuse the power it represents. When he catches himself sternly interrogating his own daughter Marie-Therese, he ruefully remarks that '[t]here's times I feel this uniform melting into me skin' (p. 10). Yet at night in his own kitchen, with the uniform unbuttoned, the authoritarian role is easily exchanged for that of petty criminal, as the Sergeant plots with a couple of local dog fanciers to pass off a winning greyhound as a known loser (Dixie's Wonder, now deceased), with the help of axle-grease and black lead, in order to fool and defraud the bookmakers.[15] Although many reviewers of the play found this plot strand fanciful and distracting, it humorously illustrates the notion that deception and disguise are inherent features of criminality and theatricality alike, in addition to perfectly capturing the local colour of the period; greyhound racetracks had begun to appear on the outskirts of towns in the late 1930s, and were 'a magnet for organised gambling, according to the loudly disapproving Church authorities'.[16] To prevent the canine deception from being discovered, the Sergeant plans to have the English actors masquerade as overseas buyers of the fraudulent dog so that it can be quickly removed from the scene without arousing suspicion. In return, the actors will receive black market petrol, so that they, too, can make their getaway.

While Kilroy intended the sudden arrival of the theatre company in Ireland during a time of war to constitute a humorous 'English invasion of sorts',[17] Madame's dwindling troupe of actors represents a diversity of British regional and personal identities. The lady herself is middle class and English, from 'the banks of the Severn' (p. 33); veteran performer Lyle Jones – imagined by Kilroy in his initial outline for the play as 'fruity, middle-aged, narcissistic, of uncertain sexual orientation'[18] – came out of 'the Welsh valleys' (p. 32); Rabe is a young Jewish actor from London's East End; and Sally joined the troupe in Belfast. Kilroy originally envisaged Madame MacAdam as 'a large fat lady, manager, ticket-seller, occasional actress and singer of light operatic songs to her own accompaniment' on the piano.[19] The French form of the courtesy title as well as some of her talents echo the characteristics and accomplishments of a stalwart of the Irish theatre scene in the first half of the twentieth century, the versatile Madame Bannard Cogley, who ran a cabaret in Hardwicke Street as well as a small studio theatre club, the Little Theatre. A friend of Edwards and Mac Liammóir, who called her 'Toto', she served on the Gate Theatre's board of directors as one of its founding members, as well as making costumes for its productions in the early years of the theatre's existence. She acted as Helen Carter and, having studied at the Paris Conservatoire, also performed as a soprano vocalist under the name Daisy Bannard. All Madame Cogley's accomplishments – acting, singing, managing a theatre – mirror those of Madame MacAdam in Kilroy's play.

As a boy in County Kilkenny, Kilroy saw Anew McMaster in some of his greatest performances; the actor also visited his boarding school to talk about *Hamlet*, performing 'a kind of one-man version' of the play in which he took on all the different parts himself, including Ophelia.[20] Fitz-Simon, in a 1991 article commemorating the centenary of the actor-manager's birth (in Birkenhead, England), remarked that many who saw *Madame MacAdam* took the character Lyle Jones 'to be his portrait – the Field Day programme certainly implied this – when it should have been clear that Jones was merely the caricature of a type'.[21] McMaster was affectionately known as 'Mac'; indeed, Harold Pinter's brief memoir of his two years touring with the company in the early 1950s bears that title. Kilroy's habit of referring in correspondence to his play and its main character as 'Madame Mac' suggests that McMaster was one of the models for Madame MacAdam as much as he was an inspiration behind Lyle Jones. But Madame Mac was also partly based on McMaster's wife. Marjorie McMaster, Micheál Mac Liammóir's sister, was always referred to by her husband as 'Mummy', and made all the business arrangements for the touring company: 'She was tough, critical, cultivated, devoted. Her spirit and belief constituted the backbone of the company. There would have been no company without her.'[22] Madame MacAdam, too, is in charge of her theatre's affairs, and Jones habitually addresses her as 'Mumsie'; indeed, motherhood is a pivotal motif in the play. But if Kilroy's Madame Mac is descended from 'Adam' rather than a 'Master', it is because the thematic emphasis of the play is not on mastery, which suggests a culmination in perfection and completion, but on human fallibility and changeability. The Sergeant points to this when he observes that fickleness is 'the curse of Adam. . . . There's a crack down the middle of the human specimen and no doubt about it' (p. 35). This human propensity to fall from grace implies the perpetual need to start anew, if only, inevitably, to fail again – albeit, perhaps, better. 'To begin once more!' (p. 77) is Madame MacAdam's final line in the play.

Shortly after their arrival in the Free State, the actors of Madame's troupe put on a cliché-ridden, truncated Hibernian melodrama about the revolutionary hero Robert Emmet, the kind of play Lyle Jones says the Irish 'simply adore' (p. 17). The performance of this little play within the play helps establish some key points Kilroy goes on to develop in the course of *Madame MacAdam*, not least about the power of deception and make-believe, since the role of Emmet, who was twenty-five when he was executed, is played by Jones, a middle-aged Welshman, while Belfast-born Sally performs the part of Sarah Curran, with the English Madame MacAdam serving as her Irish maid Annie Devlin. Emmet's hopes 'to free Ireland from the Saxon yoke' (p. 15) are dashed when he is arrested by Major Sirr on the charge of high treason, and he is led off to his trial noting that he has been betrayed by his nearest and dearest: 'Is it not ever the story of Irish patriots?' Accompanying sounds of '*uproar, shouts, hand-clapping, pounding of heels on the floor*' suggest the complete involvement of the spectators in the proceedings on stage. 'We actors are the creation of our audiences,' Jones pronounces afterwards; should they cease to believe, the show would collapse (pp. 16–17). The comment has particular relevance for what *Madame MacAdam* goes on to suggest about the theatrical aspects of the Second World War, when the costumes are uniforms, and the script is inspired by hardline ideology.

In *Madame MacAdam*, the idea that there is a 'crack down the middle' of human beings, with one side tending towards deception and darkness, the other towards positive transformation and enlightenment, is humorously brought home when Jones, as Emmet, inadvertently launches into the wrong curtain lines. Instead of the famous speech from the dock, the actor recites the last thoughts of Sydney Carton from Charles Dickens' *A Tale of Two Cities* – dramatised numerous times, including by Mac Liammóir in 1945[23] – which takes place in London and Paris during the French Revolution:

> My dear – it is a far, far better thing that I do, than I have ever done; it is a far, far better rest that I go – (*Wrong play: quick change.*) No! Think only of this when I am gone. When my country takes its place among the nations of the earth – then and not till then let my epitaph be written – (p. 17)

In Dickens' tale, Charles Darnay, a noble-minded Frenchman who has renounced his aristocratic background and left his country for London, has happily married Lucie Manette, for whom the English Carton, a reckless and alcoholic lawyer, also harbours an unrequited love. When Darnay, having returned to Paris, is arrested and condemned to death, Carton manages to rescue his rival, to whom he bears a striking resemblance, and take his place on the scaffold, motivated by his devotion to Lucie. The tale thus sets up a complex plot of doubles, of two characters and two cities that are both opposites and antagonists as well as each other's mirror image. The Hibernian melodrama about Emmet performed in *Madame MacAdam* serves to make a similar point by having the actor Rabe, who as a Jew is a member of a victimised minority, perform the part of Major Sirr, the colonial oppressor within the early nineteenth-century setting of the play. Rabe's casting against type is an instance of theatrical transformation and make-believe, but the facility with which he plays the part of the villain also hints at the complexity of his own character as revealed in the course of Kilroy's play. Victim and perpetrator are not always as easily distinguishable from each other as they are in melodrama.

Lyle Jones' quick turn back into the finale of Emmet's speech sets up a curtain line that reflects as much on the 'Emergency' as it does on the aftermath of the United Irishmen's rebellion. Emmet's defiant words – 'When my country takes its place among the nations of the earth – then and not till then let my epitaph be written' – are certainly ironic in light of the desire of the Irish government during the Second World War 'to remain outside the quarrels of the great ruling countries of the world and to rebuild her own civilisation undisturbed by world rivalries', as Joseph P. Walshe wrote in a memorandum to Taoiseach Éamon de Valera in August 1939.[24] After the end of the global conflict, however, Ireland went on, in 1955, to join the United Nations (but not NATO), and in 1973 gained membership in the European Economic Community. At the time of the play's premiere in 1991, audiences might have had reason to believe that the time had indeed arrived to write Emmet's epitaph; given the continued presence of the border, however, the extent to which the Irish themselves could be considered 'united' remained an open question.

In *Madame MacAdam*, the farcical plot line about the deception involving a painted greyhound is counterbalanced by the much darker story of Rabe, which Kilroy included to bring the Nazi horror into an essentially comic play. Rabe is one of the most complex characters in *Madame MacAdam*. The splitting headaches from which he periodically suffers are an indication of his schizophrenic personality, itself a manifestation of the post-lapsarian 'crack down the middle of the human specimen' that allows the potential for good and evil to co-exist within the same person. The disturbing involuntary memories triggered during these spells point to a history of mental illness involving confinement to padded rooms, which merge in his troubled mind with police cells and interrogation chambers. Before Rabe joined the theatre, back in London's East End, the Blackshirts had humiliated his father by forcing him to dance while they burned down his shop; Rabe's own taunting of the fascists earned him a severe beating that has left him traumatised. While he is himself a victim of racism and violence, the young actor also shares a similar attitude of intolerance with his victimisers; he cannot abide failure and is filled with hatred at his father's weakness. His inability to 'abide half-measures' (p. 18) makes him cruel, particularly to Lyle Jones, who is always willing to improvise and compromise to make the show go on. When Jones boasts to the Sergeant that he was 'in the Haymarket in twenty-seven', Rabe 'outs' him by adding that the actor was also 'up for buggery twice in Bow Street', an 'unnecessary barb' intended only to inflict hurt (p. 27). Rabe's own wounds are often self-inflicted, literally in the case of his chronic shoulder injury sustained by throwing himself at doors and walls. This double role as both victim and perpetrator plays itself out vividly in his dreams, where he imagines himself performing the part of the hunter as well as the prey. His arrest by Bun Bourke on suspicion of abducting the little girl actualises the scenario already written in his head: 'Now I know what it is! To be the knife and the wound. To be the killer and the dead child' (p. 51). Rabe's absolutism connects him with his nemesis: both he and the LDF leader lack the human quality of playfulness, the one thing Madame MacAdam tells Rabe he can learn from Lyle. While he never learns to address failings in others in a way that is neither untrue nor unkind, Rabe has moments of self-loathing when he realises that he is 'just full of shit' (p. 19), and may be 'an emotional monster, stunted, like a dwarf' (p. 23); but it is typical of his character that he always disengages himself from such insights mere moments later.

Throughout much of his career, Kilroy has been fascinated with 'artists who are actually monstrous in their private lives'.[25] Oscar Wilde as depicted in *The Secret Fall of Constance Wilde* is an example of a man in pursuit of an ideal at the expense of his family; Nell Jeffrey in *The Shape of Metal*, too, is nothing short of ruthless in her quest for artistic perfection; and in *Blake*, William Blake's fanatical traits threaten his marital happiness as well as his sanity. Rabe's uncompromising search for 'the impossible, perfect performance' (p. 65), in life as well as on the stage, illustrates the paradox that theatre is an art in which 'the most dreadful shits in the world can create moments of sublime beauty'.[26] Much like Blake in the later play, Rabe compensates for his inability to be emotionally close to others with promiscuity: brief, intense sexual encounters from which he walks away when they are over. He sleeps with Sally as well as Marie-Therese's friend Jo, and even in his final moments with Madame MacAdam can only express his indebtedness to her by making sexual advances. Madame understands that Rabe's detachment is the source of his energy and creativity; living intensely in the moment, he 'burns away everything each time to make a clean start' (p. 65). On stage, that makes for electrifying performances; as a human being, however, it makes him, as Jo observes, 'very empty' (p. 65) and something of a lost soul.

The 'lost child' motif in *Madame MacAdam* derives in part from Kilroy's love for Shakespeare's late plays, *Pericles* (Perdita), *A Winter's Tale* (Marina), and *The Tempest* (Miranda). Jo is the catalyst in the play behind the motif, which Kilroy has likened to 'a spring to unlock a series of notions, to unloose . . . one of the great primal themes'.[27] Unsettled by the absence of her parents, who are working in a factory in England, she translates her need to love and be loved into the desire to have a baby, which has led her to take a neglected toddler from her home so that she can take care of her, just for a day. She also embarks on a sexual relationship with Rabe, another damaged individual in need of healing. When the little girl disappears from her hiding place, Jo begins to understand that life's desires cannot be so easily plotted and controlled. While the townspeople search for the missing child – a Shakespearean Perdita figure – Jo, a lost child herself, harbours her secret and confesses it only to Rabe. But his problems make it impossible for him to become emotionally invested in their relationship; he channels all his nervous energy into acting. For Kilroy, the heart of the play is how Jo moves from play-acting at having a child and a loving partner into accepting the much more prosaic nature of reality. Hers is a story of survival – 'the story of a girl who, out of *loss*, comes to experience regeneration, restoration'.[28]

Suspecting the foreign actors of abducting the missing child, Bourke decides to raid their van just when Rabe and Jo are inside, making love. Bun's aggressive banging on the side of the vehicle brings on one of Rabe's turns. Recoiling in fear, he points to something Jo cannot see but the play's audience can: 'Across the back in silhouette, the figures of Bun Bourke and his LDF Men but now in Nazi uniforms' (p. 49). Part One of the play ends here; Part Two opens with the naked figures of Rabe and Jo being pushed into the light by the uniformed LDF men.[29] Bun had earlier expressed his dislike of actors: 'Pure people don't carry on, putting on the act, trying to be what they're not' (p. 46). The stark contrast between the lovers' private, vulnerable nakedness and the authoritarian uniforms of their armed captors puts that statement in a darkly ironic light.

When Rabe is eventually released through the intervention of the Sergeant, he has been badly beaten. Sally, the most practical of all the characters, decides to take him away with her to Belfast, to try and protect him from further harm. She loves Rabe precisely because, unlike Jo, she harbours no illusions about him: 'I like the way he shifts about. I like the way you never know with him. I've had me fill in me time of the other sort. Where I come from the men are all full of bibles and silence and cocoa. I like the way Rabe is always changing' (p. 44). The pair's departure is witnessed by Jo, who realises she has seen the last of Rabe. Taken under Madame's maternal wing, she quickly gets over her infatuation with him, as Madame helps her see that the idealised 'pictures' of Rabe in her head differ from the behaviour she has perceived with her own eyes: 'That is the first step towards lucidity. . . . Never romanticize failure, my dear' (p. 65). Imperfections and complications must be faced and accepted if they are to be overcome. But Jo cannot so soon forget what was done to Rabe: 'They shouldn't have beaten him like that . . . No-one should ever be treated like that, ever' (p. 67). It is her ability to show compassion for the man who has just abandoned her that makes Jo the moral compass of the play.

For Madame MacAdam, the 'glorious miracle of theatre', as Rabe facetiously refers to it, has nothing to do with costumes or make-believe, nor is it akin to a religious experience: theatre 'is built upon acceptance . . . It is built upon human error and human frailty . . . It is built upon patience with what actually exists. Not some cloud-cuckoo-land' (p. 37). This acceptance of life's imperfection also means that, in art, there may be 'no resolution', no 'victory' or 'laurels' (p. 53), but that is the point: 'If we bear witness to the steady pulse of the world there is no miracle which we may not accomplish upon the stage' (p. 37). By contrast, Squadron Leader Bourke's immorality is bound up with his rigidity and his one-dimensional belief in the power of the uniform. His final act in *Madame MacAdam* is to steal the actors' costumes from their departing van, without which he believes they will be unable to perform: 'We have 'em now, boys. Where'll they be now without their gee-gaws? Naked fuckers. Stripped' (p. 77). The statement combines the fascist's perverse desire to humiliate the powerless with his belief that a costume is an identity. 'I'm afraid that is another lesson to be learned from the theatre,' Madame MacAdam tells Jo. 'Once one puts on a uniform one is in danger of unleashing one's violence' (pp. 66–67). Unlike Bourke, the Sergeant eventually realises that the law cannot simply be put on and off with the official trappings of the office. His eyes are opened after the fateful greyhound race, when Jones, pretending to be the English buyer of the dog, disperses an angry and suspicious mob with his stentorian rendering of a speech from *Coriolanus*: 'You common cry of curs, whose breath I hate . . . Hence! Begone!' (p. 69). Lyle marvels at having triumphed 'by actually emptying the house', but Madame sees the reversal as a violation of 'the very principle of theatre' (p. 70). The performance constitutes a moment when the illusion of theatre overlaps perfectly with the deception of criminality, and as such forms 'the moral turning point' of the play.[30] The Sergeant vows to give up his dubious greyhound-related activities, and refuses to be persuaded by his accomplice's argument that the tendency to bend the rules is only human: 'Sure, wasn't the first gambler Adam and his apple?' (p. 72). Even then, he still cannot fathom that 'the very principle of theatre' does not reside in disguise and grease paint. Having belatedly rescued the troupe's 'poor looking enough' costumes from the LDF after the actors' van has departed, he wonders, much like Bourke, what the performers will do now 'without their bits of covering and their hokery pokery' (p. 78).

Kilroy saw 'the act of healing of Jo by Madame MacAdam' as the heart of the play: 'Everything else is context. We are always trying to change reality – it is our nature – through art, through war, through criminality, in our dreams. But only the action of one human on another can make a real transformation. By imitating this action theatre can share in it, if vicariously.'[31] In the theatre, costuming and performance are only a vehicle to get at 'the essential' (p. 65), which is the nakedness underneath. Madame MacAdam's main lesson to Jo, taught by example, is self-knowledge and self-reliance, for only someone comfortable in their own skin can compassionately open up to others. When Jo finds that she may be pregnant, Madame again combines maternal counsel with the advice to be self-sufficient and introspective: 'At a certain point of balance all is silence. Then one can re-emerge and face the mad tumult once more. . . . But mum's the word. Mum's the word, now' (p. 68). Jo ends the play 'preoccupied, withdrawn into herself' (p. 78). Madame MacAdam's wisdom, that 'we must never confuse theatre and everyday life' (p. 57), also applies here, since the child Jo is carrying takes the place of the stolen child, who is happily discovered as she wanders out of the wood in an appropriately Shakespearean romance resolution.

The outcome of Jo's predicament may not be so straightforward. The ending of the plot line she has set in motion is also the moment for a reality check. What *Madame MacAdam* leaves implicit (because it is a comedy) is that, just as failure should never be romanticised, the fulfilment of Jo's wish to 'have a baby' – the symbolic embodiment

Kevin Flood and Conor McDermottroe in *The Madame MacAdam Travelling Theatre*, Field Day Theatre Company, 1991. Directed by Jim Nolan. Photo copyright Field Day.

of a new beginning – should not be idealised either. Hers is, after all, an out-of-wedlock teenage pregnancy, and this is Catholic Ireland in the 1940s. Kilroy's 2010 play *Christ, Deliver Us!*, set in the 1950s, deals more explicitly with the same subject matter, and its depiction of Winnie Butler's ordeal in similar circumstances does not leave much room for optimism. In *Madame MacAdam* Jo represents the promise of the future, but her pensiveness in the closing scene may suggest her realisation that the road ahead will be bumpy, and qualifies to some degree her earlier confident statement to Madame that, after what she has been through, she can 'face anything now' (p. 57).

If the play's centre is meant to be 'the act of healing of Jo by Madame MacAdam', this ending in pensive contemplation may be too subtle to bring that point across. Anthony Roche remarks that 'Jo is the most overlooked character in the play' and 'the most clear-sighted', and that, given her centrality to the theme of healing transformation and her embodiment of the future, she 'might have had the direction of the play more fully entrusted to her'.[32] Instead, when Kilroy took *Madame MacAdam* through various rounds of revision during the 1990s, he concentrated on the play's structure and on repositioning characters other than Jo. For the 1992 New York production by the Irish Repertory Theatre, his focus was on turning Madame MacAdam into 'a Prospero-like figure' which would 'theatricalize everything'.[33] For a potential stage production in England, he proposed to make Madame 'a sort of Mistress of Ceremonies' who would conduct the entire narrative; Rabe would become 'more a prankster-performer', and the relationship between 'him and the young girl Jo, Madame and Sally . . . more overtly sexually-competitive'.[34] A possible screen adaptation for English television did send Kilroy back to Jo and Rabe, but rather than concentrate fully on strengthening the girl's perspective, he asked more questions about her lover: 'What effect does the whole experience have on *him*? . . . *Why* does he run away with Sally?'[35] Other than the revamped version of the play staged in New York, none of these revised scripts proceeded to the production stage.

On the eve of the original Field Day production's opening in 1991, the *Sunday Business Post* raised expectations by reporting that *Madame MacAdam* 'is billed as a hugely entertaining comedy' whose central device of a touring truck on stage 'is going to impress'.[36] Once the play was under way, however, many reviewers found themselves less than impressed, and were especially troubled by its many-layered and episodic structure. Christopher Murray attributed the hostile reviews from the Dublin critics to their refusal 'to see, to accept, what was in front of them', namely 'a world not of realism but of deliberate make-believe', where 'tradition, rituals, history, pain can all be miraculously transformed'.[37] Only a handful of reviewers were prepared to engage seriously with the play's intellectual and structural challenges. The *Ulster Newsletter* noted the 'distinct Fascist overtones' of the Free State and thanked Kilroy for reminding his audience that 'those tendencies are still there, cloaked under the trappings of democracy', notably in the quickness of the Irish (both north and south of the border) 'to blame others for our own shortcomings and to dispense punishment on the innocent'.[38] Joseph Woods suggested that what fascinates Kilroy is '[t]he play of paradox and the paradox of play' that involves creation through concealment; his purpose 'is not to answer questions but to provide a comic play on such ironies'.[39] Kilroy himself has said that the kind of theatre that interests him is 'one that invites you in and never for one moment pretends to be anything else but theatre, that celebrates itself and celebrates the theatricality of action and movement and the rest of it'.[40] For many reviewers, such an approach proved to be a theatrical bridge too far.

Shortly before *Madame MacAdam* went on tour and while rehearsals were still in progress, Kilroy was interviewed by Martin Cowley of *The Irish Times*. Things seemed to be going well: 'I wanted to write a play which would be fun too for the actors to work with,' Kilroy said, 'and I think it has been.' Cowley noted Field Day's ambitious programme for the near future: about to publish its 'eagerly awaited' *Anthology of Irish Writing*, the company was also planning to stage three new plays in the next year and to hold a summer school in Derry; another potential development was a series of workshops linked to a performing arts course at Derry's Northwest College of Technology.[41] When *Madame MacAdam* went on the road, however, serious problems surrounding the tour were to put a dent in those shining ambitions. In 1986, the Northern Irish tour of *Double Cross* had experienced various technical and logistical difficulties – the publicity schedule was too tight, and there were ongoing issues with sound and video equipment – but these problems were nothing compared to the troubles that were to beset the production of *Madame MacAdam*.

A farcical premonition of things to come materialised towards the end of rehearsals, when it was discovered that there was a real actor named Lyle Jones. Since the programmes had already been printed, an apologetic letter was dispatched to the thespian in question, which received no reply. (When Kilroy worked on later versions of the script, the character's name was changed to Hedley Jones.[42]) On 9 November, a letter of complaint signed by the cast and the stage managers was sent to all Field Day directors. Its immediate trigger was the sudden decision by Field Day not to take the play to the Royal Court – even though that engagement was listed on the official programme for 3–21 December – which took the actors by complete surprise. The letter's signatories also seized the opportunity to express their dissatisfaction with other aspects of the touring production, which they characterised as 'doomed' from the outset. They vented their spleen on the truck ('cumbersome, impractical and unsuitable for Irish venues'); the director ('relatively inexperienced' and cowed by the designer and the presence of the playwright); the play itself (in need of pruning and not ready for opening night); the advance publicity ('a joke'); the greyhound (a problem in the absence of a dog handler in each venue); and Field Day's handling of hiring local extras to play LDF men ('amateur and haphazard'). The main criticism was reserved for the tour itself:

> It seemed to have been badly planned. The tour took place without a Director or a Company Manager or a recognisable Artistic Director at Field Day. Yet we had an unfinished play needing cuts, polishing, tightening, and rehearsing. We felt neglected, and we played to half empty houses. The experience was most disheartening particularly when our Mecca, Dublin – rewarded our efforts with the most scathing, embarrassing bad reviews.

The letter concluded on a cautionary note:

> When we joined 'Field Day' we felt proud to be part of a company with a high profile international reputation. We were full of optimism, hopes and dreams. These were rudely shattered by our experiences on this tour. A few years ago, a 'Field Day' production was almost a guarantee of full houses. Sadly now, its reputation seems to be at an all-time low. There is something rotten in the state of 'Field Day'. Let us all hope it will rise again.[43]

Kilroy's response to the actors' letter reached the other Field Day directors on 3 January 1992. While suggesting that the document contained 'several factual inaccuracies' and that there was plenty of blame to go around for the debacle, he did not deny that 'this was a bad show, some nights a very bad show indeed'. Conceding that some of the problems were caused by the nature of the play, the inexperience of the director and the inadequacy of the lighting, design and technicals, he nevertheless placed much of the blame with the company: 'Several first rate actors wanted to do the play but declined when faced with (a) Field Day rates of pay and (b) the realities of the Field Day tour.' With regard to PR, pre-selling of seats and management, he argued, Field Day could learn from a company like Druid. '*Madame Mac*, as we all know, attracted immense hostility but would nevertheless have done better with better care.'[44] The remainder of Kilroy's lengthy letter questioned the future efficacy of Field Day, given its roots in the individualism of its participants rather than a true spirit of process and community, and the changing nature of the cultural and political climate on the island of Ireland. Seamus Deane acknowledged in a letter to his fellow Field Day directors that the company had 'let Tom Kilroy down in many important respects'.[45]

Kilroy was not ready to give up on his play. In April 1992, he sent the script to Patrick Mason, who gave him encouragement.[46] Four months later, Kilroy was upbeat about revising the play in a fax to Charlotte Moore, who was set to direct the play in New York.[47] On 21 September, he wrote to Field Day's secretary Gary McKeone: 'Just back from a good trip to NYC. If Madame MacAdam doesn't work this time, I'll personally drown her (and dog) in mid-Atlantic . . .'.[48] The American production received mixed notices. Although some reviewers thought the comedy was entertaining, others found fault with Moore's uncertain production. Kilroy himself has blamed the lack of success of *Madame MacAdam* in part on his predilection for irony. To his fellow Field Day directors, he wrote: 'I did think . . . that I was offering Irish theatre a new kind of irony. Problem with irony is that if you do not gain audience complicity you may attract severe audience hostility. Ironical perspective can suggest a superiority to characters and audience alike. Not what I intended, but . . .'.[49] He also felt that some audience members, 'fed upon realistic images', were bothered by the artifice and theatricality of the play, for which the sociological nature of much Irish theatre had ill-prepared them.[50] Kilroy's 'beloved Madame Mac'[51] meant a great deal to him and he was loath to give up on the play, but his efforts over the next decade to have it revived or adapted for television bore no fruit. In 2015, a production of the play was staged in the UK by students at the Old Vic Theatre School, Bristol.

'Do you think the amusements'll ever come back again?', Marie Therese asks Jo at the end of *Madame MacAdam*. 'Oh, they will,' she replies. '(*Pause.*) Next year' (p. 79). After the problematic Field Day tour, Kilroy vowed despondently that he would not write for the Irish stage again, although in the event, he 'got over the shock of *Madame MacAdam* quite quickly'.[52] Before the opening of the play in September 1991, Field Day had been planning a number of new plays as well as other projects. As it turned out, however, *The Madame MacAdam Travelling Theatre* was the final original play the company would produce and tour. When the actors wrote in their letter that there was 'something rotten in the state of "Field Day"', they had put their finger on a sore spot. In October 1992, Kilroy withdrew from the board of directors, not because of the problematic production of his play, but because he realised it would not be possible to 'push Field Day towards more overt political gestures', as he desired to do.[53] With Brian Friel's resignation in early 1994, the Field Day travelling theatre came to the end of its road.

The predominant themes of *The O'Neill*, *Double Cross* and *The Madame MacAdam Travelling Theatre* relate to the public sphere, and each of these plays reverberates with echoes of remote or recent historical events that are relevant for contemporary Ireland both north and south of the border. But even as *The O'Neill* parses the tragic consequences of the identity crisis that results from colonisation, *Double Cross* explores the perils of black-and-white thinking within extreme nationalism of both the global and local variety, and *Madame MacAdam* probes the dangerous consequences of the fascist's fear of otherness, each play adds depth to the psychology of its characters by focusing the political through the lens of gender and sexuality. O'Neill's political predicament is crystallised in his fraught personal relationships with the women in his life: his wife Mabel, his paramour Róisín and his sovereign, Queen Elizabeth. The fear and self-loathing underlying the absolutist attitudes of Bracken and Joyce in *Double Cross* are most overtly on display in their exchanges with their sexual partners, and in *Madame MacAdam*, Kilroy effectively exposes the blustering, one-dimensional masculinity of armed men in uniform by contrasting it with the nuanced, nurturing and creative qualities of female and sexually ambiguous theatre actors. Elsewhere in his oeuvre – beginning with the very first play he attempted to write, which eventually became *The Death and Resurrection of Mr Roche* – the politics of national identity take a back seat as the emphasis falls more squarely on individual identity, and the thematic lens focuses more directly on questions of gender and sexual orientation.

PART II

ℰ

Gender and Sexuality

4

Bachelors Gay: *The Death and Resurrection of Mr Roche*

The Death and Resurrection of Mr Roche was, according to a review in the *Evening Herald*, 'the first play by an Irish writer in which the title role is that of a homosexual'.[1] When the work was first performed at the Dublin Theatre Festival in 1968, it was imperfectly understood by Dublin critics and audiences. With hindsight, however, its portrayal of the alcoholic squalor associated with the Irish capital in the 1950s – the Dublin of McDaid's and the Grand Canal, of Patrick Kavanagh, Brendan Behan and J.P. Donleavy's *The Ginger Man*[2] – as well as the church- and state-fostered ethos of sexual purity that thwarted the development of healthy relations between the sexes, remains a perceptive reflection on how difficult it was for many individuals in mid-century Ireland to lead authentic lives. Kilroy's thematic focus in this early work on homophobia and misogyny is the first instance of what in his later plays would become a growing preoccupation with sexual identity and gender fluidity. Homosexuality, bisexuality and androgyny are important elements in *Tea and Sex and Shakespeare*, *The Secret Fall of Constance Wilde* and its companion piece *My Scandalous Life*. *Christ, Deliver Us!*, Kilroy's Irish version of Frank Wedekind's *Spring Awakening*, returns the spotlight to the soul-destroying climate of sexual hypocrisy that existed in the 1950s, but this time from a twenty-first-century perspective that takes into account the conclusions of the Murphy and Ryan reports on clerical and institutional abuse of the young and vulnerable during that period.[3]

Kilroy began writing the play that eventually became *The Death and Resurrection of Mr Roche* around 1959, by attempting to dramatise the sexual violence of the Dublin he knew in that decade.

When he was casting around for a plot line for a play that would reflect his notion that 'sexual frustration' almost invariably underlies any manifestations of physical, social or political violence,[4] he decided initially to base his script on a story he had heard about a female prostitute assaulted in a flat by a group of drunken men. When the material resisted him, he eventually concluded that the woman was the problem; her presence prevented him from concentrating fully on maleness, 'the dynamic within which the dysfunctional world of the play had its roots and grounding'.[5] The obstacle Kilroy had encountered in the writing disappeared when he placed a homosexual male in the role of the female character, which allowed him to focus on a group of men who channel their social and sexual discontent into increasingly violent expressions of homophobia and misogyny. For Kilroy, choosing to write about a gay man was also a way of freeing himself from the climate of intimidation and hypocrisy that dominated the contemporary culture: 'The writing was my way of growing up and facing the fear and guilt inculcated into me in my childhood.'[6]

A number of textual fragments and unfinished drafts in the archive indicate Kilroy's initial attempts at writing a play about social displacement and sexual frustration. These surviving scenes from abortive scripts provisionally entitled 'Where Are My Neighbours'[7] and 'House of Three Flats'[8] include elements of setting and plot retained in the play Kilroy would eventually complete. The action of these drafts takes place in a house of flats in Dublin where Kelly, a civil servant who has lived in the basement apartment for fifteen years, organises a farewell party: diagnosed with tuberculosis, he will soon be entering a sanatorium. Among the invitees are a medical student, a garage mechanic, and a teacher, as well as the occupants of the other flats: two young female civil servants and a married couple with the crudely satirical name of O'Monotony. The middle-aged husband's drinking and gambling have forced him into early retirement from his job as a bank clerk; his intelligent, younger wife is lonely and sexually unfulfilled. Just as Kelly's sickness may be indicative of a broader national malaise, his observation that the boarding house 'is haunted by all the ghosts of Ireland' suggests that the Georgian building in its current compartmentalised state is meant to reflect the fragmentation, division and lack of community characterising the nation as a whole.

In these trial pieces, Kilroy attempted in various ways to express the bitter unhappiness of the married couple. In one scene, the landlady berates Mrs O'Monotony for entertaining inappropriate men friends 'in the middle of the day behind [her] husband's back' and having 'the blinds down in the front window', insinuating that she is no better than a prostitute. Later, the unhappy wife remarks to one of the female civil servants that she 'saw two women street-walking on the Canal Bridge' who 'looked no different from you or I'. In a scene in 'House of Three Flats', the husband drunkenly tells the landlady that his wife is carrying on with Kelly: 'A regular whore-house he has down at the bottom of that stairs.' Another version has him confessing to Kelly that he gets his kicks spying on his wife's encounters with other men in bars. In this same script, Mrs O'Monotony and Kelly eventually admit their loneliness and frustration to each other, but when he urges her to express her feelings and she tries to embrace him, he recoils: 'That's . . . that's adultery.' Defeated, he recognises that he could do with his own advice: 'Because I have begun to rot – .' In a third scene, the clerk drunkenly and despairingly turns on the gas in his flat while his wife is attending a party in the basement. When the landlady raises the alarm, his wife's hysterics – 'Is he dead? Is he dead?' – break up the gathering. While some thematic elements of *Mr Roche* (sickness, loneliness, thwarted sexuality, a potential death) are recognisable in these trial pieces, only the figure of Kelly, some of his friends, and his basement flat concretely survive into the play Kilroy eventually completed.

Sometime in 1966, Kilroy gave the actor and director T.P. McKenna the script of the finished play to read, now entitled *The Death and Resurrection of Mr Roche* and featuring the gay character. While Mr Roche may have been the first homosexual to feature in the title of an Irish drama, Kilroy's was not the first Irish play to include an overtly gay character. That honour goes to Mary Manning's *Youth's the Season . . . ?*, directed by Hilton Edwards at the Gate Theatre in 1931, whose young protagonist, Desmond Millington, claims his queer, androgynous nature as his authentic self. In 1960, Hugh Leonard's play *A Walk on the Water*, staged at the Eblana Theatre during the Dublin Theatre Festival, included an ostensibly gay character among a group of 'idlers' who congregate on a Dún Laoghaire pier at the end of the Second World War. The young man, described in a review of the production as a 'potential painter and a potential homosexual', meets his companions again eight years later, having in the meantime become 'a successful interior decorator' – the profession also vainly aspired to by Desmond in *Youth's the Season . . . ?*[9] In the 1960s, however, the subject was still rare on the stage and made many people uncomfortable.

McKenna liked the script of *Mr Roche* and in August 1966 forwarded it to Kilroy's London-based agent, the formidable Peggy Ramsay, accompanied by an enthusiastic letter. He also took the play to the Abbey Theatre, but Ramsay anticipated that its board would not accept the subject matter: 'and, of course, exactly the same thing goes in England. It would never pass the Lord Chamberlain. . . . Everyone is dead scared of censure, and even the press are nervous.' She added, however, that the 'new law giving permission for consenting male adults to live together' – the Sexual Offences Act of 1967 – would affect attitudes going forward.[10] British theatre censorship would be in effect until September 1968; Ireland had no such official institution, but from the mid-1950s onwards pressure from conservative Catholic groups advocating a vigilante attitude towards all perceived expressions of anti-clericalism and obscenity was often enough to halt even mildly provocative and challenging theatrical performances. In 1955, hundreds of protesters gathered outside the Gaiety Theatre to voice their objection to what they perceived as Seán O'Casey's insults to church and nation in *The Bishop's Bonfire*. In 1957, an oblique reference to a condom in Alan Simpson's production of Tennessee Williams' *The Rose Tattoo* was enough to bring the police to the Pike Theatre's doorstep, demanding the performance be cancelled; when Simpson refused, he was arrested, and although he was eventually exonerated, the personal and financial consequences of the ordeal were devastating.[11] By the mid-1960s, however, the tide was slowly turning.

The script of *Mr Roche* was still – or perhaps again – at the Abbey in December 1966, but now in the hands of the theatre's new artistic advisor, Tomás Mac Anna, who read it with interest and wrote to Kilroy: 'It is a theme which we have never had on our stage here and it is, of course, a theme very much up to date.'[12] In February 1967, however, he reported that 'the managing director feels that it is not our line of territory. I would add to that the one word – *yet*'.[13] The director in question, Ernest Blythe, would retire later that year, but that was of little consolation to Kilroy, who decided, when the opportunity arose, to move forward with director Jim Fitzgerald of the Globe Theatre Company and stage the play at the 1968 Dublin Theatre Festival, as Mac Anna had also encouraged him to do.[14] Decades later, Kilroy wrote: 'I don't think that *Mr Roche* would have appeared, because of its portrayal of a homosexual, outside the security of the Festival', with its contingent of critics and journalists from outside Ireland.[15] He also praised Fitzgerald's 'courage and determination' without which the play with its 'sexual content' would never have been staged when it was.[16]

Kilroy made it clear to Seamus Kelly of *The Irish Times* that *Mr Roche* 'is definitely not a play about homosexuals – that's a subject on which I should be singularly ill-equipped to write' – but rather about 'the ambiguous sexuality of men who drink together and make this their way of life'.[17] Homosexuality was, he said later, a 'device to agitate the plot'.[18] Rumours about the play's theme were doing the rounds before the production opened. Colm Cronin's 'Festival Preview' in *Hibernia* announced that 'if all reports are to be believed Thomas Kilroy's *The Death and Resurrection of Mr Roche* . . . is a most exciting work dealing with sexual aberration in modern Ireland'.[19] Kilroy was annoyed that the play had been branded as controversial before it was even seen, and told an *Irish Press* reporter: 'I resent the implication that the play is cheap sensationalism and it seems to me that we spend too much time trying to decide a play is controversial or not and not enough deciding whether it is good or bad.' He described *Mr Roche* as being 'satirical of Irish society, particularly the male "jarring" element', and stressed that the play's subject matter disturbed him 'every time I read it'.[20] To *The Irish Times*, however, he characterised the drama as 'truthful' and 'very funny'.[21]

The Death and Resurrection of Mr Roche begins when the group of men who constitute its drinking fraternity – national school teacher Seamus, car salesman Myles, and an unnamed failed medical student turned morgue attendant known as 'Doc' – congregate at the basement flat belonging to Kelly, a civil servant of their number, for more alcohol after a night in the pub. Mr Roche is initially a peripheral character; he turns up late and the invitation had apparently been extended to his young friend Kevin, who accompanies him. Before he arrives, Myles has already branded him as 'the queer', but of the four men, only Kelly vehemently objects to his presence, calling him a '[d]irty, filthy pervert'.[22] Kelly's near-hysteria at the thought of having to spend the evening in Mr Roche's presence is noted by his friends, who on two occasions in Act I suggest that he is perhaps protesting too much. When this happens initially, Kelly 'exits to the bedroom where at first he stands indecisive and nervous', later bending 'to look through and listen at the keyhole' (p. 30). After the second altercation a short time later he again frantically withdraws into the bedroom where he 'wipes his face with his handkerchief, wipes his hands vigorously and then tries to listen at the door' (p. 36). These actions of self-segregation and closeting, of simultaneous aversion and attraction to the scene that includes Mr Roche or where his sexuality is discussed, signal the 'queerness' of Kelly's anxiety which the play goes on to examine.

Kilroy immediately sets the tone for the play in the opening lines, as Kelly staggers towards his front door with the words, 'Half eleven and all's well! Cripes, I'm piss-eyed' (p. 11). Kelly's subsequent references to Seamus as 'y'auld tool of a schoolmaster' and 'you auld bugger' (p. 13), indicative of the men's general tendency to sprinkle their dialogue with expletives like 'fuck', 'my arse' and 'balls', as well as a great deal of innuendo, are Kilroy's way of suggesting the frustrated masculinity and sexual dysfunction that simmer just below the surface. Reviewers of the 1968 production – virtually all male – made much of the realistic language; the *Evening Herald*, for example, noted the play's 'four-, five- and six-letter words, which taken in bulk make the banned film of "Ulysses" resemble a tale by Hans Anderson [*sic*]'.[23] Kilroy declared he understood 'this whole question of obscenity' and voiced respect for 'the people who can't take it'; he had observed that 'the men in the audience all looked at their womenfolk when the words came out and laughed only if the ladies laughed'.[24] As for the 'hysterical laughter from the audience at some of the language in his play', Kilroy told *The Irish Times*: 'The male world is an exclusive world, and most women find exposure to it frightening in the theatre.'[25] In the 1969 Hampstead Theatre Club production directed by Richard Eyre, however, it was 'some unnecessarily bowdlerized language' that caught the attention of John Higgins, who otherwise detected 'a horrid ring of truth' in the conversation.[26]

The rented, dingy, two-room flat where Kelly has lived for fifteen years is located in the basement of a Georgian house once built for the Anglo-Irish elite. He defensively refers to its 'character', but Myles is disdainful: 'Balls to you and your Georgian! Where were the likes of you and me, Kelly, when they were building your Georgian? ... Mouldering tenements!' (p. 20). Kelly's background, however, is rural; he was born in a cottage where they slept four to a bed and at dinner time would sit around the table 'waiting for one of the girls to lift the hot potatoes' (p. 59). Kilroy imagined his character as having 'large, peasant hands and a rolling, shouldering walk'.[27] The car salesman Myles, by contrast, is 'Kilroy's satiric caricature of a 1960s Ireland which is eagerly attempting to recreate itself in the image of America', but as the action develops he is 'exposed as a pathetic poseur unconvincingly trying to live up to an unnatural, borrowed image'. Kelly and Myles, then, represent 'two contrasting, yet complementary, faces of an Ireland in transition'.[28] Kelly no longer sees his family, but that very separation from his origins also allows him now to idealise the cottage as 'a natural place to live in', and to romanticise the farming activity of pulling turnips 'with the roots black and wet' (pp. 58–59), the implication being that his current state is unnatural in its aridity and rootlessness. Kelly's nostalgic fantasy coupled with his hysterical homophobia amount to what Joseph Valente calls 'a species of nationalist false consciousness, a failure to reckon with how significantly Irish cultural heritage has been implicated in and constituted through the very sorts of queer dislocations that are so often repudiated in its name'.[29]

Kilroy creates a series of symbolic displacements that show, in Anthony Roche's words, how Kelly 'is trying to live up to a variety of conflicting images and is uncertain in all of them. The past he has suppressed is not just personal but social and is addressed in terms of sexuality.'[30] The character of Mr Roche, then, serves both as an external catalyst for the play's action and an embodiment of aspects of Kelly's psyche. Reviewing the play for the *Evening Herald*, J.J. Finegan noted Kilroy's double focus on 'Mr Roche and the attitude of normal people to him', and on Kelly, who is 'full of doubts about himself and longing for the Munster he has left for ever', but had trouble working out what one theme had to do with the other.[31] In fact, while Mr Roche represents one kind of 'queerness', Kelly's 'queerness' more broadly encompasses a sense of alienation from what he has belatedly begun to conceive of as a more 'authentic' culture. In the way Kilroy juxtaposes sexual otherness with cultural displacement, the term 'queer' can be broadened outward, as Eve Sedgwick suggests in her essay 'Queer and Now', along dimensions that transcend gender and sexuality, to include 'the ways that race, ethnicity, [and] post-colonial nationality criss-cross with these *and other* identity-constituting, identity fracturing discourses'.[32]

Schoolteacher Seamus, a rural boy like Kelly who attended secondary school on a scholarship and went on to make his career in the city, has since married and moved to the suburbs. He worries that his friend has not changed in the last fifteen years: 'what was healthy then is sick now. You're sick, Kelly' (p. 55). Kelly's condition is mirrored by that of Kevin, who is 'clearly very, very ill' when he and Mr Roche arrive at the flat. Mr Roche's concerns about his young companion echo what Seamus says about Kelly: 'He is sick. The boy is sick' (p. 31). Kilroy's play, then, initially introduces both forms of 'queerness' in pathological terms. In 1968, when *Mr Roche* was first staged, homosexuality was commonly addressed – when it was spoken of at all – in the language of disease. In his *Sunday Independent* advice column of 15 October 1967, for instance, Fr Lucius McClean OFM assured his readers that, for those afflicted with homosexual tendencies, 'help can be sought and obtained and really qualified treatment can achieve a complete cure'.[33] In April 1969, a columnist in the same paper addressed a reader's question about the cause of homosexuality – 'Lack of love? Or is it caused by T.B. or cancer?' – by suggesting that homosexuals should rather be viewed as 'persons of arrested and subsequently distorted psychological growth'.[34] When David Norris, who spearheaded the Campaign for Homosexual Law Reform in the early 1970s, made an appearance on an Irish talk show the following year, billed as '[p]ossibly the first interview with an openly gay person on RTÉ Television', the opening question posed to him by Áine O'Connor was, 'David, are homosexuals sick people?'[35] Kilroy's play echoes this language in order to complicate it, ultimately suggesting that it is secrecy, lack of self-knowledge and bigotry that are the real causes of social and psychological suffering.

All the themes of sexual desire and frustration explored in the play are contained, in a nutshell, in Kelly's favourite party piece, 'The Face on the Bar-room Floor', which he performs for his friends just before the arrival of Kevin and Mr Roche,[36] particularly when that recitation is considered in conjunction with the song he reportedly sang at Seamus' wedding, ambiguously entitled, 'A Bachelor Gay Am I'. The speaker of 'The Face on the Bar-room Floor' is an artist who took to the bottle when his beloved Madelaine deserted him for the friend whose portrait he was painting, a 'fair-haired boy' whose 'dreamy eyes' on the canvas she was unable to resist. Kelly performs the piece adopting 'what he considers to be a tough, cowboy accent, but loses it from time to time' (p. 27), finishing the poem 'with great emotion' (p. 29). His recitation expresses both homosocial and heterosexual desire and loss, and the speaker's unhealthy infatuation with the now-dead lovely Madelaine, as well as his offer to draw her face on the bar-room floor – where it will be trampled and soiled by the boots of drunks – tellingly evokes the sentimental and abusive misogyny of a hyper-masculine culture. Kelly's emotional investment in the poem's sentiments speaks volumes about the state of his own psyche, as does his repression of its ending, where the speaker utters a shriek and falls dead across the picture. At this point in the play, the doorbell rings, announcing the arrival of Kevin and Mr Roche.

As the play progresses and the characters get drunker, inhibitions are discarded and Myles, Seamus and Doc start taking out their frustrations on Mr Roche. Young Kevin is in the bathroom being sick when the others start shoving Mr Roche in on top of him, holding the door closed while Mr Roche, a sufferer from claustrophobia, beats on it from the inside. Reviewers of the early productions of the play without exception took the gay man's claustrophobia at face value, but the water closet here clearly doubles as the homosexual closet, from which the revellers verbally insist on 'outing' Mr Roche while simultaneously, and literally, forcing him back in. The 'joke' shakes Mr Roche to the core: 'It's only when I feel that the door may never be opened – ' (p. 35). After more drinking, and more crude references by the men to Mr Roche's 'queerness', the gay man finally erupts into a tirade against 'this debauch' and its 'joylessness'. Mr Roche's rebuke amounts to a condemnation of the way rigidly prescriptive notions of masculinity and femininity within an unnatural climate of enforced heterosexuality drive men together into pubs – or basements – where obligatory drinking serves as a 'cover' to distinguish these inevitably close homosocial gatherings from homosexual activity. Heavy drinking, Mr Roche suggests, is 'the way we chain ourselves together, no freedom, no joy'. Kevin and Mr Roche, too, are compelled to adhere publicly to this code; indeed,

Micheál Ó hAonghusa, Joe Dowling, Eamon Kelly, Peadar Lamb, and Kevin McHugh in *The Death and Resurrection of Mr Roche*, Abbey Theatre, 1973. Directed by T.P. McKenna. Photograph: Fergus Bourke. Courtesy Abbey Theatre.

Kevin is 'only ill at night' because going out to 'have a drink' is the only legitimate way to socialise with other men (p. 41). Driven once more to engage physically with Mr Roche by this uncomfortable insight, the other men push him into what Kelly refers to as his 'holy-hole', a small cellar within his basement. When they eventually pull him out, he is not breathing and panic ensues, almost hysterically expressed by Kelly: 'How would you like to have a dead – a dead pervert discovered dead in your flat, ha?' (p. 45). Given the doubly compromising nature of the situation, calling the guards is out of the question; he therefore insists that the body be removed so that it can be 'discovered somewhere else' (p. 46).

In the small hours of the morning, while Myles, Kevin and the medical student are trying to dispose of Mr Roche's body in 'a quiet spot' (p. 47), Seamus and Kelly, alone in the flat, awkwardly end up sharing some of their most intimate concerns. Seamus confesses that his middle-class life of heterosexual conformity is a disappointment, but Kelly is barely listening and upsets his friend by remarking that his wife is 'a great woman' and that he is 'well settled there' (54).

Kelly is distracted by what Sedgwick dubs 'homosexual panic'; fearing that his sexuality may not be entirely straight, he worries that there is 'something up' with him where women are concerned (p. 57). His anxiety about the 'terrible reputation' he would acquire if his association with Mr Roche were to become public knowledge gets the better of him: 'I don't want it to come out. I don't want anything to come out' (p. 61). In voicing these fears, Kelly is inviting the double-edged sword of homosexual knowledge; while Seamus pursues a course of ignorance by refusing to know and recognise the signs of homosexuality, Kelly is adamant that he can precisely identify these traits so he can dissociate himself from gay men who 'can be seen a mile off. Sure you'd know one before he'd open his mouth' (p. 63). This comically, and disastrously, leads him to set himself up as a bit of an expert on the subject:

> SEAMUS: Who is he anyway, this Mr Roche? (*Musing*) He's a homosexual, isn't that right? I'd never have known it.
> KELLY: You know what he is. He hangs around Murray's pub.
> SEAMUS: He's the first one I've ever spoken to. Strange. (*Pause*) I didn't think Murray's was that kind of place.
> KELLY: Oh, it's changed entirely since the old days, Seamus. Sure it crawls with them after dark. D'you know they can't keep ballcocks in the men's jacks down there? . . . They carry on in there and afterwards steal the ballcock as a souvenir. (p. 60)

The slippery slope entered here by Kelly leads him eventually to reveal the secret of his previous, intimate encounter with Mr Roche: 'I let him handle me – ' (p. 63). Hitherto this private transgression had been literally unspeakable even in the Confessional – another 'closet' of sorts – where his words 'said nothing of the real thing' (p. 63). Seamus, finding his 'don't ask, don't tell' policy thus breached by Kelly's revelation, feels implicated in the act by the guilty knowledge of what he wishes Kelly had kept to himself: 'You've made me live with it as well as yourself. It's not fair, man. It's not fair' (p. 63). The uncomfortable knowledge is the trigger for Seamus to depart and assert his orthodox heterosexuality: 'Sure we'll be seeing you anyway – . . . We'll have to have you out to the house sometime too. . . . Oh, it's not too bad now' (p. 64).

When Myles, Kevin, and 'Doc' eventually return to Kelly's flat, they have Mr Roche in tow, miraculously revived by a heavy downpour that occurred just as they were depositing his body in a park by the canal. In Anthony Roche's words, 'as Kelly emerges from the closet, Mr Roche, representing that aspect of Kelly which the latter has always sought to deny, simultaneously emerges from a death-like state with his *alter-ego*'s confession'.[37] In relation to Mr Roche, who is gay, the 'holy-hole' in which he 'died', in its function as a cellar within a basement, a double 'hole' in which secrets can be buried, stands for the closet of repression.[38] In relation to Kelly, however, whose sexual identity is less starkly defined, the double cellar represents what Sedgwick calls 'the secret of having a secret', 'the closet of imagining *a* homosexual secret'.[39] But as a 'holy' retreat it is also, for both men, the sacred, liminal, timeless space of a rite of passage towards 'w*hole*ness', the transitional space between one context of meaning and another.

The ritual aspect of Mr Roche's rebirth is suggested when the returning men are seen approaching the front door 'like figures in a dance, almost linked ... to catch the mood of delirious revelry that grips them' (p. 70). Mr Roche himself describes the experience of his 'resurrection' among the trees in sacred terms and as a new beginning, symbolised by his insistence to the others that they wait in the park until dawn to see the sun rise before returning to Kelly's basement. The passage in the play where he relates what happened by the canal is marked by a dramatic change in tone:

> MR ROCHE: (*rising ecstatically, priest-like, with arms outstretched, very slowly with menace*):
> And-it-came! Like the beginning of life again.
> A great white egg at the foot of the sky.
> Breaking up into light. Breaking up into life.
> Consider the mystery of it! ...
> (*As he speaks the tone should shift radically from all that has gone before*): Breaking up over the rooftops into particles of silver and gold. And the streets opened up before it. And each tree yawned and shook, the leaves splintering. I was witness to it. (*Pause. Quietly.*) Then the clock began again. Tick-tock. Tick-tock. Tick-tock. I had come back, you see. Seconds, minutes, hours, days again, as before. I was so – so overcome to be back. The old heart-beat again. And the journey still stretching

> out ahead. (*He resumes his seat, gingerly, smiling to himself.*) (pp. 72–73)

Commenting on the script in 1968, Hilton Edwards expressed 'some puzzlement' about the reason for Mr Roche's resurrection, and confessed to being 'somewhat worried by the change of the nature of the technique'. To his mind, 'the shock of the resurrection is in itself sufficiently dramatic without taking the audience into another and un-prepared-for dimension'. In the event, however, Edwards' concerns, which he himself declared to be 'probably all poppycock', proved to be largely unwarranted.[40]

Mr Roche, Fintan O'Toole argues, is a 'richly empty figure. He is what he is perceived to be by others.' For that reason, he suggests, 'you can't play *Mr Roche* as a naturalistic drama of psychology and motivation'.[41] But that naturalistic aspect is by no means absent from the play, and the successful interpretation of the drama's several layers poses a challenge to directors and actors. Kilroy himself stressed that Mr Roche is the only character 'who steps outside the play's "realism"' and, in the last act, is removed onto 'a plane of mystery, enigma'.[42] The play in its current incarnation 'began, almost, as an academic joke about the traditional comic resurrection theme'.[43] For O'Toole, what makes the play shocking is the way in which it uses the rituals and symbols of Catholicism 'in giving us Jesus as a genteel, middle-aged Dún Laoghaire homosexual'. (Whether Mr Roche actually lives in the seaside town is another question; Myles' reference to him as the 'queen of Dunleary' is more likely a provocative nod to the fact that the harbour piers were a known cruising area for homosexuals.) But O'Toole argues that Kelly, in some ways Mr Roche's alter ego, also undergoes a rite of passage of sorts and suggests that, at the end of the play, after he has been abandoned by his friends, he should be seen to go through 'a moment of utter nakedness, of emotional truth'. The irony on which the final part of the play turns 'is the fact that Kelly (not Roche) is alive at all. To feel that wonder we have to feel that at some stage he had died.'[44] 'Resurrection equals new life, shedding of old personality,' Kilroy later wrote in his notes. 'What does Mr Roche offer Kelly? . . . New chance to grasp life? To understand self? I think something like that.'[45]

Almost forty years after the 1973 Abbey production of *Mr Roche*, John Devitt remembered being stunned by the play in that it 'dealt with things everybody knew about and nobody had previously exhibited in the theatre'.[46] Kilroy has said that he did not know in writing *Mr Roche* 'where the gay thing came out of'.[47] At the time of the play's premiere several reviewers remarked on Kilroy's fondness for the comedies of Ben Jonson, whose works, like many of Kilroy's own, convey 'a rigorous moral sense, against normal morality and with an ambiguous resolution', or an ironic reversal, at the end.[48] One of his favourite Jonson plays, *Epicoene, or the Silent Woman* (1609), may have contributed to his thinking about the comedic treatment of anxiety about gender and sexuality. In the comedy, a wealthy old man named Morose, who is particularly sensitive to noise, has been tricked by his nephew Dauphine, who expects to profit from the deal, into taking Epicoene, the 'silent woman', as his wife. After many shenanigans engineered by Dauphine, the marriage turns out to be null and void because the wife is revealed to be a boy, which not only shames Morose but also two other foolish characters who had earlier claimed to have slept with the woman.

A more intriguing – and perhaps unconscious – inspiration behind the scapegoating and ritual 'sacrifice' of the gay character in *The Death and Resurrection of Mr Roche* may have been David Rudkin's play *Afore Night Come*, which has a plot line that bears a broad resemblance to Kilroy's material and features an Irish character also called Roche. Kilroy does not remember seeing the play but acknowledges he may have read it, or read about it. The working title of his own drama was initially 'The Death and Resurrection of Mr Rice';[49] all he remembers about his eventual choice of the name Roche is that he was pleased by the alliteration in the title of his play.[50] *Afore Night Come* was first produced by the Royal Shakespeare Company in London in 1962 and revived at the Aldwych Theatre in 1964, in repertory with, among other plays, Peter Brook's production of Peter Weiss' *Marat/Sade*, which had such a profound impact on Kilroy's thinking about theatre and its possibilities.

Set in an orchard in the Black Country on a day in early autumn, Rudkin's *Afore Night Come* revolves around a group of seasonal fruit pickers, including three newcomers: schoolboy Jeff, a student called Larry and an eccentric Irish tramp named Roche. During the day the atmosphere grows increasingly menacing as the established workers' frustrations about aspects of their personal lives and various mishaps in the orchard begin to drive them towards finding a scapegoat to blame for the ills they cannot otherwise address. On more than one occasion they turn on Roche because he is Irish, for class reasons, but generally because he is eccentric, contrary and elusive. Some of the men push him around more and more aggressively until, eventually, he is attacked, killed and beheaded. Roche's corpse is then respectfully wrapped and buried in a hole off stage. Hints are dropped throughout the play that such a 'sacrifice' has occurred annually for the last number of years.

From the opening scene onward it is clear that the men are preoccupied with notions of masculinity and sexual potency, and that their victim will be someone who threatens their sense of manhood or is likely to expose their sexual insecurities. To them, Irishness and an advanced education are signs of effeminacy. Irishmen like Roche are 'hopeless' at fruit picking which is, the foreman stresses, 'a man's job',[51] while the student Larry is at a disadvantage because his pen-pusher's hands are 'like a woman's' (p. 3). Scapegoats are typically outsiders to a community and violence against them is often justified by accusations of sexual transgression, such as adultery, incest or homosexuality. In the orchard, much is made by the established workers of selecting the fruit for health and size, particularly of removing 'bitter pip' as well as what one worker refers to as '[t]wisted types. Bloody perverts' that will 'spoil the sample' and need to be thrown out (p. 7). Roche is troublesome to the men in part because he finds the 'segregation' process arbitrary and unfathomable and puts all the fruit he picks into the boxes regardless of quality or size (p. 17).

In *Afore Night Come*, Roche is triangulated with two other 'outsider' characters, Larry the student and Johnny, a tractor driver. Roche also refers to himself as a student, albeit of humanity, while Johnny first mistakes Larry, who hails from his own home town, for an Irishman. Johnny likes Larry very much while Jeff, a young newcomer eager to fall in line with the established ethos of masculinity, suggests that Larry, to whom he refers as 'Rosie', is 'soft on Roche' (p. 39). Aware of what will inevitably happen to Roche, Johnny tries to lure Larry away to protect him from witnessing the imminent violence by suggesting that he is the intended victim. In the course of persuading Larry, Johnny embraces him protectively, to which Larry reacts at first with pleasure and then with a violent gesture of repugnance. Later he returns and explains to Johnny how the feelings released in him by his touch had made him afraid; he gives Johnny his fountain pen in acknowledgment of their mutual understanding. Johnny, however, is soon blamed by the orchard's 'gaffer' for various calamities and re-committed to the institution where his mother had first placed him because he 'had no father' and she was 'ashamed' (p. 63). The foreman's lack of sympathy shows that he regards Johnny as one of the 'perverted' fruits that spoil the sample and are better removed altogether: 'Homo-bloody-maniac, they calls them blokes, or something' (p. 64).

Kilroy's Mr Roche has several traits in common with Rudkin's Roche. Both Roches are slightly elusive and mysterious characters about whom little is known by the others or revealed by themselves during the play, though Seamus says of Kilroy's character that he is 'no tinker. You can tell that' (p. 62). Both appear more genteel and educated than the men around them, although in the case of Rudkin's character (nicknamed 'Shakespeare' by the orchard workers) this may be more bluff than substance. In each instance, the murderous attack on the Roche character occurs shortly after he has been baited to such a point of infuriation that he bursts out with 'the truth' in the form of a withering diatribe on his current companions' innate rottenness. In both plays, the Roche figure operates on a naturalistic as well as a symbolic plane. In the case of Rudkin's Roche, the character's abstract quality is reflected in the other men's uneasy sensation that the tramp is from 'another planet', a ghost or a zombie (p. 29) who will keep coming back 'to plague us: never shake him off. Hang on to us. Blight us. Never shake him free' (p. 41). Before things turn ugly, Roche initially plays along: 'Perhaps I am gone. Perhaps I'm not. Ha!' (p. 28). In Kilroy's comedy, Mr Roche keeps turning up in Kelly's life and returns alive after Kelly thought he had been killed. Mr Roche teases Kelly: 'Ah, but I'm not here at all! I'm only a ghost, old chap. . . . I'm dead, remember? . . . Dead and won't lie down, as the man said' (p. 78). Neither Roche is really gone, because the problem each is made to represent lies elsewhere. A scapegoat is a 'sacrificeable' victim upon whom a community projects its own shortcomings and towards whom it deflects the violence that would otherwise be vented on its own members. In this way, the sacrifice of the scapegoat deprives the community of 'knowledge of the violence inherent in themselves with which they have never come to terms',[52] and which, therefore, has not been removed at all.

Like Kilroy, who claimed to be disturbed by the subject matter of *Mr Roche* 'every time I read it', Rudkin has talked about how the 'transgressive' nature of his own writing in *Afore Night Come*, his first play, made him uneasy, not only because of the language, which was 'stronger' than he had ever heard in a play, but because of the nature of the sexuality. In such a male play, 'inevitably the erotic dimension had to be homosexual. . . . In plays at that time, anything or anyone homosexual was very rare, and heavily coded. I think this was the first British play in which this fact of life was handled candidly and straight.'[53] *Afore Night Come* caused strongly negative reactions in the theatre when it was first performed, but some influential critics praised it and noted links to Artaud's 'theatre of cruelty' (of which Rudkin had never heard) and John Osborne's *Look Back in Anger.* Ramsay, who was Rudkin's agent as well as Kilroy's, found the savage murder of *Afore Night Come* 'startling' but its tone of menace 'a little too dark'.[54] Although Rudkin had conceived of his play as a comedy, the RSC unsurprisingly refused to bill the bleak drama as such. Kilroy's *The Death and Resurrection of Mr Roche* is, of course, a comedy in a truer sense of the word, albeit a satirical one; nobody dies, the sun rises and foolishness and hypocrisy are eventually exposed.

By the spring of 1973, when *Mr Roche* was revived at the Abbey Theatre, Dublin had seen, or was about to see, other plays that employed the theme of homosexuality. Some months before the play premiered in 1968, Kilroy had sent the script to Hilton Edwards, who commented that the drama was not his personal cup of tea, and that it revealed 'a side of life that I prefer to dismiss as I would the contemplation of my natural functions'.[55] A year later, however, when he had occasion to write to Kilroy on a different matter, he graciously conceded that his was a minority view that was 'probably quite wrong', and that he had heard from many people whose opinion he respected how much they admired the play.[56] In October 1973, the Gate premiered a new play by Micheál Mac Liammóir called *Prelude in Kazbek Street*, which Edwards directed. As Éibhear Walshe points out, in the repressive decades following independence

Mac Liammóir and Edwards 'survived, and even flourished, as Ireland's only visible gay couple'; this was possible in part because they were 'unwilling to highlight the homoerotic in their theatrical work'.[57] In *Prelude in Kazbek Street*, a play about a homosexual ballet dancer, Mac Liammóir eventually, and only to a degree, overcame this reticence.

Like *The Death and Resurrection of Mr Roche*, *Prelude in Kazbek Street* is about loneliness, a condition frequently ascribed to gay individuals by commentators of the time. In his *Sunday Independent* advice column of October 1967, for example, Fr McClean cautions that homosexuality, if left to 'fester', can lead to 'great loneliness and despair'.[58] In his 1968 review of Kilroy's play, Leslie Faughnan portrays Mr Roche as 'a gently fading queer . . . whose ready wallet when the next round is due buys him temporary relief from his loneliness'; both Roche and Kelly, he suggests, are 'deeply lonely'.[59] The plays of the period reflect the reality that gay people in Ireland were careful to maintain a neutral profile. Kilroy noted that Mr Roche is not a camp character but 'a very typical Dublin homosexual, of good, sober background, a self-employed business-man perhaps'.[60] Indeed, in the play Seamus remarks to Kelly that he would never have known that Mr Roche was a homosexual (p. 60). Throughout *Prelude in Kazbek Street*, Mac Liammóir is at pains to dissociate homosexuality from effeminacy, and Christopher Cazenove, who played the ballet dancer in the Gate production, stressed that his character 'is not a pansy; he's outwardly quite straight'.[61] Mac Liammóir was seventy-four when his play premiered. He would have been conscious that homosexuality was still controversial and, indeed, technically an offence; decriminalisation would not happen until 1993.

Kilroy's treatment of the subject and his drama's favourable reception in 1968 paved the way for – and inspired – his friend Brian Friel's 1971 play *The Gentle Island*, which revolves around the complex interaction between a gay couple from Dublin vacationing on an island off the Donegal coast, and members of the island's only remaining resident family. *Mr Roche* meant a great deal to Friel; he once called the work 'as perfectly shaped as a Brancusi; . . . A very cool play of whispered affections. Respect sounds grudging. Envy is closer.'[62] In an article considering the similarities between *Mr Roche* and *The Gentle Island*, Shaun Richards argues that what unites the two plays is their public engagement 'with one of the founding faiths of the state: hegemonic masculinity and its subsequent contemporary discontents',[63] which is to say that, as Fintan O'Toole puts it, 'Mr Roche's homosexuality is there to make the "normal" maleness of the characters visible. And with this light shone on it, we can see it as troubled, insecure, full of mistrust, terror and sheer downright misogyny.'[64]

In *The Death and Resurrection of Mr Roche*, Myles' treatment of the gay man says much of his attitude to the women he claims to be sexually conquering by the score: 'Oh, you dirty devil. *(Whips behind and catches Mr Roche about the chest)* Are you wearing your bra tonight, Agatha?' (p. 41). Earlier he had spoken of women in terms of the cars he sells for a living: 'Make sure they're serviced often. Right? Well tuned-up, the ignition firing, keep the cylinders clean and keep the headlamps shining in the darkness' (p. 23). The fact that Myles lives with his mother, who will have his breakfast on the table for him the next morning oblivious to the fact that he has been out all night, completes the picture of the immaturity of these men whose relations with women are abusive and unhealthy (and, here, essentially non-existent). Kilroy sees much of the sexual frustration of mid-century Ireland as stemming from the fear and guilt the Catholic Church instilled in people from a young age, particularly through the education system: 'I think that the whole relationship between the sexes was totally abnormal. We were . . . imprinted with a very deep fear of [sex] long before the physical thing had any meaning.'[65] Kelly's admission to Seamus, that he has never had a serious girlfriend because he cannot stand the 'skittering and giggling' of women (p. 57), suggests that when they do meet, both sexes have trouble behaving like adults in each other's company.

Interviewed in 1972, Kilroy explained that the world of drinking and fear of women portrayed in *Mr Roche* had its origins in his student life of the 1950s, and that by the time the play finally reached the stage in 1968, he had already distanced himself from it. When the Abbey staged the work in 1973, five years after its premiere, critics likewise seemed eager to point out how much attitudes had changed in the meantime. J.J. Finegan reflected that the play 'is now almost a period piece', and that its language 'which then seemed raw and untamed now falls on the ears without a flicker of an eyelid'.[66] Gus Smith expressed the view that its 'dated' material 'failed to carry over to the permissive seventies with any impact whatsoever'.[67] However, when the Abbey revived the play in 1989, the general critical view was that the issues it raised remained relevant and that their poignancy had, in fact, increased with the passing of time. *Irish Times* critic David Nowlan, who had himself somewhat controversially referred to Mr Roche as 'a queer' in his 1973 review, acknowledged in 1989 that the play 'has survived well its very specific early sixties origins when lads were lads . . . drink was drink, women . . . birds or mots, and homosexuals were queers'.[68] Almost another decade later, Emer O'Kelly, too, affirmed the play's staying power when she declared in the *Sunday Independent* that, while Kilroy's plays are often 'too cerebral for broad popular appeal', *Mr Roche* will still be applauded 'when we are dust'.[69]

At the end of *The Death and Resurrection of Mr Roche*, after his dark night of the soul, and for all his efforts to pretend that nothing has happened, Kelly can no longer completely ignore the 'queerness' of his existence. It being Sunday morning, he proposes that his friends accompany him to the church of 'St Mary's, Gayfield', of the Carmelite order, located 'down there beside the Royal Hospital for Incurables. . . . It's very peaceful. They're enclosed – ' (p. 81). The mass-going was intended by Kilroy to constitute 'an empty habitual ritual at the end',[70] with the linguistic play on 'enclosed' and 'incurables' suggesting that Kelly and his friends are closing themselves off again from the truth of their lives and will not fundamentally change. But 'Gayfield' also implies that 'gayness' is inexorably part of the fabric of Irish society; the orthodox perspective has been queered, and the closet door cannot be completely shut again. If Kelly is to overcome the sickness of his life, its 'queerness', in all senses of the word, will have to be acknowledged. Mr Roche, therefore, is not going anywhere. He will be waiting in the flat – 'not necessarily in the flesh'[71] – until Kelly returns, while young Kevin symbolically sleeps off his nausea in Kelly's bed. A more wholesome Irish society, too, requires that fear and bias be overcome in favour of greater openness and inclusiveness with regard to a person's origin, gender or sexual orientation.

Male anxiety about the expression of gender and sexuality remains a central issue in Kilroy's third play, *Tea and Sex and Shakespeare*; there, however, the emphasis falls more heavily on documenting the mental breakdown of the central character, who is a writer, than on mirroring the queer state of the nation. From the mid-1970s onward, the theme of madness runs like a thread through Kilroy's oeuvre. Brien, the protagonist of *Tea and Sex and Shakespeare*, undergoes a personal and artistic crisis that in many respects resembles the psychological breakdown suffered by Rabe in *Madame MacAdam* and William Blake in *Blake*; although the individual conditions of their lives and the manifestations of their problems vary, in each instance the character's mental turmoil is connected to the way his artistic temperament is inexorably bound up with his sexuality. Out of Kilroy's own troubled private and artistic circumstances around the time he began writing *Tea and Sex and Shakespeare* emerged his growing preoccupation with the artist as emotionally deficient 'monster', and with the ambiguities and complexities of masculinity and femininity, what a character in a later play calls the 'sexual zoo'.[72]

5

Psychological Baggage: *Tea and Sex and Shakespeare*

'The word "sex" has appeared for the first time in an Abbey play,' the *Evening Herald* proclaimed when *Tea and Sex and Shakespeare* premiered in October 1976 as part of the Dublin Theatre Festival.[1] Kilroy's third play had been some years in the making, since he was already working on it when his novel *The Big Chapel* was published in 1971. The play's focus, Kilroy told *The Times* in November of that year, was 'the isolation of the artist. The withdrawal you get – which at least you get in me. Sometimes I think it's the artist's crime against art.'[2] Six months later, the work was still in progress. 'I don't know what it's about until it's finished,' Kilroy admitted to Elgy Gillespie, other than that it 'takes place inside the mind of one man; it's a fantasy play and a marriage play . . . and about the alienation of the intellectual, too'.[3] In more recent years, Kilroy has spoken about the crisis in his personal life in the early 1970s, when giving up his lectureship at UCD to concentrate fully on writing coincided with other, difficult private circumstances. This confluence of upheavals negatively affected his creative ability and triggered the fear that he might never write again, but also formed the starting point for *Tea and Sex and Shakespeare*, a work about a writer who suffers a psychological and creative breakdown. The play, while giving Kilroy 'enormous difficulty', at the same time became one of the means of overcoming his own crisis of confidence.[4]

Sex and marriage are at the forefront of *Farmers*, a television script on which Kilroy worked during the same period he was writing *Tea and Sex and Shakespeare*. Between 1973 and 1977 he tried, unsuccessfully, to get the drama accepted by the BBC or RTÉ; the Irish broadcaster eventually produced it in 1979. Its setting is metaphorical: a dilapidated farmhouse in the West of Ireland exuding a sense of 'total decay',[5] rented by two couples in an attempt at communal living. Nuala and Seán are married and have two small children; Americans Peter and Judith are unwed and childless. There are suggestions that Peter pressures Nuala into having sex with him, and that Seán eventually gives in to Judith's desire to sleep with him to conceive a child. Kilroy's frank treatment of its subject matter provoked a Cork priest into dispatching an angry letter to the *Irish Independent* in which he labelled the rather bleak drama 'crude, distasteful and revolting', its values 'pagan and degrading', its language 'lewd and repulsive', and its attitude to sex flippant and irreverent.[6] *Farmers* approaches the theme of marital complexity from a grimly realistic, if slightly lurid perspective; by contrast, *Tea and Sex and Shakespeare* turns its subject matter into a farcical comedy of desperation.

That kind of comedy, Kilroy argues, 'draws on hysteria and the hysterical' and is therefore 'working close to disintegration'.[7] The material of *Tea and Sex and Shakespeare* took him very close to home, as he was translating his own sense of failure into the experiences of his protagonist, a struggling writer named Brien, whose inner turmoil is made visible on stage in the 'surrealistic' quality of the room where he lives with his wife Elmina in Mrs O's boarding house. At the start of the play's opening scene, characters in strange apparel move in and out of the wardrobe and back and forth through a section of the wall, but Brien pays little attention, having 'seen it all before'.[8] The tension he feels between his need for solitude and the emotional isolation created by that need is made evident when he steps onto the landing and announces to the empty space: 'OK, everyone! I don't want to be interrupted before midnight. OK? Got to work. Going to do a bit of the writing now. Get that first act going' (p. 14). He then locks himself into the room and sits at the typewriter, but no words come. Tormented by writer's block, Brien instead finds himself assaulted by figures conjured up by his imagination in the form of his wife, her parents, and his neighbour, who serve as expressionistic devices to perform his anxieties about his marriage, talent, class and economic status.

Elmina works in an advertising agency, but nevertheless keeps popping out of the wardrobe in the room where Brien is trying to write, each time wearing a different hat, to berate her husband about his inability to pay the bills and his sexual inadequacy. This, as Brien exasperatedly and coarsely explains to her, is a direct result of his creative endeavour: 'When I'm writing I can't fuck' (p. 16). As the play progresses it transpires that the couple are childless, and there are suggestions that Elmina may have suffered a miscarriage or false pregnancy. Her well-heeled, disapproving parents keep barging in through the walls of Brien's room to have tea and to remind him that he is not 'one of them'; their condescension creates in him feelings of inferiority and rebelliousness. Mrs O, the landlady, is forever in and out of his room with cups of tea and sweeping brushes, while her attractive teenage daughter Deirdre keeps asking for Brien's advice about her studies of William Shakespeare's plays. Brien suspects his elusive neighbour Sylvester – whose outfits range from a long black coat and hat to a series of increasingly flamboyant combinations – of conducting a torrid affair with his wife, notwithstanding the ambiguity of his sexuality. Sylvester performs several parts in Brien's fantasies but in one of his guises keeps insisting on parking a number of suitcases in Brien's apartment – the 'baggage' of his marriage which Brien is, in the end, no longer able to ignore. Brien must eventually acknowledge all these personified anxieties preventing him from writing his play and, to some degree, exorcise them.

For Kilroy, the process of writing *Tea and Sex and Shakespeare* was 'like cutting through immense, tangled undergrowth and it meant numerous wrong directions'.[9] Some core elements, however, were in place early on. Kilroy's notes for a draft version called 'Inmates' reveal his search for a device to express the psychological state of his main character: 'The sense of enclosure within a room. The room as mind. The house as "experience". A day in the life of – .'[10] He had used a similar concept in 'House of Three Flats', the early attempt at the script that would eventually be completed as *The Death and Resurrection of Mr Roche*. There, the basement of the compartmentalised house stands for the fragmented state of the nation as well as its occupants' sense of displacement and stagnation. In *Tea and Sex and Shakespeare*, a more intimately personal play, the device of the room as mind lacks the broader implications of the earlier drama; in both plays, nevertheless, the confined space indicates lives and minds that are stalled because social or psychological traumas have not been fully addressed and are preventing a move forward into a healthier and more productive future. In 'Inmates', Kilroy had also already found the central metaphor for his protagonist's mental baggage. In one of the drafts, Brien claims to be pursued everywhere by a man with two suitcases; in an alternative version of the same scene, Brien has started writing a novel but has been unable to progress beyond this initial premise involving a man in possession of two suitcases, which somehow seem essential to the plot.[11] In all versions of the play their hidden contents serve as a metaphor for the suppressed causes of Brien's psychological troubles, which he needs to confront before he can move on with his life. In the finalised version of the play, Brien eventually discovers that the suitcase contains a dead baby.

Once Kilroy had a complete draft of *Tea and Sex and Shakespeare* he sent it to the playwright Mary Manning for comments. While she found the dialogue 'brilliant', the drama's 'total lack of exposition' frightened her; the curtain, she wrote, 'will rise on total confusion[.] What *is* wrong with Brien?' The repeated references to 'fucks and screws' in the text struck her as 'very boring', while she also felt the play needed the addition of 'one small scene of genuine agony'. This suggestion perhaps led Kilroy, in his notes, to emphasise to himself the importance of the 'suitcase and foetus scene', by reiterating 'suitcase' and 'the suitcase + baby'.[12] Manning urged that any production should have 'a high powered actor' as Brien and 'a director who understands it', but did not think such a person could be found in Dublin.[13] Donal McCann, however, would eventually play the part with impeccable 'intelligence of apprehension and timing'.[14] Having accepted the play to be presented at the 1976 Dublin Theatre Festival, but realising that the text was still in need of revision, the Abbey's artistic director Tomás Mac Anna approached English freelance director Max Stafford-Clark to work with Kilroy on rewriting parts of a script that was, as Kilroy himself concedes, 'much less structured', 'freer' and 'much less neat' than that of his previous play, *The Death and Resurrection of Mr Roche*. In particular it lacked, as Kilroy acknowledges, a workable shape to contain the surrealistic projections of Brien's imagination: 'I submitted a very shapeless manuscript, and I'd never have got it into shape if it hadn't been for Max Stafford-Clark and the cast.'[15] Stafford-Clark, who considered himself 'Kilroy's hired gun' in the matter,[16] adopted an optimistic and workmanlike approach to the revision process, which Kilroy saw as a mixed blessing. As rehearsals were progressing (with Donal McCann as Brien, Aideen O'Kelly as Elmina and Kevin McHugh as Sylvester) he wrote to Brian Friel: 'M. Stafford Clark is extremely professional. I do worry, at times, on his insistence upon a *LITERAL* basis for everything . . . but it has had the good effect of making me *THINK* about the play which I've tended to avoid – and to do some good re-writing which has focused the play more.'[17] The rehearsal script in the Abbey Theatre archive reveals something of the extent to which the text was revised at this stage.[18]

In a 2004 interview, Stafford-Clark ruminated that the difficulty with *Tea and Sex and Shakespeare* was that 'it was quite coded', which was 'both the point of the play and what was hard about it'.[19] Choosing to read the coding as non-personal, he situated the play among a number of other Irish works of the time, including Friel's *Faith Healer* and Tom Murphy's *The Gigli Concert*, which were, 'in a way, about writers' block, or about the inability of Irish writers to write directly about the things that were going on in their country: the Troubles'.[20] Each of these plays features a couple (Frank and Grace in *Faith Healer*, JPW King and Mona in *The Gigli Concert*) whose problematic relationship involves unresolved questions concerning impotence, infertility and a dead or phantom baby. In her letter to Kilroy, written before *Tea and Sex and Shakespeare* was produced, Manning read its cryptic nature in a different way: 'I feel there are sad autobiographical strains of distant music in your play and that maybe you should have been braver and indulged in more indecent exposure.'[21] In 1991, Kilroy acknowledged in a letter to Friel that the coded nature of his writing tends to be a source of difficulty: 'I know how problematical my work is, perhaps because I unload so much personal crap, perhaps because I write at such an angle to my presumed subject.'[22] In *Tea and Sex and Shakespeare* this quality is exacerbated because the work originated in uniquely difficult personal circumstances and went through several rounds of quite drastic revamping that, each in their own way, affected the play's tone and direction.

Some draft scenes of the script in Kilroy's archived notebooks contain overt references to ambiguities of gender and sexual orientation that have been toned down in the published version of the play, which is based on the substantially revised text of the 1988 production by Rough Magic, directed by Declan Hughes. In one of Kilroy's initial attempts at an opening scene, Sylvester's conversation with Elmina subtly emphasises their mutual awareness of his sexual otherness:

> ELMINA: . . . Never support a husband, Sylvester.
> SYLVESTER: I'm unmarried.[23]

Sylvester's masculinity is subsequently brought into question by Brien when he quotes the well-known lines of a song from Shakespeare's *Two Gentlemen of Verona*:

> SYLVESTER: Life is so – so extremely difficult.
> BRIEN: (*Loud declamation*) 'Who is Silvia? Who is she? That all our swains commend her?'
> SYLVESTER: To whom, may I ask, is he referring?
> ELMINA: Pay no attention to him, Silvia – I mean Sylvester.[24]

In the version of the play staged in 1976, Brien tells his landlady: 'My wife's in the closet! Everyone in the closet! Door locked.' Mrs O's reaction to this statement, deleted from the prompt script by Stafford-Clark, suggests that her lodgers have been experiencing ongoing marital difficulties: 'He hasn't been as bad since the night she threw everything out the window and into the street.'[25] In his subsequent revisions of the text, Kilroy amended the phrase, 'my wife's in the closet' to, 'my wife's in the clothes-closet', and then changed the word 'closet' to 'wardrobe', further erasing any reverberations of closeted homosexuality.[26] In the published text of *Tea and Sex and Shakespeare* that gender-bending aspect of the relationship is projected exclusively onto Sylvester. 'The best jokes are private,' the latter, in the guise of a psychiatrist, cryptically tells Brien in the original version of the play.[27] In this first iteration of the script, the couple's childlessness is barely mentioned, which largely detaches the scene towards the play's end, when Brien cradles the 'naked, dead infant' he has taken from the suitcase, from the context of his marital crisis. Also lacking in this version are the numerous references to Shakespeare's *Othello*, which have been strategically inserted into the 1988 text of the play to express Brien's sense of jealousy and suspicion towards Elmina and Sylvester.

Donal McCann and Aideen O'Kelly in *Tea and Sex and Shakespeare*, Abbey Theatre, 1976. Directed by Max Stafford-Clark. Photograph: Fergus Bourke. Courtesy Abbey Theatre and James Hardiman Library, NUI Galway.

Shortly after completing the play in 1975, Kilroy discussed with Caroline Walsh of *The Irish Times* his interest in the themes of self-confrontation and 'the confusion of sexual roles: male and female elements being mixed in every person'.[28] This expression of a fundamental preoccupation with gender performance and sexual orientation goes much further than his characterisation of homosexuality in *The Death and Resurrection of Mr Roche* as a mere 'device' to set the plot in motion. In the novel on which he was working in the late 1970s – the unpublished 'Angela, Falling from Grace' – Kilroy also explored the same issue from various angles, including a personal one. Angela is, as the opening paragraphs of a published extract make clear, a version of Kilroy himself: 'Why I've had to concoct her at all must wait for the moment. It is certainly not enough to say that by making me into a her when in fact I am a he, allows me to conceal the personal. Something of that, yes, as always but more, much more.'[29] A description of the novel-in-progress Kilroy wrote in 1985 for a grant proposal summarises its three parts.[30] Section One, set in the 1970s, deals with Angela's sojourn in a Dublin psychiatric clinic after her breakdown and disappearance. Section Two takes place in 1956 and focuses on twenty-two-year-old Angela's relationship with the owner of the Swiss private school where she is teaching, a middle-aged man described as 'an inventive hypochondriac, a bisexual'. (Kilroy himself was twenty-two in 1956, and taught for a year in a finishing school in Switzerland, between completing his bachelor's degree and starting his master's.) Section Three is a retelling of the myth of Hermaphroditus and Salmacis which appropriates androgyny 'as a metaphor of the relationship between Angela and the writer-narrator'.[31] Speaking to Walsh, Kilroy said of these mythical characters: 'In their double form they are neither man nor woman; they seem to have no sex yet to be of both sexes.'[32] The sections of the unpublished novel, in their focus on mental breakdown and self-confrontation, androgyny and the artist's endeavour to transform lived experience into art, extend the themes that are more cautiously evident in *Tea and Sex and Shakespeare*. Androgyny and artistic endeavour are likewise core issues in Kilroy's later, more mature play *The Secret Fall of Constance Wilde*.

Kilroy himself was not entirely satisfied with the 1976 production of *Tea and Sex and Shakespeare*, telling Brian Friel that he felt it was 'more leaden in performance than it should have been',[33] and made extensive revisions to the text for the play's revival by Rough Magic in 1988. By then, he had come to see the play as being about 'the dangerous consequences of Brien's misguided and excessive passion for control'.[34] In collaboration with director Declan Hughes, who agreed with the author that the new version 'should be more self-consciously theatrical and surreal',[35] Kilroy rewrote substantial sections of the second act, imposing a shape whereby the action starts out 'in some sort of pedestrian normality' and re-enters that normality at the end. Kilroy regrets that the printed text of the play continues to suggest that the setting should be 'a surrealistic version of the top floor of Mrs O's house' and would like to see that altered to a scene that is 'absolutely naturalistic'.[36] Indeed, when the Cork-based Brown Penny Theatre Company mounted a touring production of the play in 2001, their use of a surreal set 'caused a lot of problems at the beginning of the play because the audience did not know where it was'.[37] Reviewers liked the energy of the 1988 Rough Magic production, but generally detected what Ronan Farren described as 'an excessive drift into the conventions of farce'.[38] Amidst the 'crazy fun' that was 'perhaps . . . a little too far over the top', David Nowlan missed 'the despair of creative impotence' McCann had brought to the main character in the 1976 production, and felt that the new version of the play lacked a 'resting point of sanity'.[39] Patrick Burke agreed that Hughes' interpretation 'cauterized much of the pain in Kilroy's text', which meant that 'the most effective moment in the production' – when Brien holds the baby to his chest – 'felt like a scene from another play'.[40] Fintan O'Toole summed up the 'knowing subversiveness' of *Tea and Sex and Shakespeare* in this production as 'a brilliantly clever but arid exercise in talking shop'.[41]

In the opening tableau of both versions of *Tea and Sex and Shakespeare* we see Brien hanging by the neck, as if he is dead, until we notice that he is furtively smoking a cigarette he is hiding behind his back. This performance of the writer's feelings of suicidal despair in the face of his inability to write is interrupted by the emergence from the wardrobe of Sylvester, dressed entirely in black, who cuts the rope above Brien's head with 'a gigantic scissors' (p. 13). As the embodiment of various aspects of Brien's psyche, Sylvester is a complex figure who is made to perform several different roles. As the unmarried neighbour across the hall who resents Brien but likes Elmina, he serves as the figure onto whom Brien projects his anxieties about his wife's fidelity, which in turn are a product of his sense of failure as a husband. On the other hand, as a creation of Brien's jealous imagination, Sylvester keeps presenting himself to Elmina as an ardent lover and to her parents as a model husband for their daughter. But in those capacities, Sylvester may also represent the part of Brien's psyche that would like to be that person for his wife. Sylvester is a man who lives a lonely and isolated existence in a room identical to Brien's own, and as such is also the alter ego of Brien the artist, who craves solitude and isolation, but whose peace and quiet is forever being intruded upon by the other occupants of the house.

In the 1976 script of the play, Kilroy suggests that the set in Act II should be exactly as it was in the previous act, except that 'Brien's room is now painted a brilliant clinical white', as if to suggest an actual or internalised psychiatric hospital.[42] Stafford-Clark's production merely suggested this effect by draping white bedsheets on the walls of the room. Sylvester's role in the initial tableau of Act II, as a surgeon who 'chops at Brien's hands' with a knife while his patient is asleep, suggests that it is a psychological block, a dark or 'monstrous' subconscious secret, that is preventing Brien from beginning his play. Sylvester refers to himself in a later scene as 'merely the shadow on the wall' (p. 55); that version of Sylvester is dressed in a long black coat and hat and is suspected by Brien of being in the 'KGB – CIA – Special Branch' (p. 18). This black-clad Sylvester with his suitcase full of secrets is Brien's shadow self, something that is particularly evident in the scene with the baby: 'The wardrobe opens: SYLVESTER, in long black coat, black hat, as in the beginning of the play, carrying a suitcase. BRIEN stands still. Something wrong? Turns quickly. SYLVESTER has turned as quickly behind him. They begin a slow circling, BRIEN in panic' (p. 74). In the opening moments of Act I, the same alter ego's sabotaging of Brien's 'suicide' indicates that Brien knows, on some level, that the cause of his failure to write lies buried deep within himself, and that he will have to face that hidden obstacle sooner or later. Sylvester's cutting of the phone line used by Brien to appeal alternately to God or Shakespeare for assistance during his most despairing moments is likewise an act of positive sabotage, in that it forces Brien to dig within himself for the means to unblock his creative powers rather than appeal to external forces that are only aggravating his problem.

Brien is typical of what psychologists call the 'dysphoric/avoidant type of blocked writer', the type that expresses 'a wide variety of acute emotional distress' including anger, fear, confusion, self-criticism and fatigue, and a variety of anxieties. Such writers 'possess vivid imaginative capacities', which in the present circumstances they are unable to turn effectively towards creative production. Instead, they generate negative thoughts. As a result, they enter a vicious cycle in which 'past interpersonal losses and humiliations' contribute to the writer's depression, causing a negative state of mind that then also interferes with the writer's ability to concentrate on his creative work. To aggravate the matter, the writer's sense of equilibrium is further threatened by 'the loss of writing as a means of self-soothing and self-empowerment'.[43]

Psychoanalysts often consider writer's block to be the product of an unconscious conflict within the artist. Joan Acocella summarises the argument: 'the artist trawls his unconscious for his material, but every now and then, in that dark estuary, he encounters something so frightening to him that he simply comes to a halt, and no one ever knows why'.[44] During the course of *Tea and Sex and Shakespeare* Brien's psychological journey is towards uncovering and acknowledging what it is that unconsciously frightens him so much that it stops him from writing. On numerous occasions in the play, characters conjured up by Brien's imagination make a connection between his biro (his pen) and his penis, both of which have failed to be creatively productive. Indeed, Brien's inability to produce a play is increasingly connected to Brien and Elmina's failure (or Brien's unwillingness and Elmina's inability) to produce a child. Brien is only able to refer to this conflict facetiously when, early in Act I, he calls the Elmina who has popped her head out of the top of the wardrobe 'the mother of our children', which evokes from her the response, 'Monster!' (p. 15). This Elmina, while being wooed by Sylvester in the presence of her husband, confesses that '[t]here is – a baby', but that there is a problem: 'I think – I – I lost it' (p. 61). During a nightmarish tea party with Elmina's parents in a later scene, 'Mummy' expresses her disappointment with Brien and suggests that he 'emigrate' without his wife: 'I think we may be thankful now that there are no children' (p. 71). Childlessness is located at the heart of Brien's problematic relationship with Elmina in this version of the play, but because the two are unable to discuss the trauma effectively, it has stalled Brien's creative energy, and thereby also becomes the metaphor for his lack of creative productivity.

The crisis in Brien and Elmina's marriage can only begin to be resolved when they both acknowledge the traumatic reality that has led each away from the other. Elmina eventually faces her deep anguish at the lack, or loss, of a child:

> ELMINA: *(Low, monotone)* There is no baby, then? No baby, he said. No quickening, no show, no ripening, no bud, no blossom, no life, no blue babe on the white bloodied sheet, no rounding apace. Nothing. (p. 73)

Brien, left alone on stage, realises that his self-obsession has prevented him from responding adequately to his wife's pain. Prompted by his alter ego Sylvester he opens the suitcase and 'takes out a naked, dead infant form. Bending his head, he sits cradling it, weeping. He puts the infant back in the suitcase, closing it' (p. 74). The moment of loss and mourning captures Brien's recognition of the origins of his failure to communicate as a creative artist and to commiserate as a human being.

In the script as Kilroy originally wrote it, the ending following the scene in which Brien discovers the baby differed considerably from that in the rewritten text created with Stafford-Clark. In the earlier version, the lights dim and go up again on 'the white room of the beginning of Act Two', which represents the space of Brien's madness. Elmina and Brien are there, surrounded by all the suitcases of the play, and as they embrace and begin to talk, Brien gradually detaches himself from his fantasy world. His wife encourages him to 'just take things as they are', and he assures her that he has 'come back'. Elmina reveals that she has changed her job and found a new flat, offering a fresh start for the two of them. As they leave for home, she offers to help Brien with his bags and picks up the suitcase of the previous scene:

> BRIEN: No, no, no! I'll take that!
> ELMINA: What's in it? It weighs a ton.
> BRIEN: Nothing.
> ELMINA: Nothing.
> BRIEN: Just some – some – personal – effects.
> *They go out with the suitcases and the play ends.*[45]

The emphasis in this ending rests on the couple's reconciliation but the conclusion does not overtly address the problem of Brien's stalled creativity.

Working with Stafford-Clark on finalising the script, Kilroy wrote a new closing scene, in which Brien and Elmina's conversation in the white room takes an entirely different turn. Elmina tells Brien of her visit to her parents, who 'look so old now', and muses that her father, who was such a strong man once, now needs her mother's help. Since her parents express their love for each other through bickering, their words of annoyance are also 'words of assistance'; Elmina confesses to being moved by this 'strange language of affection'. She explains that, when she left the old couple, she could not look back because she felt that 'the child inside [her] had finally died'.[46] The sentiment seems designed to give added value to the preceding scene with the baby in the suitcase. In his review of Stafford-Clark's production, Des Hogan commended Kilroy for turning the mood from comedy to thoughtfulness by making the play, in the end, 'a study of aging, of the horrors of losing love in personal relationships . . . and of the fear of losing creativity'.[47] Kilroy returns the white room of Brien's feverish imagination to a realistic context by having Elmina remark that, whatever her husband has been up to during the day, he should 'take down these sheets' or else Mrs O 'will have a fit'. Brien explains that he has been on a journey, 'exploding through tunnels, white faces at windows and staggering, muffled figures in the corridors, thundering through the undergrowth down, down into the dark and luggage, luggage stuffed with possessions'. While Elmina goes downstairs to make them both a cup of tea Brien lingers, looks into the wardrobe, shakes his head, pauses at Sylvester's door to wish him 'Good-night, Sweet Prince', and then delivers his exit line: 'Good God. I forgot to tell her that Mrs O has given us a weeks notice' (*sic*).[48]

In collaboration with Declan Hughes, Kilroy once more rewrote the play's conclusion for the 1988 production. At the end of the scene in which he has held the infant, Brien 'cowers with his suitcase, downstage, like a refugee' (p. 74). The moment of catharsis is raw and painful, hardly conducive to producing the upbeat conclusion to the as yet unwritten drama Brien has been trying to coax out of Shakespeare's example since asking about the Bard, at the play's beginning: 'How the fuck did he manage all those happy endings?' (p. 14). Brien's confrontation with his inner demon (or monster) is here abruptly and shockingly followed by a hysterical finale in which the characters of his imagination perform a conflation of happy endings – a marriage, a lost child found, a family reunion – cobbled together from Wilde's *The Importance of Being Earnest* and Shakespeare's *A Midsummer Night's Dream* and *The Winter's Tale*. In this crazy concoction it is revealed that it was Mrs O who left the suitcase in the cloakroom of Kingsbridge station, and that the infant contained in it was Deirdre, her attractive daughter, who rapturously recognises Brien as 'Daddy' (p. 76). The scene reflects both a kind of willed resolution to Brien's agony and his attempt to block out with forced comedy the new-found dark knowledge of what is in his personal suitcase, which he physically 'pushes . . . away from himself, towards them' as he 'cringes and tries to hide himself in thin air' (p. 75). Once the dangerous contents of the suitcase have thus been comically defused, Sylvester takes the bag out of the room, followed through the wall by all the other figures of Brien's overwrought subconscious. Left alone, Brien gives 'a wild, savage, sardonic and prolonged laugh' intended to have the effect of 'a shocking, conclusive end to the proceedings', which amounts to a form of exorcism. Then he once more sits down at the typewriter and 'tries to type. All lights down to a pool about him' (p. 76).

The contrived 'happy ending' of the scenario in Brien's imagination, in which the tragic central adultery-and-death plot of *Othello* is replaced by plot ingredients from Shakespeare's and Wilde's comedies, is happy only insofar as it finally ends the riot in Brien's head. This conclusion is really a tentative beginning, a cathartic change of mood in the writer that will allow him, finally, to clear his mind and start his play. Kilroy has said that 'playwrights write plays in order to populate an empty space. . . . For a playwright, there is no place as moving, as imaginatively exciting, as an empty stage. There is also no place more desolate.'[49] Brien's psychological breakthrough is that he is now able to face that desolation. O'Toole, however, felt that Brien's moment of self-confrontation in Hughes' 'formidably energetic production' was just 'another ghost in a machine that is thundering along at a ferocious pace'. The character's core problems remain unresolved, since 'there is no sense that Brien has been re-born from his descent into the purgatory of madness, and if anything the revision of the second half of the play cuts off this sense of development, leaving Brien in his room rather than have him exit with his wife'.[50] The revised ending does indeed move away from an overt sense of rebirth, but it nevertheless involves a shift in Brien's attitude towards his predicament, whose subtlety may have been overwhelmed in the Rough Magic production by the madcap craziness of the play's final hullabaloo.

The more subdued comic irony of the actual ending of *Tea and Sex and Shakespeare* – that is, the conclusion of Kilroy's play as opposed to the Shakespearean-Wildean finale of Brien's dysphoric imaginings – is created in the 1988 version by the return of Elmina to Brien, who has exchanged his pyjama top for an old sweater and sits at the typewriter in his room:

> Suddenly: the distant voice of ELMINA calling 'Brien! Brien! Are you there, darling?' BRIEN, tense again, sits up, waiting. ELMINA has entered into the light, relaxed, affectionate, coming back from work. She wears an elegant coat, carries stylish shopping bags. She kisses him on the top of the head, ruffling his hair, and behaves with great warmth towards him. She drapes herself across his work area, with a sigh. (pp. 76–77)

Most commentators have read Elmina's return as a healing moment for Brien. Christopher Murray, for example, argues: 'His anxieties clearly have no basis. His wife inhabits his writer's space at her ease; she has the walk of a Muse. Suddenly their being together cancels all that went before, leaving a transformed icon. . . . The audience is brought to experience the very process of creation, its victory over the void.'[51] The irony of the play's final moment, however, when Elmina asks Brien, 'Hiya! Well? *(Pause)* And how was *your* day?', whereupon 'BRIEN looks at audience, raises an eyebrow, and the play ends' (p. 77), goes beyond the mere discrepancy between Elmina's affectionate behaviour upon her return home and the anxieties about her that dominated Brien's psyche all day, as witnessed by the audience. Brien's ironic eyebrow also points to the dilemma posed by Elmina's return. If facing the darkness within himself has dispelled the block that stopped him from writing, that writing process is now once more interrupted by his wife's presence. However, the psychological process that unblocked his writing has also led Brien to face the real communicative block at the heart of his marriage: his refusal to acknowledge his role as a husband and Elmina's desire for a child. With that issue 'unblocked' as well, Elmina's seductive presence on his writing desk, next to the typewriter, poses a question: will Brien still have to choose between writing and making love to his wife, or will he be able to do both, now that he has faced the contents of his psychological baggage? Brien's acknowledgment of the audience in this dilemma acts as a device to indicate that he is no longer locked within his own psyche, as he was in the play's opening scene. Instead, in the play's final moment, Brien is able to distance himself from himself and look upon his predicament with ironic amusement rather than despair. The ending of Kilroy's play hangs comically suspended in the unwritten (because impossible?) moment of reconciliation between Brien's life and his art. The typewriter beckons; so does his wife. Kilroy's conclusion suggests that the way forward, both in human and artistic terms, lies in the embrace of such incompleteness and imperfection.

The reception of *Tea and Sex and Shakespeare* in 1976 exposed the fault line evident in Ireland at the time between theatre traditionalists and modernists: the play 'had a very ambiguous success, attracting a cult following and total rejection in equal proportions'.[52] Many reviewers were of the same opinion as Seamus Kelly, who detected the spirit of Denis Johnston, James Joyce and Flann O'Brien in the radically innovative play and concluded that Kilroy deserved 'a golden cap and bells' for his desperately comical depiction of the human condition.[53] Desmond Rushe, however, introduced a sour note by frowning upon the play's 'tricks, gags and pretensions', 'crudities, vulgarities and cheap titillations', as well as 'four letter words, double-meanings and a couple of attempted sex scenes'; he urged the Abbey Theatre to return to the manifesto of its founders 'in the hope of dredging something that might set its values straight'.[54]

The Death and Resurrection of Mr Roche and *Tea and Sex and Shakespeare*, like so many plays written in the 1960s and '70s, approach questions of gender and sexuality mainly from the perspective of their male protagonists. Another decade later, Tom Murphy became the first male playwright of his generation to acknowledge, after being taken to task by a female audience member, that his work until then had been preoccupied almost exclusively with masculine themes and characters. He redressed the balance with *Bailegangaire* (1985), a play featuring three strong women characters: two sisters and their mentally and physically declining grandmother who, through the shared telling of a story, gradually come to terms with the hidden traumas of their past and present. Friel followed suit in 1990 with *Dancing at Lughnasa*, set in Donegal in 1936 and centred on the struggles of five sisters, who were modelled on his own mother and aunts – a subject that had first been suggested to him by Kilroy. In Kilroy's case, a similar awareness was evident in his creation of Madame MacAdam, the pivotal figure in his 1991 play about the misfortunes of the travelling theatre named for her. But it was in the focal character of *The Secret Fall of Constance Wilde* (1997) that Kilroy found a protagonist whose experiences – her marriage to Oscar, motherhood, her suspicion as well as understanding of her husband's lover Alfred Douglas, and her response to the scandal of Oscar's trial and imprisonment – allowed him to explore, from a female perspective, a broad spectrum of questions relating to parenting, gender roles, sexual orientation, as well as sexual abuse – the 'secret' behind Constance's 'fall' in Kilroy's creative interpretation of her life.

6

The Wound of Gender: *The Secret Fall of Constance Wilde*

In *The Death and Resurrection of Mr Roche*, Kilroy employs the central character's homosexuality as a device to explore how deeply insecure masculinity expresses itself in verbal and physical aggression. *Tea and Sex and Shakespeare* examines the psychological link between a writer's inability to write and his sense of sexual and emotional inadequacy within his marriage. *The Secret Fall of Constance Wilde* brings together many of these same thematic elements – an artist and his wife within a complex marriage, a homosexual relationship, psychological trauma – in a more intricate and maturely considered matrix. When Kilroy decided to write a play about Constance Wilde, he was particularly interested in examining her place within 'the whole psycho-sexual network' of herself, Oscar (whom he imagines as bisexual), and Lord Alfred ('Bosie') Douglas, as he wondered when she learned about her husband's sexuality, how much she knew, and what attracted her to Oscar in the first place.[1]

Kilroy has often noted that a playwright can only write about historical characters by filling lacunae in the biographical record with invention and imagination. In 1995, at the time when he was beginning to compose the play, the news media were saturated with reports of clerical sexual abuse cases such as those brought against Fr Brendan Smyth and Fr Seán Fortune, who had molested numerous juveniles from the 1970s onward. Kilroy saw the exposure of these crimes as 'a great cathartic revelation', which led him to re-read the Wilde story from the perspective that something similar had happened to the three principal characters: that Constance, Oscar and Bosie 'were deeply traumatized growing up by the actions of their own fathers', and that this affected their sexuality.[2] Kilroy speculates that, at some level, Constance knew all along that her husband's sexual nature was fluid – indeed, that she 'fell in love with Oscar's bisexual nature, the full, mercurial, brilliant expression of it, the double nature of it, its need for role-playing and its peculiar, if destructive empathy with women' – and that he 'would have to make such a doomed love credible out of the character of the woman invented for the play'.[3] However, the genesis of the work that would become *The Secret Fall of Constance Wilde* was by no means as straightforward as these retrospective comments make it appear.

In early 1994, Patrick Mason approached Kilroy to see if he would write something for the centenary of Oscar Wilde's 1895 trial and subsequent imprisonment in Reading Gaol. Mason had been appointed artistic director of the Abbey Theatre in 1993 and had successfully collaborated with Kilroy in 1977, when he directed the very well-received production of *Talbot's Box* at the Peacock. For the commemoration, he suggested that Kilroy base his contribution on Wilde's novel *The Picture of Dorian Gray*, perhaps by exploring the connections between the fictive and the biographical: Alfred Douglas as Gray, Oscar as Henry Wotton/Basil Hallward, and Constance as the tragic victim, Sybil Vane. Kilroy liked the idea, although he was well aware (as perhaps Mason was not) that writing to a deadline was hardly his forte. His intentions were certainly good, and he began immediately; only a week after Kilroy had informed his agent of the commission, Mason expressed his delight at the seven pages of material the playwright had already compiled for what they agreed to call, for the moment, 'The Untitled Wilde Play'.[4] Kilroy had recently completed his version of *Six Characters in Search of an Author*, also commissioned by the Abbey (which would be staged in May 1996), and Mason detected a touch of Pirandello in the Wilde material, although he thought the way the characters were finding their voices was 'pure Kilroy'.[5]

Kilroy's notes for the play in progress and several drafts for the opening scene suggest a focus on both theatrical and gender performance from the very beginning. One of the earliest outlines envisages a raised platform at centre stage to serve as an 'inner stage' which 'challenges the outer'.[6] Another draft juxtaposes a tableau featuring a number of the novel's characters and the painting of

Dorian on an easel with, stage left, Oscar Wilde late in his life, seated at the outdoor table of a Parisian café. Kilroy's notes, which include references to classical mythology – Zeus holding the double axe, symbol of the goddess; Hercules in women's clothing – make it clear that one of his goals in the play was to try to 'understand what it is to be female/male'.[7]

Oscar's opening monologue in these early versions harks back to the days when he had it all, to his 'vision of perfection in this all too imperfect world', embodied as 'Dionysos, the man-woman',[8] or, in a variant, 'Ovid's androgyne'.[9] In this latter draft, Oscar's speech is followed by the revelation, on the inner stage, of 'Dorian and Taylor' under a scarlet sheet – Dorian being Alfred Douglas' alter ego in Wilde's novel, while Alfred Taylor was a friend of Bosie's in real life and his liaison to the world of male prostitution to which Douglas later introduced Wilde. A subsequent iteration renders these themes in a more stylised and suggestive manner: on the raised platform centre stage is a Victorian conservatory, in semi-darkness, but dimly visible within are rich foliage and 'a reclining "statue" of an Androgyne. . . . To either side stand four attendants clothed in black with black hoods covering their heads in the manner of assistant operators of Bunraku puppets.' Stage right is the picture on an easel covered with drapery. Stage left shows the outdoor café, but Wilde's words now stress his straitened circumstances as he asks an English passer-by to 'help out a fellow countryman in distress'.[10] The attendants, the Androgyne and Oscar are retained in the play Kilroy eventually completed; Dorian Gray was about to be replaced by Constance Wilde.

In January 1995, when the first draft of the Dorian play was due, it was clear that Kilroy would fail to meet the deadline, in part because the '*Dorian and Melmoth* project', as Mason now referred to it,[11] had reached an impasse. While doing research for the play Kilroy had not only 'come to the conclusion that there were already far too many adaptations of *Dorian Gray*', but had also become more interested in the position of Constance, whom he saw as 'a shadow in the familiar story' that he wanted to bring into the light.[12] Mason, who sensed Kilroy's excitement at this new angle, encouraged him to pursue the idea for a different play whose working title now became 'Wife to Mr Wilde'. In a 1997 interview with Eileen Battersby, Kilroy observed about the drama's long gestation process that it had taken him 'quite a while to see what [he] was writing about',[13] but when 'the Constance thing', as Mason called it, became clear to him, the writing went quickly.[14] By November 1995 he had finished a complete draft. The extant opening scene and the setting of this version owe much to the earlier *Dorian* drafts, but the raised platform has been replaced by 'a large white circular disk, an actual wooden acting space but now hanging on the back wall, stage left, like an abandoned wheel or gigantic wafer. It will be rolled into place later.'[15] In his notes, Kilroy wrote emphatically: 'Create an unfinished element in the opening with O + C.'[16] To do this he moved Oscar and the café to the very end of the play, and by the time rehearsals began the Victorian conservatory was gone, leaving only the 'great white disk, a performance space like a circus ring'. Oscar and Constance, both at the end of their lives and leaning heavily on sticks, are led on by attendants to perform on the disk.[17] The play's working title was now 'Ode to Mrs Wilde',[18] but by opening night this had become *The Secret Fall of Constance Wilde*. It was 8 October 1997. The year marked the centenary of Wilde's release from Reading Gaol, where he had served a two-year sentence, with hard labour, for gross indecency.[19]

According to Mason, two biographical facts about the historical characters were pivotal in the development of the play: Constance's refusal to allow Oscar to see their children after his release from prison, and her crippling fall down the stairs of the Wildes' London home in Tite Street,[20] when she badly injured her arm and subsequently developed a spinal condition that became increasingly debilitating. Medical details of Constance's ailment discovered in family letters by the Wildes' grandson Merlin Holland in 2015 – which describe a condition that 'progressively robbed her of the ability to walk, riddling her body with pain and leaving her with excruciating headaches and extreme fatigue'[21] – have now been interpreted by experts as symptoms of multiple sclerosis. Constance turned to eccentric treatments and surgeries by a German 'nerve doctor' that would eventually lead to her death. Kilroy writes that one of the most moving experiences he had in researching his material was reading Constance's letters in the Clark Library in Los Angeles and seeing her gradual physical degeneration reflected in her worsening handwriting. For Kilroy, her fall down the stairs became

> a kind of flight as well as a fall, a launching out into space by a woman at the end of her tether, in stage terms a choreographed movement of white falling into blue. 'I saw blue and began to fly.' And in the larger scheme of the Wilde story I saw her falling or flying between two other figures, also falling, the figures of Oscar and Bosie.[22]

To round out his theme, Kilroy seized on two other snippets of information gathered from his reading about Wilde that have a much shakier historical foundation: an account of the arrest of Constance's father for public indecency (Robert Ross wrote that he was charged 'for exposing himself to nursemaids in the gardens of the Temple'[23]) and André Gide's unreliable suggestion that Douglas had expressed an erotic interest in Oscar's young son Cyril when he 'whispered with a self-satisfied smile, "He will be for me"'.[24] As Mason puts it, Kilroy's focus became 'the sexual, psychological conundrum of fathers, children, husbands, wives and lovers'.[25] Constance denying Oscar access to their two sons had, Kilroy felt, 'something to do with her own hidden terror of her dead, disgraced father'.[26]

'I'm writing a lot now about family,' Kilroy told interviewer Christopher O'Rourke in 1997, 'about the relationship between generations and the transmission of guilt, or suffering . . . between one generation and the next.'[27] The lost or absent child and the overbearing or abusive father are recurring motifs in Kilroy's theatrical oeuvre. Oscar obsesses about his children in the opening scene of *The Secret Fall*, crying that he 'must see them!' (p. 20). The private solace he finds in Cyril and Vyvyan's innocence is offset by his own public post-trial status as a 'corruptor of young men' (p. 41) deemed unfit for paternity, and by his memory of the promiscuous and cruel behaviour of his own father, William Wilde, whose two extramarital and unacknowledged daughters died horribly in a fire when Oscar was sixteen. It was Alfred Douglas' 'monstrous father' (p. 32), the Marquess of Queensberry, who called Wilde a 'sodomite'; it was partially out of hatred for this 'mad little man' (p. 43) that Bosie encouraged Oscar to bring the fateful libel action against him that eventually led to Wilde's arrest and conviction for the very crime of which Queensberry had accused him. In Kilroy's imaginative reconstruction, Constance's need to protect her children's innocence by keeping them away from Oscar after his release from prison –

or rather, from the dubious attentions of his young companion, Douglas – has roots in her own father's record of 'corrupt[ing] the innocent' (p. 23), most devastatingly herself as a young girl – the 'secret fall' at the heart of the play.

In *The Secret Fall*, the symbolic function of the child is indicated by the representation of the Wildes' sons as puppets, manipulated by attendants who accompany the main characters as 'stage hands and puppeteers, dressers, waiters and Figures of Fate' (p. 11). Constance's father and the judge who sentences Oscar to two years' hard labour are also represented by puppets, while both Constance and Oscar in their later years, although portrayed by actors, are 'on sticks' which serve as naturalistic walking aids but also evoke the control rods of marionettes. Such devices are an integral part of modernist thinking about theatre, allowing as they do for experimentation 'with the possibilities and the limitations of anthropomorphic and psychological representation'.[28] Puppets can draw attention to 'the strange, the uncanny, to the fact that humans . . . are the only creatures who can be "strange to themselves"'.[29] Mason notes that one source for Kilroy's deployment of puppets and their attendant figures was Wilde's description in *De Profundis* of Douglas as an instrument of doom: 'It makes me feel sometimes as if you yourself had been merely a puppet worked by some secret and unseen hand to bring terrible events to a terrible issue. But puppets themselves have passions. They will bring a new plot into what they are presenting, and twist the ordered issue of vicissitude to suit some whim or appetite of their own.'[30] As characters manipulated by impersonal outside forces, but with their own overt or hidden motivations, the child and father figures in the play express one of its overarching themes: the tensions between fate, societal expectations, and individual responsibility. Through their symbolic stylisation, the archetypical figures of the child and father also come to stand for abstract and contrasting notions of innocence and purity versus power and corruption.

The use of puppets stemmed as well from Kilroy's interest in classical Japanese theatre – Kabuki dance drama and Bunraku puppet theatre – with which he had become familiar during visits to Japan in 1990 and 1992. Kabuki involves stylised performance and elaborate costumes and make-up. Female roles are traditionally played by male actors, with a performer known as the *onnagata*

Jane Brennan and unidentified actors in *The Secret Fall of Constance Wilde*, Abbey Theatre, 1997. Directed by Patrick Mason. Photograph: Joe Vaněk. Courtesy Abbey Theatre.

specialising in the portrayal of female characters. Frequent elements of Kabuki include a sudden, dramatic revelation or transformation, 'magical' costume changes, and special effects such as an actor who 'flies' over the stage suspended from wires. Scenery and prop changes are commonly executed by black-clad stage hands. Trap doors are used for dramatic effect, as is a revolving stage: originally this involved a wheeled platform that was pushed around manually; later the platform was embedded in the stage. In Bunraku puppet theatre, which shares elements with Kabuki, the characters are manipulated by three puppeteers dressed in black robes and hoods. In *The Secret Fall of Constance Wilde*, the attendant figures, the performance space in the form of a white disk, the quick transformations and costume changes, the 'statue' of the Androgyne which is magically 'flown in or elevated in' (p. 20), Constance's choreographed 'fall' onto the raised hands of the attendants, and elements highlighting the performance of gender, are all related to or have their origin in Kabuki and Bunraku – although, as Kilroy points out, they ended up as 'something else' by the time the play was finished.[31]

In *The Secret Fall*, Oscar's obsessive need to see his children has a counterpart in his insistence that he 'must have' and 'will have' the figure of the Androgyne (p. 20). The latter appears on stage towards the beginning of the play, 'in a moment of white magic to Oscar's wand', as a naked, living statue posing in front of the great white disk. For Oscar, this 'man-woman' embodies 'the undivided Adam, whole and intact, where there is no man, no woman, no duality, no contrary, no grotesque fumbling towards the Other because the Other resides within oneself' (p. 20). Oscar's contention that this dream of perfection has haunted authors from Leonardo to Shakespeare and Balzac suggests that he is speaking as a creative artist about an artistic trope. These artists and many others, in order to free themselves from the traditional concept of external inspiration in the form of a female muse, adopted an androgynous creative model and shared the 'common belief . . . that to be artistic one must have the unique combination of masculine and feminine elements found in hermaphrodites and homosexuals'.[32] In the play, Oscar is speaking as one of these male authors who 'represent their creative minds as if they are characterized by a balance of sexually charged energies, fueling their artistic impulses with oppositional tensions'.[33] One of the questions Constance poses to her husband is how this ideal can be reconciled with his relationship to his wife and children.

In virtually every draft of *The Secret Fall* Kilroy describes the 'statue' of the Androgyne as 'reclining, naked, rear view, on a classical plinth' (p. 20), but in the earliest versions he specifies that the figure's pose should be 'as in Museo e Galleria Borghese, Rome or in the National Museum, Athens'.[34] The works of art he has in mind – the Sleeping Hermaphrodite in Rome and the Statue of a Sleeping Maenad in Athens – deliberately obscure the sex of the figure, which is lying prone on a couch. In her book on androgyny and aesthetics, Catriona MacLeod points out that many classical statues of androgynes are 'modeled after adolescent boys, puberty being the critical moment of sexual indeterminacy and liminality' when 'the youth occupies the middle position between feminine softness and masculine hardness and rigidity, between feminine passivity and masculine activity, between the contourlessness of the female and the clear outlines of the male'.[35] Such descriptions evoke both the Constance with whom Oscar first fell in love, described by him as 'a grave, slight, violet-eyed little Artemis',[36] 'white and slim as a lily',[37] and Bosie, worshipped by Oscar while lying 'like a hyacinth on the sofa',[38] his 'slim gilt soul' that of 'Hyacinthus, whom Apollo loved so madly'.[39] MacLeod suggests, however, that the androgynous ideal seems tangible only 'in the tantalizing contours of a marble statue',[40] being 'an aesthetic construction, outside nature and beyond human understanding'.[41] Kilroy's Oscar nevertheless sees Douglas as the androgynous inspiration incarnate, the 'man-woman descended . . . as a golden boy in whites into a London drawing room' (p. 20) – a construct that suggests 'the primacy of the "masculine" side' of Oscar's androgynous equation,[42] which complicates the position of his wife. That the idealised androgyne of Oscar's vision is, in Pacteau's phrase, an 'impossible referent' becomes ironically evident when the 'statue' on stage is transformed into the less than perfect flesh-and-blood Bosie, who competes with Constance for her husband's attentions.[43]

In the final rehearsal draft of *The Secret Fall*, Kilroy stipulated that Douglas (and hence the Androgyne) should be played by a woman. In her notes on the Abbey production for Mason and Kilroy, associate director Judy Friel wondered 'if more might be lost than gained . . . by this inversion', including 'the larger, homosexual dynamic between Bosie and Oscar'.[44] Mason, too, while declaring androgyny 'a nice idea', envisaged it would be difficult to identify a suitable actress. In the event, Andrew Scott received the part because the director liked his 'febrile energy' and 'boyish androgyny'.[45] Since the figure's nakedness worried Scott, a costume was created for the 'statue' that suggested nudity without leaving the actor's body exposed; it gave the impression of metal body armour, comprising a face mask with classical male features and a torso with breasts and a phallus. The explicitly hermaphroditic frontal effect was quite far removed from the much more ambiguous rear view of the classical models Kilroy had originally in mind, and from the slim, flower-like shape Oscar admired so much in young Constance and Bosie. Pacteau comments on the problem of the physical representation of androgyny: 'From its contradictory position – both "this" and not "this", a position therefore logically outside systems of signification, the androgyne demands not to be talked about, not to be represented.'[46] The representation as a hermaphrodite exacerbates the problem: 'incarnated, seen, it is effectively a man with breasts or a woman with a phallus' rather than a being representing the 'fantasized abolition of sexual difference' which is so clearly present in Oscar's dream of Paradise restored.[47]

In line with the spectacular effects used in Kabuki theatre, Kilroy's script imagines that the 'statue' of the Androgyne, reclining nude on its classical plinth, is 'flown in or elevated in'. It then rises before being hidden behind a scarlet sheet held up by the attendants, who transform the figure into Douglas by dressing him in 'startling whites' (p. 20). In a production, the desired effect may be hard to achieve without drawing undue attention to the technical feat or making the scene, to quote Mason, 'self-consciously arty in the wrong way'.[48] The 2008 Guthrie Theater production instead used a lift in one of its two trap doors to bring Bosie, standing naked on a pedestal, up to stage level – another very common effect in Kabuki theatre. For the final moment of the play, Kilroy's script envisages a grand transformation scene in which the figure of Oscar, who has been seated at a café table in a Parisian street, rises to full height and throws both hands in the air, whereupon 'all the costume, together with the hat and wig, fall off to reveal the naked Androgyne who now poses before the white disk' (p. 69). Rather than attempt to achieve this effect, both the Abbey and Guthrie productions omitted the scene altogether.

Kilroy has written that one of the great paradoxes in the history of art is 'how persons who are capable of monstrous behaviour are also capable of creating sublime beauty upon the page or stage'.[49] These are also the questions Constance wrestles with: 'What is the connection between [Oscar's] foul behaviour and the beauty of what he writes? Can anyone ever answer that question?' (p. 39). The action of the play and its theatrical devices are used to explore that tension. *The Secret Fall* opens with the tormented couple shortly before their deaths, waiting to re-enact pivotal scenes of their lives. They perform these scenes on the white disk, where they are put through their paces and applauded by the attendants. In this context, the disk is used to represent the confining nature of the public arena, the realm of the social or the 'real'. In his script, Kilroy conceived that, at other moments in the play, for example when the Androgyne appears on stage, the movable disk stands or hangs against a wall, as a moon or wafer, where it suggests an image of wholeness and perfection – the realm of art or the 'ideal'.[50] Constance suggests to Oscar that in the narrative of their lives, the 'real' has not received the attention it deserves; she wants to tell the events from a new perspective, 'to face myself, to face, finally, what it was that made me end up like this. . . . I want myself restored to me now. As I really am' (pp. 12–13). Oscar's story has received much attention, 'but this time there has to be mine as well! You and I. Our – marriage. Our – children' (p. 17). Constance's quest to face herself as she 'really' is, however, is complicated by the play's Brechtian emphasis on performance, through its use of puppets, masks, costume changes and choreographed movement. Paradoxically, the 'real' self can only be discovered and faced via a process of ritual re-enactment, which allows the historical characters to be removed from their actual experiences even as they experience the events all over again. During a process of ritual unmaking-and-becoming, one reality is dismantled and another is put together. This performance is cathartic; it eventually allows the characters, at least to some degree, to come to terms with their lives and even to envisage a possible future. At the time of the play's first production, Irish society was going through a similar process of revisiting the past, confronting hidden traumas, considering how past abuses might be redressed, and addressing possible ways forward.

What Constance wishes to explore with her husband is 'what it was that made me end up like this. Here. With you' (p. 12). This is her most pressing question: 'Why did I marry you, Oscar?' (p. 15). Constance is dimly aware that something 'Unspeakable. Evil' (p. 16), something she has 'sort of – blotted out' (p. 23), is connected with her initial attraction to her husband. Significantly, during the re-enactment of their courtship scene, Constance confesses to Oscar that her father, a respectable barrister, had been arrested for trying 'to corrupt the innocent' (p. 23), a revelation that anticipates her acknowledgement later in the play of her father's abuse of her as a child. Oscar remarks in turn that he despises his father, and tells Constance the story, disguised as a fairy tale, of his sister and two half-sisters (three 'princesses') and the cruel father who sent them 'away to die' (p. 25). For Constance, Oscar embodies a dark side of her psyche she can barely allow herself to acknowledge: 'It was . . . as if I were meeting someone out of my most disturbing dreams, half-realized, but now here it was, the thing itself. I immediately decided I was going to marry him' (p. 21). Conversely, Oscar sees in Constance the real-world fulfilment of a 'dream of perfection', a phrase he had used in the earlier scene to describe the figure of the Androgyne. He is 'ecstatic' that Constance is not 'contaminated by life' (p. 22). Whereas the marriage allows Constance to embrace a darkness Oscar denies she possesses, for Oscar the union constitutes the ideal and symbolic merging of male and female principles where there is no 'grotesque fumbling towards the Other' (p. 20). His strange request at the time of his marriage proposal to Constance, that she be his 'sister' (p. 25), has its roots in that dream of 'Paradise restored' (p. 20) as much as in his wish to find a replacement for the idealised 'princess' sisters of his childhood.

Constance's compulsion to construct her sons as innocent, unspoilt creatures who must be fiercely guarded against corrupting influences emanates as much from her own childhood trauma as from an objective assessment of the actual circumstances. However, in keeping the boys away from scandal – from 'all that – filth!' (p. 58) – she also harms them by denying them the genuine love of their own father. Indeed, Douglas and Oscar both suggest at different times, the 'filth' may be 'in [her] own mind' (p. 58). The children miss their father and when Constance explains that 'sometimes one's Papa can be cruel', Vyvie puts his finger on her secret motivation for separating the boys from Oscar when he asks, 'Was your Papa cruel, Mummy . . . ?' The futility of her protective impulse is shown when 'the puppeteers whisk the puppets away in a wild, childish run and they are gone'. The invalid Constance complains that the children 'keep running away from me and I cannot follow'. For her, there will in the end be 'nothing left' (p. 62).

Just as Constance in many ways serves as a screen onto which Oscar can project his dream of uncorrupted perfection, Cyril and Vyvyan are to him almost more symbol than reality. While both

Kilroy's play and the historical record do show Oscar to have been a loving and dedicated father, his desperate need to see Constance and the boys as pure, innocent and 'not of this world' is also shown to be a selfish desire. Oscar's quest for wholeness also explains the vision he imparts to Douglas after his release from prison, at the end of the play, that the boys will come and visit and the four of them will have 'such fun' (pp. 60–61). This fantasy, of possessing both the idealised Androgyne and the innocent Child, is immediately exploded by Bosie, who furiously rejects the image of the 'holy family' and cruelly declares that the boys are 'gone forever'. Soon afterwards, he himself abandons Oscar because there is 'nothing left here' (p. 64).

Bosie's ambiguity is the pivot around which the conflict between Oscar's idealism and Constance's realism revolves. Lover and tormentor to Oscar, potential brother and rival to Constance, beautiful androgynous boy and pathetic monster, Douglas is perilously poised between innocence and its corruption, unable to stop himself from betraying what is most dear to him. MacLeod points out that, while in classical antiquity the androgyne was a symbol of perfection in art, the birth of a hermaphrodite in the real world was cause for horror. This paradox presages 'the uncanny doubleness that will mark the androgyne's future: monstrosity in the real world versus perfection in the aesthetic realm. . . . This unsettling link between the beautiful and the grotesque will underpin the concept of the androgyne in its literary incarnations.'[51] As the paradoxical incarnation of the androgynous ideal, Douglas is beautiful as well as grotesque, monstrous as well as perfect. This is borne out by his ambiguous attitude to the Wildes' beautiful boys. In Part One of the play, as Constance escorts the children up to bed, watched by Oscar, Douglas addresses the audience: 'And then there were those two children. Made things frightfully complicated, the children. (*Short pause)* Adorable things – ' (p. 26). A few moments later he adds: 'And that's another thing! This frightful slander that's being passed about everywhere. I never interfered with those children. Never!' (p. 27). Constance's angry refusal in Part Two to allow Bosie to see the two boys before he goes abroad sparks the same vehement protest: 'I would never harm a child. Never! . . . If Oscar were here he would be pleased that I admire the beauty of his sons. Very simple. Very pure' (p. 58). But it is precisely by protesting too much that Bosie undermines the veracity of his denial.

Douglas explains the artist's position to Constance: 'there are no absolutes except in the desperate imagination of men and women. No black. No white. No good. No evil. No male. No female. Everything runs together and runs in and out of everything else.' But he also notes how such indeterminacy is resolved in the world of social reality; since 'human beings cannot abide such glorious confusion' they 'invent what is called morality to keep everyone and everything in place' (p. 56). Constance, who is at the mercy of public moral scrutiny for her social survival, insists on drawing a firm line. For her, the erasure of boundaries and the absence of private morality open the door to child abuse. In aesthetes like Oscar and Bosie, the beautiful child inspires rapture – 'a riveted and passionate glance' – of the kind that, 'in the sexually normative ideology of our contemporary world, induces only panic'.[52] Kevin Ohi argues that a child's innocence 'becomes meaningful, legible, perceptible, only in the retrospective light of its demise; it is something one can "have" only at the moment of its loss. Paradoxically, then, the protection of innocence can bring it into being only by securing its ruin'.[53] The much older Alfred Douglas as depicted by Kilroy in his 2000 one-act play, *My Scandalous Life*, is acutely aware that 'Once we try to possess innocence, then all is – destruction!'[54] In *The Secret Fall*, such insights are left implicit, not only in relation to the Wildes' opposing attitudes towards the children, but also in the tension between Oscar's insistence on Constance's purity and her own awareness of the corrupting childhood incident that constituted her secret 'fall'. To borrow Ohi's language, the child – Cyril, Vyvyan, as well as young Constance – is made 'to embody an improbable innocence' that signals an uncontaminated origin, an uncorrupted autonomy that, inevitably, 'presupposes its breach', and therefore implies 'a narrative of a Fall that has always already taken place'.[55]

In *The Secret Fall*, as the ritual re-enactment of Oscar's public disgrace unfolds, Constance gradually makes the connection between her marriage and the childhood trauma she has blotted out in her memory: 'It was as if I married him a second time in that disgusting prison but this time not the bride in cowslip yellow . . . oh no, this time naked in the bed of filth. You see, I saw Papa, too, in that cage, degraded, loving, generous, reviled, monstrous Papa. I loved two criminals, you see. Papa-Oscar. Oscar-Papa' (p. 47). It is through Oscar's prison degradation that Constance is led to her own epiphany: 'Christ came in the dirt, obvious, isn't it? I followed him! Followed him down into the dirt. And loved him there in my bowels' (p. 50). Her marriage to Oscar allows her to relive her most disturbing 'dream', the violation of the innocent child she was by the father she loved: 'you were drawing me into horror, step by step, like a dangerous guide, the horror of myself. You have made me brave, Oscar' (p. 66). Constance's confrontation of her attraction to the father who abused her destroys Oscar's fairy tale construction of her but also, disturbingly, reveals an element of self-accusation and self-loathing: 'You're uncontaminated by life, Constance. That's what you said. What utter rot! You needed to invent me because you couldn't face life as it really is. Uncontaminated! How more contaminated could I be?' (p. 66). Constance faces the paradox that her own 'loving, generous' father can be 'monstrous' at the same time, but can only translate that recognition into an imperfect compromise where her own children are concerned, given that '[t]hey and I have to live in the real world' (p. 67) – the 'real world' being the social and moral realm of late Victorian England.

At the end of Part One, after Oscar's imprisonment, Constance addresses the audience: 'People keep asking me questions: What will you do now, Constance? And what will you tell the children?' (pp. 47–48). At the end of Part Two, once the secret reasons behind the Wildes' marriage have been exposed and faced, these questions can be answered. Constance will refuse Oscar access to his children, but she will remain married to him, as his 'sister' (p. 67). Her final words of the play, just before her death, are addressed to her sons, in a letter in which she strongly defends the father whose love she found it imperative to deny them, and the 'terrible, strange vision' for which he sacrificed everything: 'All his troubles arose from his own father, from the way his father crushed something within the soul of his own son. But your father is a great man' (p. 68). Oscar's final thoughts about his sons – 'Cyril is the one I worry about most. He is such a perfectionist that he may do something terrible with his life' (p. 67) – reiterate the tensions between fate and agency, between impersonal force and personal responsibility, at the heart of the play.

The Secret Fall of Constance Wilde embodies the tension between the surface demands of society to perform certain roles (husband, wife, father) and the private depths of the individual psyche in a series of theatrical metaphors that stage a complex interplay between actors and audience. The attendants who prepare the characters for performance and applaud them with clappers after each scene highlight the play's structural and thematic emphasis on performativity. Their presence brings out the ritual function of theatre as well as the inexorability of fate. The events in the scenes re-enacted by the characters have, after all, already happened, just as the events in Kilroy's play that contains them are scripted from beginning to end and are repeated with each performance. This structure makes visible Kilroy's assertion that 'as writers we are all puppeteers. . . . It is simply a question of how we hide our hands.'[56] Within the play's re-enacted scenes, Oscar, Constance and Bosie observe each other's performances. For example, during the strange courtship scene between Oscar and Constance, Douglas 'poses, an "audience" to what is going on' (p. 21), and 'applauds daintily' at the conclusion of the scene (p. 26). When Constance takes her children upstairs to bed, and assures them that their absent father loves them very much, 'Oscar, away to one side, watches all this' (p. 26). When Oscar and Bosie make love in the next scene, Constance stands facing out into the audience and 'pays no attention to this' (p. 27). In these instances, the 'public' reactions of the witnessing characters serve as depictions of their conscious or repressed awareness of the hidden or private aspects of their own and others' lives. Perhaps this again serves as a metaphor for the collusion of ordinary individuals in the abuses perpetrated at official levels of the Irish state, as they passively turned a blind eye to what was, in many instances, hiding in plain sight.

By having Oscar and Constance re-enact scenes from their past lives, Kilroy draws attention to the self as having both inherent and performative aspects. The playwright places his actor-characters both within and outside of the play's action. In the former role, as 'actors', they acknowledge the presence of the theatre audience; in the latter, as 'characters', they are unaware of being watched. The doubleness of the device also has the effect of making the theatre audience aware of their own passive-active position as spectators. In the sense that they are hidden public observers of the intimate details of the private lives of others, Kilroy's play offers a study 'of theatre itself as accomplice to voyeurism and exploitation';[57] but the audience are also invited to experience theatre as communal ritual, whereby they collectively act as witnesses to the cathartic healing and transformation of the characters on stage. Constance acknowledges the coercive presence of the audience at the beginning of *The Secret Fall*, when she alerts Oscar to the demands of public expectation: 'They're waiting for us, Oscar. Back there. In the darkness.... Waiting to put us through our paces' (p. 17). By the end of the play, however, the role of the audience is positively transformed, along with the characters, when Oscar, in the year of his death, anticipates the moment of the vindication of his sacrifice: 'There are times when I see the mist of the future lift. I see them there, in rows, standing. And, you know something? They are applauding me – ' (p. 68). Since the play ends shortly hereafter, the applause upon its conclusion actualises Oscar's vision in the present moment of performance, serving as a sign of public approval as well as private understanding of that vision.

Murray has noted that at the core of Kilroy's work lies the notion of 'theater as community, as image of the very healing process which the drama itself indicates is necessary if the alienated state of modern man and woman is to be addressed',[58] or indeed, less abstractly, the fragmented state of Irish society. At the end of *The Secret Fall of Constance Wilde*, both main characters are dying; they have reached an approximate understanding of each other, an uneasy truce in which they agree to disagree about life and art. Yet even Constance acknowledges the power of Oscar's 'terrible, strange vision' that will outlive them both (p. 68). In art, the ideal of perfection prevails, even (or especially) in the face of life's compromises and failures. In the final moment of the play, the artist's vision is made flesh when the human figure of Oscar is transformed, via a magical *coup-de-théâtre* derived from Kabuki theatre, into the symbolic figure of the Androgyne. Even as the applause that follows the blackout actualises Oscar's anticipation of a time in the future when his 'terrible, strange vision' will be acclaimed, the play's imagined final theatrical moment also underlines the impossibly utopian nature of that vision. The transformation in the final scene of Oscar into the Androgyne, Oscar's 'dream of perfection', must needs be a failure, and can only draw attention to the figure's inevitable doubleness. While the Androgyne is an emblem of fluidity and transcendence of boundaries, the embodied figure simultaneously depends for its effect upon the audience's recognition of a stable opposition between male and female. Since 'sex and gender boundaries are always fluid and not fixed, the androgyne remains a body continually at war with itself. Constantly poised between self-enunciation and self-erasure, this figure never attains the ideal state of harmony toward which it gestures.'[59] The final theatrical moment of *The Secret Fall of Constance Wilde* therefore embodies not only Oscar's artistic triumph, but also his all-too-human fallibility.

Kilroy thinks of theatre as a collective effort and leaves a great deal of room for the imagination of the director and the designer in the physical execution of the play in an actual theatrical space. During the gestation phase of *The Secret Fall* he had been in close touch with Mason and made considerable changes to the script based on their discussions. For the director, achieving the playwright's vision also meant not taking everything in the script literally; Kilroy's aspirations 'could be more fully realized' by executing them in ways that are 'only potential in the script'.[60] Mason argues that Kilroy's theatre poses immense challenges on every level because 'he wants to speak in so many different languages' but also achieve unity and integrity. As works of 'immense subtlety' his plays require a similar response in a director and designer – and, one might add, in an audience.[61] Kilroy is well aware that his plays are not 'particularly easy to do'.[62]

Given both the late-Victorian historical context and the influence of Japanese classical theatre, Mason and designer Joe Vaněk aimed to give the Abbey production 'a very clean aesthetic' considering the emphasis Wilde himself placed on purity of concept and the 'importance of "line"'.[63] The Wildes' 'house beautiful' in Tite Street famously featured an all-white drawing room and dining room. When working on 'Wife to Mr Wilde', Kilroy came to imagine the desired effect as black and white, reflected in the finished play by Bosie's reference to Constance's 'desperate need to have everything black and white' (p. 56). These leads prompted Vaněk to create 'an essentially monochrome' and 'skeletal' world,[64] to which colour – blue, scarlet and gold – could be added through lighting. While many reviewers felt that the stylish production failed to engage the emotions, Hugh Leonard praised the collaborative effort that refused to separate 'veins, sinews, heart and head', and pronounced it 'one of the most stunning marriages of text and direction' he had ever seen.[65] Indeed, within their rather stark interpretation of Kilroy's script, Mason and Vaněk had looked to provide 'moments of extraordinary passionate ritual'.[66] Ritual and emotion certainly informed Merlin Holland's request that Jane Brennan wear his grandmother Constance's wedding ring on the play's opening night while performing the title role.[67] For Kilroy, the hostility to a more 'intellectual' form of theatre is 'simply a failure to recognize the depth of passion which can be conveyed through thinking'.[68] Looking back, however, Mason observed it was hard to create moments of great intimacy in the Abbey given the production's 'epic scale', and believed that the visual effect was, perhaps, over-refined. He suggested that, were he to do it again, he would opt for a 'much rougher kind of aesthetic', something, he conceded, Kilroy might have preferred.[69]

For Kilroy, the collaborative nature of theatre means that, while there can be disappointment 'when things do not quite jell the way you want them to jell', some of the most effective stagings of his work have happened after the opening production and have at times come as a 'terrific surprise', especially if the new interpretation moved radically away from the concept he started out with.[70] The production of *The Secret Fall* at the Guthrie Theater in 2008 could certainly not have been more different from its Abbey predecessor. In 1997, Joe Dowling was in his second year as the Guthrie's artistic director when he saw the play at the Abbey. Very impressed with it, he nevertheless held off on a Minneapolis production until he had both a suitable stage and a director who would be able to 'bring out the variety of elements that make the play so special'.[71] With the opening of the Guthrie's new theatre centre in 2006, presenting *The Secret Fall* at the McGuire Proscenium Stage became a realistic option. In Marcela Lorca, meanwhile, Dowling had also found a director who, he felt, really understood the complexity of Kilroy's work.

Interviewed in 2004, Mason imagined the design of a future production of *The Secret Fall* as 'much more rough and ready' than the relatively austere look Vaněk had created at the Abbey.[72] The set of steel and grimy brick walls designed by Tony Fanning for the Guthrie production evoked 'an old warehouse, a railway station or a prison',[73] but behind the concept was the intention to create 'something that Oscar would have appreciated and found beautiful'.[74] Lighting and texture were used to keep the black-clad attendants from 'disappearing' against the dark set, the idea being to render them 'almost ghost-like'. Paul Tazewell designed their costumes to underscore the play's theme of androgyny, using 'a mixture of clothing items typically considered "masculine" or "feminine"';[75] top hats and spats were paired with parasols and skirts, while some attendants wore cage crinolines on top of rather than underneath skirts in an analogy of the way the play's characters are led to expose the hidden layers of the subconscious.

The use of puppetry in the play underlines one of its central concerns, that the three people at its core 'were to some extent puppets of fate'.[76] In Kilroy's script, however, those three people are portrayed by actors; it is the children, the father and the judge who are represented by puppets. In the Abbey production, the two boys were small, white, blank marionettes. By contrast, the Guthrie production used 'life-size puppets intended to resemble Victorian dolls as closely as possible', with real hair and painted faces, wearing the sailor suits that were Vyvyan's favourite apparel.[77] The much larger size of the father and the judge, measuring over ten feet in height, was meant to convey something of their impersonal, archetypical force. In the Guthrie production the figure of the father, a grey, faceless, looming shape, literally overwhelmed Constance on the landing at the top of the staircase. In the Abbey production, 'a monster in the form of a gargantuan judge' heard Oscar speak the words that condemned him to prison, and subsequently engulfed him.[78] At the Guthrie, by contrast, a cut-out cartoon version of a courtroom was moved in front of Matthew Grier, the actor playing Oscar, who transformed himself into the judge by donning a wig and robes. While the actor's metamorphosis into the judge hinted at Wilde's own part in his downfall, Oscar's replacement by a small puppet, a few feet high, simultaneously suggested his inability to control the trial's inevitable outcome.

Precisely because Kilroy's material is highly theatrical as well as deeply considered, his scripts frequently strain at the limits of what can be represented on stage. In a 2011 lecture entitled 'The Intellectual on Stage', the playwright acknowledged that there may be 'an implied conflict' between complexity of thought and the simplicity of form by which drama is often best served, which he identifies as one of the technical problems faced by Shaw, Yeats, Beckett and, perhaps by implication, himself.[79] Theatre, however, involves risk, and in Kilroy's case the risk may be increased because he never plots his plays with any kind of absolute precision. Intellectuality in the theatre, he contends, is not 'the imposition of a strong, single vision upon others'. Much of what can or cannot be done on stage is left to the imagination of the director and designer in a collaborative effort: 'Intellectual expression has to find its place in that group, if it is to survive.'[80] Few things illustrate that better than the development of the text of *The Secret Fall of Constance Wilde* and the two very different productions the play has received to date.

At the time when Kilroy was writing his play about Constance, Oscar and Bosie, instances of clerical and institutional child abuse were just beginning to be exposed in the Irish media. By 2010, when he was finalising *Christ, Deliver Us!* for the Abbey stage, these earlier revelations had led to official investigations culminating in the publication of the Ryan and Murphy reports, which documented the extent of the abuse perpetrated in institutions such as orphanages and industrial schools over a period of many decades. In *Christ, Deliver Us!* Kilroy returns to the 1950s, the time period of *The Death and Resurrection of Mr Roche*, in order to consider again the climate of fear and repression in which ordinary citizens were held to almost impossible standards of sexual purity by the rigid moral dictates of church and state, while some members of the clergy were covertly allowed to get away with the most heinous transgressions.

7

No Such Thing as Love: *Christ, Deliver Us!*

When Kilroy decided to embark on an interpretation of *Frühlings Erwachen* (1891, hereafter referred to as *Spring Awakening*), the first and most famous, indeed notorious play by the German playwright Frank Wedekind, he had already written versions of classic dramas by Anton Chekhov, Henrik Ibsen and Luigi Pirandello. Each of these renderings retains the title of the original work: *The Seagull*, *Ghosts*, *Six Characters in Search of an Author* and *Henry* (after *Enrico IV*). These earlier, more straightforward adaptations Kilroy regards as, in many respects, commissioned 'journey-work' that pertains to 'the practical business of making theatre'.[1] Taking his cue from a remark once made by his agent Peggy Ramsay, he considers such projects 'a form of privileged conversation with an author', in which he also allows himself the licence to 'take off imaginatively'.[2] In *The Seagull* and *Ghosts* he used that freedom to transpose the action to Ireland, as he also does in *Christ, Deliver Us!* In turning Chekhov into 'O'Checkov', as he jokingly wrote to Friel, Kilroy's aim was to move the language away from what director Max Stafford-Clark regarded as a misplaced English gentility often found in Anglophone adaptations of the Russian playwright. The Irishness of Kilroy's version, then, is not first and foremost intended as an original dramatic intervention into an Irish cultural or historical debate. His adaptation of *Ghosts*, too, is moved to an Irish context, a provincial town in the 1980s, and employs contemporary equivalents for Ibsen's concerns with the long-term consequences of marital unhappiness; however, Phyllis Ryan, who commissioned the play, expressed disappointment that it nevertheless remained 'too much Ibsen, in his time, and not enough Tom, in *our* time'.[3] *Christ, Deliver Us!* completely reverses that balance, as the drama's new title also indicates. The play was not a commission; it was Kilroy himself who opted to write a work inspired by *Spring Awakening*, and while he (loosely) retains that play's episodic framework he makes the material entirely his own by refocusing it through the lens of 1950s Ireland. The play's reception likewise reveals the degree to which *Christ, Deliver Us!* was regarded less as Kilroy's adaptation of Wedekind than as his response to contemporary revelations about past abuses in industrial schools and Magdalen laundries.

In her book on Wedekind's 'Theatre of Subversion', Elizabeth Boa suggests that the issues centrally explored in his work are the clash between the outer world of social relations and the inner world of dreams and illusions, the generational and sexual connections between parents and children and men and women, and the position of the artist in the world.[4] Given Kilroy's engagement with very similar concerns throughout his playwriting career, it should come as no surprise that he has had a long-standing fascination with Wedekind. The latter's *Spring Awakening* is a work Kilroy says he was haunted by 'for many, many years' before he attempted to write his own version of it. One of the aspects of the play that fascinates him is that it 'fails consistently to achieve anything like a coherent finish'.[5] That sense of provisionality and lack of closure, itself a frequent theme in Kilroy's own work, is one of the features that make *Spring Awakening* a challenging play, not only for theatre producers, but for critics, translators and adaptors as well.

Christ, Deliver Us!, Kilroy's free interpretation of Wedekind's drama, premiered at the Abbey Theatre in February 2010, after the playwright had worked on it, on and off, for a decade. In 1998, Kilroy had 'balked' when asked by director Joe Devlin to write a version of *Spring Awakening*, but having re-read the play he concluded that 'it could be done in "our" fifties – boarding schools, priests, orphanages, nuns, Fr Brendan Smyth – the lot'.[6] In late 1999 Ben Barnes, then preparing to take over the artistic directorship of the Abbey Theatre, expressed his excitement about Kilroy's plans for a new work loosely based on *Spring Awakening*, and told him he would 'provisionally hold a slot in late spring 2001' for the production.[7] In early 2000 he mentioned the planned adaptation to Victoria White of *The Irish Times*, and suggested that Kilroy, given 'the background of his schooldays, . . . can't help but refract it through what we know now about those times. We do have a responsibility to interrogate the past.'[8] When Kilroy submitted the first draft of the play, however, Barnes felt that the script, while 'theatrically daring', read too much like a 'highly theatricalised threnody on the subject of repression in Ireland in the middle of the last century'. Feeling that the work failed to 'add anything new to what we understand of those repressive and depressing times', he relinquished the Abbey's interest in the play so that Kilroy would be free to pursue other options to have the work produced.[9]

An opportunity to put *Christ, Deliver Us!* before an audience did not arise until some years later, when Andy Hinds, artistic director of Classic Stage Ireland – a Dublin-based company devoted to performing classic works of world dramatic literature – conceived a plan to develop the play for an eventual staging at Dublin City University's Helix theatre. The envisaged production was to involve young people from Smashing Times, a theatre company with a community-based approach to drama, but the project fell through in early 2007 when the Arts Council turned down a request for funding, partly on the grounds that the proposal was too ambitious.[10] In 2010 the Abbey Theatre, now under the artistic management of Fiach Mac Conghail, decided to stage *Christ, Deliver Us!* after all. The production was directed by Wayne Jordan, a promising young talent for whom this was his Abbey debut.

Begun as a straightforward English-language version of Wedekind's play, *Christ, Deliver Us!* increasingly became an Irish work as the adaptation process progressed. The parallels Kilroy perceived between the late nineteenth-century German provincial society portrayed in the original play and the Ireland of the 1950s that became the focus of *Christ, Deliver Us!* were, in his words, 'very striking'.[11] In both, a climate of sexual repression prevailed; ignorance and timidity were confused with innocence; moral standards were at times brutally enforced by patriarchal authorities; and transgressors of the moral code were punished or became tragic victims of fear and self-loathing. In *Spring Awakening*, however, that morality is largely the expression of a petit-bourgeois mentality hiding self-interest behind the mask of propriety and respectability. For the adaptation to work in an Irish context, Kilroy needed to play up the role of the Catholic Church. He had already expressed his feelings about the role of religion in Ireland in a 1991 essay entitled 'Secularized Ireland', where he diagnosed it as a cause of widespread fear: 'a kind of timidity before life itself in all its mortal glory and all its dreadful horror, its inexpressible variety. People who are afraid of life will always try to restrict the lives of others. We have many examples of individuals and institutions which seek to control and restrict the actions of others.' Such fear, he went on to argue, 'has its source in education, particularly that directed by the two most politically assertive churches on this island, the Roman Catholic and Presbyterian'. While *Christ, Deliver Us!* broadly follows the plot outline and episodic structure of Wedekind's play, its emphasis on the role of the Catholic Church in the mid-century Irish Republic affects the play's tone. The kind of fear described in Kilroy's essay, which 'generates violence' and 'perverts and distorts moral values',[12] is the motivating force behind the characters, whereas in Wedekind the driving factor tends to be self-interest 'distorted by the prevailing moral philosophy'.[13] Wedekind's emphasis is on mocking that philosophy; indeed, he commented that he had resolved, while writing *Spring Awakening*, not to lose the humour in any scene, no matter how serious it might be.[14] Kilroy's play, which is more piercingly psychological and less ironically distant than its model, focuses on young individuals who are adversely affected by moral tyranny, and therefore uses a darker palette.

When Wedekind set out to write *Spring Awakening*, he drew upon his personal experience. During his time at the gymnasium, for example, a number of his fellow students buckled under the pressure of homework and exams and committed suicide, as does Moritz Stiefel in the play. Kilroy stays true to that spirit of authenticity in that he, too, tried 'to write a play drawing upon [his] own growing up in the 1950s'. In Kilroy's version, the secular gymnasium of *Spring Awakening* becomes a diocesan college, loosely based on St Kieran's College in Kilkenny, which Kilroy attended. St Kieran's, like the school in Wedekind's play, was academically very demanding and 'examination results were all that mattered'. In addition, however, its strict religious ethos put 'an awful lot of pressure on children', who consequently experienced a great deal of 'guilt and fear'.[15]

In *Christ, Deliver Us!* Kilroy based the reformatory school to which Michael Grainger is sent on St Conleth's Reformatory School for boys in Daingean, County Offaly, but changed its name to St

Joseph's Industrial School. His stage direction paints a grim picture of deprivation and abuse:

> A shivering line of Industrial School boys, in old nightshirts, with towels around their waists, standing impassively, facing the audience. A Christian Brother, in his full clerical garb, carrying a leather strap, stands on guard, also facing out. The boys are different from the college boys, shaven and bruised heads, black eyes, one or two with dirty bandages. Behind their backs we see three cubicle showers with doors closed.[16]

Behind the Brother's back, the boys perform sexually suggestive gestures. Kilroy's depiction of the industrial school is no exaggeration. In 1966, *Irish Times* journalist Michael Viney – an Englishman resident in Ireland who became '"almost a one-man department of sociology" exploring "Ireland's dark corners"'[17] – visited St Conleth's and was given a harrowing account by one of its teenage inmates of 'multiple floggings, always being hungry, "baldy haircuts", countless fruitless attempts to run away followed by more beatings, a shower once a month, and being forced to work in the fields in winter' without adequate clothing. Viney's eight articles in *The Irish Times* sparked a single letter to the editor: 'Nobody commented on them. Nothing happened.'[18]

Christ, Deliver Us! premiered in the wake of the public debate concerning the injustices done to women – often unmarried mothers – confined in Magdalen laundries, and only a short time after the publication of the Ryan and Murphy reports that finally brought the extent of institutional child abuse to light. Kilroy explains that he did not write about sexual abuse in his play because he himself never experienced such a thing as a child, although the physical abuse he foregrounds was 'violent and systemic' in his school days and 'seeped through the whole culture'.[19] His work should therefore be seen as a drama 'behind' rather than about 'the current clerical scandals'.[20] Different from *Spring Awakening*, *Christ, Deliver Us!* immediately emphasises the pervasive presence of violence. In the play's opening moments, a group of boys in the college are caught smoking and receive a caning on the hands from one of the priests. One reviewer noted that quite a few older audience members tittered in recognition at this form of punishment.[21] The caning of the pupils is immediately followed on stage by 'a highly choreographed sequence of boys hurling' (p. 11) – a sport for which St Kieran's College is well known and at which many of its pupils have excelled over the years. The excitement of the scene in the Abbey production reflected the 'theatrically daring' quality Barnes had noted in the script in 2001; but the loud clash of the hurleys and the spectators' shouts egging on the players to 'bate the hell outta' their opponents (p. 11) also served to suggest that sport can be an extension of a culture of violence as much as a healthy outlet for youthful aggression.

In method, Wedekind's *Spring Awakening* looked back to Georg Büchner's *Woyzeck* in its use of caricature and the strange juxtaposition of humour and horror, and anticipated some of the distancing effects used in Brecht's epic theatre. As Boa points out, the title *Spring Awakening*, 'evocative of love in life's springtime, is contradicted by the subtitle, *A Children's Tragedy* ("Eine Kindertragödie") with its message of young lives blighted'[22] – a subtitle which, moreover, suggests that the tragic aspect of the play itself is scaled down and not taken fully seriously. Although tragic things do happen – Moritz commits suicide, Melchior is sent to a reform school for teaching Moritz the facts of life and for getting Wendla Bergmann pregnant, and the girl dies after an abortion – the melodrama (rather than horror) of these events is subtly undercut by 'a vein of mocking humour [which] undermines the pathos'.[23] Boa suggests that Wedekind's disturbing vision of the fragility of social institutions is 'rendered all the more unsettling through the . . . comical-lyrical-satirical-tragical-farcical-melodramatic mixing of the modes', in which 'the conventional is set against a fantastic flouting or eclectic mix of styles collapsing into absurdity'.[24] This effect is visualised at the end of the play, when the ghost of Moritz appears to Melchior with his head under his arm, which is simultaneously funny, sad and surreal. Boa concludes that: '[l]ike the dismantled Moritz, the play as a whole can be taken apart into pieces which do not fit together neatly to form a mimetic representation of a closed world, whether a lyric realm of nature and young love or a fatally determining social environment'.[25]

While Kilroy is, as Anthony Roche affirms, 'one of Ireland's most technically adventurous writers', whose 'experimentation' and 'restless innovations' always serve to articulate 'the troubling vision of a modern Ireland undergoing ever greater social and ideological stress',[26] his approach in the Wedekind adaptation is largely a move away from the stylistic eclecticism of the original towards greater realism. This shift was dictated by the sensitivity of the subject matter in an Irish context, especially in the climate of ongoing revelations and investigations at the time of writing. Fintan O'Toole describes Kilroy's approach to the adaptation as 'a process of double refraction, of contemporary Ireland strained through a European classic and then shifted back into an Irish past'; the play, then, 'is not essentially about a socially realistic 1950s but about our present need to confront the psychic legacy of the culture that was at its height in that decade',[27] the kind of double vision Kilroy also aimed for in a historical work like *The O'Neill.*

Wedekind used humour as a kind of alienation effect, 'to make the horror more palatable'.[28] Even his teenage boys speak in comically elaborate and pompous phrases, while many of the adult authority figures are little more than ridiculous stereotypes. Principal Sonnenstich (sunstroke) supervises teachers with names like Knochenbruch (brokenbone), Knüppeldick (bigstick) and Zungenschlag (tonguetwist); the custodian is called Habebald (bringquick). In Kilroy's version, the teachers, all members of the clergy, have regular names, but the canon knows what the boys call them behind their backs: Fr Jimmy, the science teacher, is referred to as The Spirit Lamp; Fr Seamus as Stutters; Fr Joseph as Fishy; and the canon himself as Big Dog. There is also humour here, but of a different kind than Wedekind's satirical mockery, and its effect is to add psychological insight into the characters rather than create caricatures. Reviewers of *Christ, Deliver Us!* recognised these lighter moments but, on the whole, found the play very dark, and close to being 'an austere, even hopeless work'.[29]

The play's new title, *Christ, Deliver Us!*, indicates the shift in focus 'from the bloom of desire to the frost that kills it'.[30] The reference to the phrase from the Lord's Prayer ('lead us not into temptation, but deliver us from evil') raises questions about the source and nature of that 'temptation' and 'evil'. *Spring Awakening* presents characters who are all tragi-comically entangled in a web of obfuscation, as the teenagers have questions about their developing bodies and confusing desires, and parents keep the unspeakable truth at bay with lies and fairy tales. Kilroy recalls with dismay that in his own school days, 'the whole relationship between the sexes was totally abnormal', and that 'a very deep fear' of sex was instilled in young people 'long before the physical thing had any meaning'.[31] Every equivalent scene about sexual relations in Kilroy is darker and less comically abstract than in Wedekind. The latter gives us a scene in which Hans Rilow melodramatically throws a picture of a naked Venus down the toilet because she is distracting him too much from his homework and exhausting him in her painted unresponsiveness. In Kilroy's play it is the clerics at the diocesan college who gather around to look at the 'filthy pictures' of 'naked hussies' they have confiscated from their pupils' desks, which the only sensible teacher, Fr Seamus, identifies as (hardly voluptuous) images of the goddesses in 'The Judgement of Paris' by Lucas Cranach the Elder (p. 38). In *Spring Awakening*, Moritz confesses to Melchior that he once saw a naked girl – when he sneaked into a forbidden part of the anatomical museum – and that she was 'oh, so true to nature!'[32] In *Christ, Deliver Us!*, when Mossy shares with Michael that he, too, once saw a girl 'without a stitch', the context has changed:

> MOSSY: 'Twas dark. 'Twas behind the Duffy circus caravan. A lot of the lads were there.
> MICHAEL: Oh, I heard about that.
> MOSSY: She was wan of the wans outta the circus. *(Pause)* She charged us all tuppence each. For to look.
> MICHAEL: Go 'way! And did ya get to touch?
> MOSSY: She was the other side of the barrier from us. (p. 22)

While Wedekind's play stresses the artificial and clinical divide between the sexes, Kilroy's scene not only emphasises the 'barrier' between boys and girls, but also evokes an entire culture that fosters sexual and social division, marginalises outsiders, and leads to hysteria, exploitation and perversion.

These pervasive sexual and social divisions are everywhere in *Christ, Deliver Us!*, much more so than in *Spring Awakening*. Kilroy shows abuse of power at all levels and in many different contexts. In the industrial school, boys are abused by the staff and in turn abuse each other. Those who are not bullies become victims, unless, as in the case of Michael, the parcels they receive from home can serve as bribes to ward off violence. Parents use their authority to pitch child against child: Mrs Butler tells Winnie she cannot see Michael Grainger again because he is stuck-up and 'not your class of boy' (p. 32); Mrs Grainger wishes that Michael wouldn't 'consort with that fellow' Mossy, because he represents 'the riff-raff of this town' (p. 36). The main power lies with fathers, however. Michael's father is 'an important man, not only in this town but beyond' (p. 39). Even the canon, who is not a bad man but weak in the face of social pressure and authority, is afraid of antagonising him and browbeaten into agreeing that Michael should be punished with a brief spell in the industrial school – 'a good, sharp shock to the system' – for his 'degenerate' behaviour (writing down for Mossy the facts of sexual intercourse), even though the standard remedy would be 'a retreat for the boy, a period of reflection and silence' (p. 53). Mossy Lannigan worries that his father, an army man, will 'lather' him for failing his exam: 'He's a killer, so he is, me father!' (p. 16). The canon is aware that Lannigan is '[n]ot a nice man' and '[d]angerous' (p. 26), but underestimates the seriousness of the situation. Mossy is an only son and unable to live up to his brutal father's expectations, which he mimics just before he commits suicide: 'No son of mine – no son of mine will let me down in front of everyone' (p. 45). Winnie Butler's father, who was 'a good man' (p. 32), is dead, which in this patriarchal society puts the girl at an immediate disadvantage. 'Wouldn't he stand up for ya, Winnie? Ways that I can't,' Mrs Butler exclaims when Winnie's pregnancy is discovered: 'No wan'd talk about ya behind yer back if yer Daddy was alive. I guarantee ya that' (p. 56). Only men have the power to punish and defend; women are kept ignorant and passive and are told to 'offer up' their lives: 'All women has to do that. Tha's the beginning and the end of it' (pp. 32–33).

Spring Awakening also concerns itself with society's enforcement of rigidly coded male and female identity markers. Wedekind depicted male sexuality as active and inclined towards sadism, and female sexuality as passive and masochistic, characteristics broadly displayed by Melchior and Wendla, although they also share a sense of curiosity and inquisitiveness. This dichotomy leaves the fearful, insecure, soft-hearted, and intellectually less gifted Moritz in a predicament. While the girls praise Melchior's ability to swim and his 'beautiful brow', they consider Moritz 'a stupid' even if his eyes have a 'soulful look'. One of them recalls with distaste the time he offered her some sweets from his pocket which were 'soft and warm' (p. 48), like Moritz himself. Unable to embody masculine and intellectual leadership, Moritz identifies with the headless queen in the story his grandmother used to tell him: 'When I see a pretty girl, I see her without a head – and then presently, I, myself appear to be the headless Queen' (p. 70). Schönborn argues that Moritz shoots himself in the head because it does not match his body: only in death can he become like the headless queen of the fairy tale. Mossy in *Christ, Deliver Us!* is also 'a right auld softie' (p. 15), but when he kills himself it is with a shot through the heart, the symbolic seat of love and the emotions, and Vivie – who is much more upset at Mossy's death than her German counterpart Ilse is at Moritz's – describes Mossy's mortal wound looking 'as if a big red flower had opened up on the front of his shirt' (p. 49), suggesting a blossoming that should have occurred in life rather than in death.

In *Spring Awakening*, Ilse is a village girl who spends most of her time in the city drinking in cafés and cabarets, modelling for (and sleeping with) an exotic group of painters, and generally transgressing all social and moral codes. She is alive, even if she is living on the edge. Moritz is jealous of the exciting freedom she represents, but too timid to emulate her example, which only adds to his suicidal despair. In his initial drafts of *Christ, Deliver Us!*, Kilroy had cut Ilse, 'the local "hot" girl', because she did not seem to belong in the world of 1950s Kilkenny,[33] but after working on the script with Hinds in 2007 for a potential Classic Stage Ireland production he reintroduced the character in the guise of Vivie Hackett. Vivie is subtly different from her German counterpart. She and her family have recently returned to Ireland from London, where she experienced the Blitz, which was terrible and frightening but also made her feel 'alive'. (Many of the play's characters only feel alive, or feel anything at all, in painful or life-threatening situations.) Vivie's father is an artist, notorious for painting 'naked women' (p. 24), which renders the family suspect in the eyes of the other characters. Whereas Wedekind's Ilse has freely chosen a wild and bohemian existence, Vivie is much more pathetic. When she runs into Mossy shortly before his suicide, she is swigging from a bottle, and the grandiose future she envisages for herself – 'I'm going to Paris. I'm going to model for all the great painters in their studios! I'm going to be every kind of woman you can think of!' (p. 42) – sounds less like wishful thinking than the cry of desperation from someone who knows she is trapped without any real options of escape. Her drunken offer to '[m]ess around' with Mossy in the bushes (p. 42) has none of the playfulness of Ilse's teasing invitation to Moritz: 'I will singe your hair and hang a little bell around your neck' (p. 100). Kilroy shows that there is no healthy way for sexuality to find expression in a culture that sees all such expressions as uniformly evil.

Wedekind uses a further example of unorthodox behaviour to question the rigid moral code and compulsory binary division between genders in a scene late in the play, where Hans and Ernst are seen kissing each other while lounging in the lush surroundings of a vineyard. Their decadent indulgence is not so much a celebration of gay love as a statement about the rejection of conventional behaviour. The boys are simply seizing the day while cheerfully, if somewhat cynically, planning a future where God will go hand in hand with Mammon. Ernst sees himself as a clergyman, his life of privilege made even cushier by 'a good-natured little wife' and 'a well-filled library', while Hans foresees a life of sensuality and riches, which he will use to 'erect a monument to God'. Both fully intend to 'skim off the cream' even as they will finally be forced by adulthood to put on the costume of virtue (p. 143). Along with Ilse, Kilroy had also omitted these two boys from the first version of his script, but Hinds said he missed the love scene, which to him was 'part of what makes the original so courageous and complete'.[34] Kilroy therefore added a new moment earlier in his play where the college prefect teaches the boys an awkward lesson in ballroom dancing. The moment the instructor is called away the pupils begin making crude sexual innuendoes, but once they, too, have vacated the room, two boys expertly waltz onto the stage. As the music dies down, they kiss. The effect of Kilroy's scene is to emphasise the misogyny fostered by an all-male environment, and the irony of the invisibility of homosexuality within the context of the homosocial and potentially homoerotic situation in which the prefect is obliviously placing the boys. Many reviewers of the Abbey production saw the scene of the two boys dancing and kissing as the play's most moving moment, and the only genuine expression of love and affection in it. It is, of course, a poignant reflection on a society in which all forms of sexual expression are demonised as lust, and men and women are taught to regard each other with fear and suspicion, that the most touching expression of sexual love is the love that dare not speak its name, the love that is invisible and disavowed by mainstream society.

Mossy's calling out of Michael's name after he has inadvertently witnessed the kiss can be read as both a clamouring for enlightenment of what he has just seen and a longing for the same kind of gentle closeness. It is also a plea for help. Kilroy's Mossy is different from Wedekind's Moritz, who sneaks into the teachers' conference room to see if he has passed his exams, petrified as he is to let down his parents after all the sacrifices they have, supposedly, made for him. Mossy secretly changes his answer in the mock maths exam because he is terrified of his father's physical violence, should he fail. These differences in motivation also set into motion different trains of events.

Wedekind's Moritz melodramatically decides that killing himself is preferable to failing his exams and giving his father a heart attack and his mother a nervous breakdown. After his suicide, which takes place off stage, Moritz's father delivers to headmaster Sonnenstich the twenty-page treatise explaining the facts of life, 'illustrated with life-size pictures' (p. 110), written by Melchior for his friend. In an absurd scene, the headmaster questions Melchior in convoluted terms regarding the offending document. The boy eventually agrees that he is the author, protesting, however, that what he wrote is 'neither more nor less than what are well-known facts to' the teachers (p. 113). At that moment Sonnenstich notifies the custodian that it is time for 'the three hours' exercise in agglutive Volapuk' (p. 114), a precursor to Esperanto. Wedekind's joke underlines Melchior's point; the facts of life are a universal language spoken and understood all over the world, but here they amount to evidence of what Melchior's father, a lawyer, calls 'moral imbecility' (p. 125), curable only by a spell in the reform school. Mrs Gabor is reluctant to follow her husband in this conclusion, but changes her mind after she learns that Melchior has written a letter to Wendla, offering to stand by her should there be consequences of what he has come to see as his 'sin' against her. Since Mr Gabor now has possession of Melchior's letter, which is the only evidence of his son's involvement with Wendla, Mrs Bergmann no longer has a legal leg to stand on to make her pregnant daughter respectable again in the public eye, and resorts to procuring a backstreet abortion.

In *Christ, Deliver Us!* the priest who has heard Mossy's confession about changing the exam uses that information against him outside the confessional. Mossy's desk is searched and Michael's document is found, but even under great pressure, Mossy refuses to reveal its author. Michael is too self-absorbed to see that Mossy's brave attempt to do the honourable thing – 'I'd never tell on ya, Michael. Never!' (p. 35) – is a thinly veiled appeal for Michael to stand by him and share the blame. Afraid of his father and abandoned by his school, the church, and his best friend, Mossy concludes that '[e]very door is shut on me' (p. 43). The one shut door we see him trying to open at the beginning of Act II, that of his father's large wardrobe, becomes, once Mossy succeeds, what Schopenhauer called the 'always open door' of suicide:

> A full army officer's uniform hangs inside, facing out like a disembodied presence. . . . Draped across the uniform is a Sam Browne belt and holster. He reaches for the holster, flaps open the cover and removes the revolver. Pause. He pushes the gun into his chest, bending over. As the lights come down: a single shot. (p. 46)

Mossy's death takes place at centre stage. In a play exposing the repressive and abusive regime of the past, whose effects are still being dealt with in contemporary Ireland, it is important that the tragic consequences of that system not be dissimulated: they must be shown in all their horror.

Kilroy establishes a clear connection between Mossy's fate and what happens to Winnie Butler by showing the extent to which the church is in control of the social sanctioning of both birth and death. In 1950s Ireland, suicide and extramarital pregnancy were equally taboo. At Mossy's funeral, one of the girls notes that he is being buried in a corner of the cemetery, 'with the unbaptised babies', and comments bitterly that they 'might as well put him down in an open field, so they might' (p. 49). Coming just moments after Winnie has told her best friend that she is 'going to have a baby' and will soon be sent to a convent 'to be hid away' (p. 47), the juxtaposition of 'unbaptised babies' with 'open field' subtly evokes the events of 1984, when the discovery on the beach at Cahirciveen, County Kerry, of a newborn child that had been stabbed to death led to a bizarre and insensitive murder investigation; eventually, Joanne Hayes falsely confessed to the killing, only for it to be revealed that she herself had secretly given birth to a stillborn baby around the same time and buried it in a field on her family's farm. What came to be known as the 'Kerry babies' case was one of a series of events that sparked an unprecedented and ongoing public debate in Ireland about 'terror and hypocrisy and misogyny'[35] that broke open a long-standing culture of silence.

There had certainly been earlier attempts to break that silence. In September 1964, *The Irish Times* published Michael Viney's series of seven articles collectively titled 'No Birthright', which investigated the plight of unmarried mothers and their treatment in Ireland. That same month, Máiréad Ní Ghráda's play *An Triail* (later translated into English as *On Trial*) premiered at Dublin's Damer Theatre, produced by Tomás Mac Anna. Using Brechtian techniques, Ní Ghráda, too, explored the terrain covered by Viney, but from the perspective of Máire, a schoolgirl impregnated and abandoned by her married lover. Refusing to give up her child for adoption when pressured by the Mother and Baby Home where she gave birth, Máire ends up taking her own life and that of her daughter. In a retrospective assessment of the play and its social context published in 2015, *Sunday Business Post* columnist Colin Murphy commented that *On Trial* has 'one of the most striking openings ever in Irish theatre: "I killed my child because she was a girl".' Although the play's subject matter caused controversy, and some people were shocked, even outraged by it, both its Irish and English language performances were enormously successful. So why then, asks Murphy, was nothing done in response, and why did the play end up disappearing from the public eye for thirty years after its initial impact had worn off? The answer is complex and includes 'the cultural consensus around motherhood and morality' in Ireland as part of a wider community ethos that 'inhibits dissent', as well as a general lack of resources at the time to improve social services for single-parent families.[36] While, in its day, Ní Ghráda's play constituted a relatively isolated protest, in 2010 *Christ, Deliver Us!* formed one of many expressions of outrage in a widespread public debate.

Winnie, the pregnant young woman in *Christ, Deliver Us!*, dismisses her friend's dismay about Mossy's funeral with characteristic forth-rightness: 'It don't matter where ye're buried. . . . When ya rise up ye're all perfect and together again as if nothing had happened to ya' (p. 49). Optimistic as she may try to be, however, what remains unspoken is that it is life before death that routinely leaves people crushed and broken. Winnie and Mossy do rise again at the end of the play, literally on stage and figuratively as haunting memories in Michael's mind. For each performance of Kilroy's play, too, Winnie and Mossy come back to life, only to die horrible deaths once more, to remind the audience that the social traumas of the Irish past have not yet gone away. To echo the central metaphor of *Tea and Sex and Shakespeare*, this historical baggage has to be opened and fully acknowledged in all its ugliness before society itself can begin to come together and move towards some form of wholeness.

Fairly early on in his career, Kilroy said that his works were an attempt to 'acknowledge a failure to achieve a wholeness of community in the Irish experience which they describe'.[37] That the society depicted in *Christ, Deliver Us!* is fragmented is made clear in the name of the special place by the river where Michael and Winnie sometimes meet in secret. Whereas in Wedekind's play, Melchior and Wendla encounter each other accidentally in the woods, as in a fairy tale, Kilroy's young couple seek out a location called 'The Gash', named for 'the white water out there over the rocks at the fork in the river. Golawn Gash' (p. 28). The Irish name, *Golán Gais*, suggests a weeping, gushing stream (white water), while the anglicisation and Michael's description of the location call to mind a gaping wound or divide: a forked gash. More specifically, the image evokes Winnie's rape, which occurs there, and the bloody childbirth scene that follows. The place, moreover, is known for its 'swallow hole', an area that sucks in anything that floats by, from objects to dead bodies, which is symbolic of the culture of repression and secrecy stifling these two inquisitive characters, who both long for straightforward knowledge and openness of expression. 'It'd be wild if we could see what was down in that swally hole beyond,' Michael says to Winnie. 'If it suddenly threw up everything in a gush, like the geysers in Iceland, prams and bed springs, Ma Healy's chamber pot, and Biker Coady's old bikes, bones and saucepans and somebody's old nightshirt . . . ' (pp. 29–30). But Winnie recognises the dark side of this kind of free thinking: 'You know, when I laugh at them all I think I'm going to be punished for it' (p. 30). The scene following this conversation (taken from Wedekind), in which Winnie makes Michael hit her with a switch, and his initial reluctance to do so turns into an uncontrolled outburst of physical and emotional frustration, has the effect of showing the extent of the gash created by the culture of repression, whose codes have been internalised even by those who are trying to resist them.

While *Spring Awakening* emphasises a bourgeois culture of respectability that renders certain topics unmentionable, Kilroy shows the extent to which the Catholic Church is in charge of monitoring sexuality, especially female sexuality, within the family. Wedekind's tone is wickedly ironic throughout. Mrs Bergmann cannot bring herself to tell Wendla the facts of life, even though the fourteen-year-old makes it clear that she finds it hard to believe that her sister's new baby was delivered by the stork. It is only when Wendla threatens to ask the (obviously disreputable) chimney sweep about the bird's means of access to the house that her mother, with much hand-wringing and after considerable dithering, agrees to reveal the truth: 'In order to have a child – one must love – the man – to whom one is married – love him, I tell you – as one can only love a man!' (p. 82). When Melchior initiates sex with Wendla, she applies her mother's advice literally and cries, 'Don't kiss me, Melchior! – Don't kiss me! . . . People love – when they kiss – Don't, don't!' Melchior asserts, in his detached, philosophical manner, that 'there's no such thing as love! – Everything is selfishness, everything is egotism! – I love you as little as you love me' (p. 88), and although Wendla keeps saying 'don't' as Melchior proceeds beyond kissing, her protests taper off as she appears to be consenting to the act. Indeed, Wedekind shows the girl walking in the garden the next morning, blissfully smiling at the memory of what she still cannot put into words. In *Christ, Deliver Us!* the tone is much grimmer. Mrs Butler wants to wait until Winnie is getting married before telling her about sex and, in the meantime, refers her for answers to the priest, who, on a past occasion, had told her 'to pray for all the women of the world' (p. 32). Later, Michael responds to Winnie's expressions of affection with the bleak statement that there is '[n]o such thing as love' (p. 43), his black mood resulting from his recent conversation with Mossy about his role in his friend's terrible predicament. When Michael bluntly tells Winnie to lie down, she appears to be blind-sided. The scene is more obviously a rape than in Wedekind's play, since Winnie makes it clear that she is not sure what is happening and that Michael is hurting her. While this is taking place on stage, '[t]he canon and a line of impassive priests, soutanes and birettas, appear, looking out into the audience' (p. 44), a juxtaposition that is silently made to speak for itself.

In *Spring Awakening*, Wendla does not know she is pregnant and believes she has some dreadful disease until her mother lets the news slip out: 'You haven't the dropsy, you have a child, girl!', to which Wendla responds, quite logically in view of what she has been told, 'But it's not possible, Mother. I'm not married yet!', allowing her mother to deliver the punchline: 'that's just it, you are not married! That is the most frightful thing of all!' (pp. 139–40). This comedy of errors ends ominously when Mrs Bergmann admits old Mother Schmidt to the house, after which Wendla is not mentioned again until the play's final scene, when Melchior stumbles upon her gravestone, whose inscription states that she died of anaemia and piously proclaims, 'Blessed are the Pure of Heart' (p. 147). Only when the Masked Man appears in the graveyard is the hypocrisy unmasked, as Melchior learns from him that he was not responsible for Wendla's death but that 'she was killed by the abortives given by Mother Schmidt' (p. 155). The gentleman also belatedly points out to Moritz's ghost that it might have done his parents good to get a little upset with their son, and that very few people die of shame.

In Kilroy's version, Winnie bluntly tells her friend Monica that she is going to have a baby. Monica, who is regularly beaten by her parents, reacts with panic: '*(In tears)* Me father'll murder me when he hears about all this!' (p. 48). In 1950s Ireland, an abortion would have been out of the question; Winnie will be sent to a convent '[f]or to be hid away. Till it's all over' (p. 47). Kilroy here complements Winnie's first appearance in the play (a scene taken from Wedekind, in which she resists having her dress adjusted to a more modest length by her mother) with a second scene in which the mother is letting out the dress in the front and sides. Mrs Butler will only tell her daughter that '[i]t's all arranged. The doctor 'n everything. The – baby. Afterwards. Everything's settled and paid for' (p. 56). Kilroy does not have to use the phrase 'Mother and Baby Home' or 'Magdalen asylum' to make his audience understand that this is where Winnie will be sent. Investigations into what was done to thousands of women behind the doors of such institutions by religious orders of nuns were very much in the news around the time of the play's premiere. Winnie does not know what fate awaits her, but her reaction to the news that Michael has been 'put . . . away for good' in the industrial school – 'God Almighty! St Joseph's! That place!' (p. 57) – reverberates with a foreboding of her own future. As it happens, Winnie goes into labour before she can be sent away, and as in the case of Mossy's lonely suicide, her ordeal plays out shockingly on stage:

> Lights up on WINNIE in the darkness by the river bank. She is already in labour, groaning and breathing heavily. For a moment she stands, holding up an old towel and a scissors. She tries to settle herself on the ground, with difficulty, shifting about from position to position. Finally she lies down, her back to the audience, and removes her underwear. She gives birth with a single scream and holds up a bloody foetus. She cuts the cord and collapses back, the dead foetus in her arms. (p. 61)

The scene, described by one reviewer as 'an appalling and downright unnerving few minutes of theatre',[38] amounts to a glaring exposure that counteracts the decades of silence and secrecy that surrounded the reality of extramarital pregnancy in Ireland.

Kilroy's stage direction echoes in its details the horrifying case of Ann Lovett, the fifteen-year-old schoolgirl from Granard, County Longford, who kept her pregnancy secret until she gave birth alone, on the last day of January 1984, in a grotto dedicated to the Virgin Mary behind the town's Catholic church; discovered with her stillborn baby wrapped in a coat and a pair of scissors beside her, which she had used to cut the umbilical cord, she died in hospital a few hours later. Like the Kerry babies case in the same year, the tragic death of Ann Lovett has since become 'an event used to define the growing pains of a country caught half-way between past and progression'.[39] In the scene that follows Winnie's ordeal in Kilroy's play, Michael is told by a Brother in the industrial school that 'that girl' has been found dead: 'Down by the river, they say' (p. 62). Michael identifies the place as Golawn Gash, but the phrase used by the Brother also evokes the title of Edna O'Brien's 1997 novel *Down by the River*, whose plot was based on the 1992 'X case', which involved a fourteen-year-old girl who was raped and impregnated by a family acquaintance.[40] The Irish state obtained a court order forcing the suicidal girl and her parents to return from England where they had travelled to procure an abortion, until the Supreme Court reversed the decision under the pressure of citizen outrage. In the course of his play, then, Kilroy subtly but unmistakably evokes three tragedies involving young women with crisis pregnancies, placing Winnie's predicament in the context of recent Irish social history.

The mysterious masked man Wedekind introduces in the slightly surreal final scene of *Spring Awakening* is a personification of 'the instinct for survival, even life itself',[41] intended to guide Melchior towards life and a viable future, away from the ghost of Moritz who appears to him in the graveyard and is the embodiment of death. Wedekind used the figure – a role he himself liked to play on stage – because he was reluctant to conclude the play among schoolchildren, without any perspective of the life of adults.[42] According to the masked man, each boy ends up with his proper share: Moritz, the nihilist, with 'the consoling consciousness of having nothing'; Melchior, the free-thinker, with 'an enervating doubt of everything' (p. 159). The deus-ex-machina solution of the masked man does not feel particularly out of place in *Spring Awakening*, which employs such an ironic and eclectic mixture of theatrical styles, including numerous references to myth, fairy tale and allegory. Kilroy saw the figure as representing 'the spirit and magic of theatre itself in the cabaret style of the time that Wedekind loved', but decided that 'this very German scene' had to be changed radically for his own Irish story.[43] Because *Christ, Deliver Us!* is more psychology-driven, Kilroy ended up substituting a kind of dream sequence for the supernatural scene that ends Wedekind's play.

In Kilroy's conclusion, Michael escapes from the reform school by dropping down from the dangerously steep side of a tower, a route no escapee has ever taken before, and all the more symbolic for that: 'Never again in my life will I do what they expect me to!' (p. 63). Some reviewers felt that the play should have ended with that resolution, rather than with the 'experimental ending' that follows it, which was seen by some as a 'cop out',[44] as lacking punch, or as being out of synch with the rest of the play. The *Sunday Times* reviewer, however, called the scene 'majestic' and its sentiments representative of 'that probing, fearless credo that runs through Kilroy's work'.[45] After Michael's terrifying crash from the tower, the mood changes, as if the physically injured and mentally scarred boy is entering a psychological twilight zone: 'The effect is of a dark cave or tunnel opening up. MICHAEL appears within and staggers forward downstage into light. He is injured and bedraggled' (p. 63). The 'figure of a white-faced Winnie' and the 'bloodied figure of Mossy', both appearing in the tunnel behind him, are here to be taken as projections of Michael's psyche, a device Kilroy used before, for example in *Tea and Sex and Shakespeare*, and to depict Rabe's mental trauma in *The Madame MacAdam Travelling Theatre*.

The masked man's place is taken by Fr Seamus, the decent, stammering teacher who, in an earlier scene, had responded to his fellow priests' hypocrisy by tearing off his clerical garb in a gesture of ineffectual frustration that left him at the time 'a shivering old man in a ragged white shirt and braces' (p. 39). Appearing to Michael at the end of the play, Fr Seamus is transformed into the personification of honest humanity and made 'whole', wearing 'a decent layman's suit, collar and tie' (p. 64), and speaking without a stutter, an indication that it was always the church that was putting restrictions on his speech. Michael never looks at Fr Seamus directly because he is hearing the man's common sense in his own head, knowing that he must get past the ghosts of Winnie and Mossy even as he vows he will never forget them. This strategy for coping with past trauma has broader implications for a society trying to come to terms with harrowing aspects of its own history. Kilroy wrote in 1991 that transformation can be a positive outcome of fear, since 'fear is a signal to us that we must change or calcify', whereas a negative outcome of fear 'solidifies [a sense of] . . . helplessness and hopelessness'.[46] Mossy is someone who has allowed fear to overwhelm him to the point of despair, whereas Michael is pushed by it towards risk and change. Fr Seamus advises Michael to be true to his own mind and body, and above all, to mistrust the deadly certainty of authority: 'Know nothing! A clean slate! . . . We are born under the sign of a question-mark, Michael. And that's how we end, too. Questions, questions!' (p. 66).

In 'Was ich mir dabei dachte' ('what I was thinking at the time'), Wedekind comments that *Frühlings Erwachen*, which he had intended as an ironic critique of bourgeois morality, was initially considered by many to be sheer pornography. Later, when the shock value had worn off, the work was dismissed as arid pedantry.[47] Kilroy's *Christ, Deliver Us!* also evoked reactions that ranged from shock to mild disappointment. Its premiere came at a time of extensive media coverage of clerical and institutional child abuse, and new revelations about the maltreatment and detention of women in Magdalen laundries. Perhaps as a consequence of this media saturation, some audience members felt that the play's material seemed familiar, and that aspects of what they saw on stage verged on cliché. Others, however, who had personal experience of situations analogous to those depicted in the play, were deeply affected by the performance, leaving the theatre with renewed anger, or in tears. Some who did not live through the 1950s wondered if the darkness of that decade could really have been 'that unrelenting'.[48] Had the play been staged ten years earlier, Emer O'Kelly argued, 'there would have been an outcry against its "exaggeration" and "vicious anti-clericalism". Now its depiction of the horrors of children's lives in small-town Fifties Ireland appears almost mild.'[49] Longman Oz similarly suggested that the events shown in the play might seem far-fetched to some, but that 'the frightening thought is that Mr Kilroy's depiction of the time may not go far enough'.[50] Whatever people thought and felt about the play, they were not afraid to express their views. The open debate sparked by *Christ, Deliver Us!* was itself an indicator that much has fundamentally changed in Ireland since the 1950s, even if the hurt and injustice referenced in the play still have not been fully confronted and redressed.

PART III

Art and Mysticism

8

Relations with the Absolute: *Talbot's Box*

An important strand in Kilroy's work deals with the notion that the single-minded focus of artists and mystics on their inner vision at times makes them behave 'monstrously' to their nearest and dearest and places them, in a sense, beyond the bounds of common humanity. Kilroy first tentatively examined this obsessive quality in *Tea and Sex and Shakespeare* as an aspect of the writer Brien's personal and marital predicament, and subsequently developed it more fully in relation to the figure of Oscar Wilde in *The Secret Fall of Constance Wilde*. In the three plays discussed hereafter, *Talbot's Box*, *The Shape of Metal*, and *Blake*, the uncompromising nature of the creative genius or mystical thinker and the consequences of such absolutism in their personal lives takes up a more central thematic position. In the earliest of these works, *Talbot's Box*, Kilroy examines the extreme individualism of Matt Talbot, Dublin's twentieth-century 'working-class saint', whose unworldly behaviour alienated him from his family and his community, but also made him an easy target for exploitation, both by those with a religious agenda to promote and by those who politicised his actions for their own ends. Unlike the central characters in *The Shape of Metal* and *Blake*, Talbot is not a control freak; rather, he feels driven by a spiritual force greater than himself. While Kilroy was troubled by the extreme qualities of Talbot's spirituality, he gradually also gained a greater appreciation for the man's uniqueness and for the ultimately unknowable nature of his personal faith.

Interviewed by Aodhan Madden in July 1969, when *The O'Neill* had recently been staged at the Peacock and *The Death and Resurrection of Mr Roche* had just opened at London's

Hampstead Theatre, Kilroy observed that he had for some years been contemplating writing a play he wanted to call 'A Mass for Matt Talbot'. It would focus on the conflict between the spirit and the flesh, a religious theme that he would treat 'intellectually' in a way not often seen in Irish theatre.[1] Kilroy began writing the play that would be staged in 1977 as *Talbot's Box* with the intention of satirising both the absolutist nature of Talbot's religiosity, which involved self-inflicted suffering and extreme asceticism, and the unquestioning esteem in which most Irish people held this essentially sado-masochistic icon. Talbot's zeal may be partially explained by the fact that he was a reformed alcoholic. Born in 1856 in a Dublin slum, the sixth of twelve children, he was already a heavy drinker by early adolescence. At the age of twenty-eight, however, he took a pledge of total abstinence and from then on, guided in his resolve by Dr Michael Hickey, a professor of philosophy at Clonliffe College, he lived a life of fasting and prayer – all the while working as an unskilled labourer. After his sudden collapse and death while on his way to Trinity Sunday Mass on 7 June 1925 it was discovered that, underneath his clothes, he had bound his body with chains and cords as a form of penance and to express his devotion to Mary, the Mother of God. A movement to have him canonised quickly emerged. In 1931, an inquiry into Talbot's life was opened by Archbishop Byrne of Dublin, and the official Apostolic Process was set in motion by the Vatican in 1947. In 1972 his remains were removed from Glasnevin Cemetery to Our Lady of Lourdes church on Seán McDermott Street, where his coffin is displayed in a glass case; also preserved are his pledge certificate and the heavy chain he wore around his waist. Pope Paul VI declared Talbot 'Venerable' in 1975, the second of four steps necessary for canonisation, which requires evidence of a physical miracle. Although *The Kerryman* reported early in 1977 that signs from the Vatican appeared to indicate that Talbot's beatification was imminent, he has not been declared a saint to this day.[2]

While regarded by many as a saintly man, Talbot was reviled by others (including by Seán O'Casey, who referred to him as 'Mutt' Talbot) for refusing to accept strike pay during the great lockout of 1913, on the grounds that he had not earned the money with his labour. In 1975, the fiftieth anniversary of his death brought a certain amount of Irish media attention to the controversy surrounding his legacy. In a sermon covered by *The Irish Press*, the Auxiliary Bishop of Dublin eulogised Talbot as an honest and 'shy Dublin workingman' and characterised him as 'a true patriot, who lived rather than died for his country', a man who was no strike breaker, and whose example served as 'a lesson to us all'.[3] Reporting in *The Irish Times*, John Cooney cited the opinion of Fr Morgan Costelloe (the leading figure in the Irish movement to have Talbot canonised) that there is a lesson to be found 'in the fact that a poor man, who was utterly unknown in life, may become one of the most famous Dubliners of this century because of his union with God'.[4] Cooney's article provoked a number of letters to the editor, two of which disapproved of his reference to the Venerable Matt Talbot as 'a Dubliner whose anti-intellectual devotionalism is at variance with the theology of the second Vatican Council'. J.P. Murphy, General Manager and Secretary of the Dublin Port and Docks Board, testified in another letter that Talbot went on strike when employed by the Port and Docks in 1900,[5] and Sé Geraghty of Henrietta Street (then still an area of tenement housing) wrote that, far from being unknown, Talbot 'was in fact extremely well-known' in not-so-pious areas of the city and would, to the Dublin people, 'always be the Scab Talbot'.[6]

When *Talbot's Box* opened at the Peacock Theatre in October 1977 as part of the Dublin Theatre Festival, Dublin audiences found the play in many ways a theatrical revelation. In his *Irish Times* review, Kane Archer praised Patrick Mason's direction for giving unity to 'an almost unimaginable diversity of means'.[7] John Devitt, who confessed to being of a generation for whom 'Matt Talbot was a very special figure, . . . the exemplary sinner who redeems himself', remembered in an interview late in his life the 'very vivid production' at the Abbey Theatre and Kilroy's unusual angle of approach; his impression was of 'a playwright handling radioactive material', and he noted 'a certain kind of coldness and rigour about the play, and about the production' which startled him.[8] Declan Hughes was a very young director when he revived *Talbot's Box* in 1984 as the first evening show staged by Rough Magic, the company he had founded that year with Lynne Parker; he considered the play's 'sheer theatricality . . . unusual, perhaps unprecedented, on an Irish stage', in the way its style 'shifts continually and fluently from realistic to music-hall, absurdist to expressionist, pastiche to post-modern'.[9] For Kilroy himself, it had come as a discovery that, stylistically, 'you could do this, and at the same time write a play which would reflect history'.[10]

Kilroy's 'intellectual' approach to his material led him to adopt a broadly Brechtian technique in which the various characters representing Talbot's antagonists – employers, trade unionists, members of the religious and medical establishment – are played by four actors referred to in the script as 'First Man', 'Second Man', 'Woman' and 'Priest Figure', the latter also to be played by a woman. Talbot is the only figure to remain 'himself' throughout the play. While working on the script, Kilroy became less interested in mocking Talbot and began to focus instead on exploring 'the way individuals of exceptional personality invite manipulation and the projection of the needs of others'. Talbot, then, came to represent a type as much as a specific historical individual; such a figure, Kilroy argues, 'transcends any one profession or belief'.[11] *Talbot's Box*, then, in its concern with the fate of the visionary within the public realm, could be considered to be 'as much about art as religion'[12] and as much about the artist as the religious mystic. Kilroy would explore the specific connection between art and mysticism more overtly in his later play *Blake*.

In the summer of 1974, Kilroy sent the completed script of *Talbot's Box* to his agent, Peggy Ramsay, who was less than enthusiastic about the distancing effects used in the play – indeed, she 'loathed' Brecht, Kilroy would later recall.[13] Ramsay disapprovingly likened the techniques used in *Talbot's Box* to those employed by James Saunders, another of her clients, in his 1972 play *Hans Kohlhaas*, and was of the opinion that the style of Kilroy's play would not be warmly welcomed by professional theatres in England.[14] At the time, Saunders was considered one of the leading British exponents of the theatre of the absurd, and his work, like Kilroy's, was often considered cerebral. Undaunted by the critique, Kilroy sent *Talbot's Box* to the Abbey Theatre; Tomás Mac Anna was still in charge, and he accepted the play with a projected production date of August 1975, which turned out to be optimistic; it would not open until over two years later. After its initial Dublin run, the play transferred to the Royal Court Theatre and therefore did make it to the English stage after all. Perhaps Ramsay's disapproval three years earlier had rankled with Kilroy, for as *Talbot's Box* was moving to London he made a point of telling the *Guardian* newspaper that, apart from

John Arden and Edward Bond, the English playwright he admired most was James Saunders.

Kilroy suggests that the experimentalism of the technique he used in *Talbot's Box* presented itself as right for the subject: 'You have to match the experience with its appropriate style and in matching it you expand and illuminate the experience,' he told an interviewer.[15] His attempt in *Talbot's Box*, he said elsewhere, was 'to use the stage in non verbal ways'.[16] The opening stage directions of the play indicate that, when the lights go up, they should reveal 'a huge box occupying virtually the whole stage, its front closed to the audience. The effect should be that of a primitive, enclosed space, part prison, part sanctuary, part acting space.' The front of the box is opened out from within to reveal 'Three walls, perhaps with daubed signs and objects of a religious shrine. All the actors, costumes and props required in the play are already within the box.'[17] Archer praised the interpretation of the concept in the Abbey production:

> From the moment that the crazy timber gates of Wendy Shea's magnificently simple setting swing open, to let us enter the world, the times and even the mind of Matthew Talbot, we are caught in a kaleidoscope, whirled through patterns of history, a hundred attitudes, riding on great waves of laughter to be cast upon a beach of quietude, of mystery, of something that even in the text itself goes far too deep for speech.[18]

To Caroline Walsh, Kilroy explained that the play 'is an attempt to take the stage as pure space into which you put the kind of happening that has a historical base but that in fact doesn't belong anywhere except on the stage. It is an attempt to dramatise metaphysics or the idea of spirituality.'[19] In his review of the 1988 Red Kettle production, which did not use a box at all but nevertheless managed to maintain the style of the play, Fintan O'Toole called *Talbot's Box* 'complex, expressionistic, full of play-acting', and 'one of those plays where the form and the content are inextricable'.[20]

Although Kilroy claimed that, by the time *Talbot's Box* was staged at the Peacock, he had moved on to other ideas and was no longer that interested in the subject of Talbot,[21] the timing of the production was right. Notwithstanding Ramsay's misgivings, the play received favourable reviews in both Dublin and London. Irish audiences in particular would have recognised that many of the opinions about Talbot aired in the Irish press in the years leading up to the play's production are echoed and satirised in *Talbot's Box*, where Kilroy is interested in the way visionaries of one kind or another attract hostility as well as 'the projection of other people's needs'.[22] In the play, the pro-Talbot side prays 'for the Beatification and Canonisation of this holy Dublin working man, that in these troubled times the people might have a model of Christian loyalty and obedience, to fight off the false doctrines, subversive influences, dangerous and foreign practices, that threaten our faith – ' (p. 17). The anti-Talbot faction spit on him and call him, 'Scab! Strike-breaker! . . . Where was he in 1913? . . . Why didn't he go on the picket with the men?' (pp. 29–30). The First Man, speaking as a business leader, becomes frustrated with Talbot's prayerful silence: 'What use is a saint if he doesn't stand up for us? Good, decent, ordinary, normal, god-fearing, law-abiding, cash-paying customers – I mean people.' The Priest Figure assures him that the church will decide in time whether and how to quote Talbot, once he has been claimed as a saint, winning over the businessman: 'Canonisation! You think it'll work? . . . A saint of our own, one of ourselves, begod. That's an idea!' (p. 33). The Priest Figure insists on protocol, 'Death – apostolic enquiry – sacred process – ', while the First Man cannot wait to get down to business: 'Where's the Pope?' (p. 34). All the while, Talbot has been on his knees, praying, but at this point he suddenly rises to his feet and utters an anguished cry: 'Oh, Gawd! I seen Satan in the streets!' (p. 34). His visionary mind has foreseen the violence inflicted on the strikers during the lockout, but to an audience his words also reflect indirectly on the colluding figures of the priest and the businessman, to whom Talbot himself is oblivious.

While he was working on *Talbot's Box*, and as he moved away from his initial concept of mocking Talbot for his sado-masochistic obsession with mortifying the flesh, Kilroy became increasingly fascinated by the impenetrable nature of the mystic's private experience. As he felt himself compelled to find 'some kind of respect' for Talbot, his focus came to rest on the tensions between the extreme individualism of an inaccessible man and the claims made on him by family, community and society. 'Saints must be very difficult people to get on with, like great artists and eccentrics,' Kilroy said in an interview at the time of the play's first performance.[23] This is the paradox to which the playwright returns time and again in his work: that without such extreme figures the world would also be without greatness. Kilroy is fascinated by this kind of double perspective. As O'Toole has observed, what is persistent in his work is a sense of 'things turning into their opposites, or being different things at the same time'.[24] Such a paradox also lies at the heart of Talbot's saintliness, for his religious vision 'unites all opposites'.[25] 'Blessed be the dung o' the world,' he says, 'For on it is built the City on the Hill!' (p. 36). The recognition of the kinship between mystic and artist made it impossible for Kilroy to be completely dismissive of Talbot, however much the man's visionary qualities differed from his own artistic obsessions. The issue then became to capture a seriocomic note that would convey not only Talbot's taxing eccentricity but also his simple sincerity, as well as the troubling nature of his religiosity and of the forces that manipulated the man and his image for political and religious ends.

Talbot's Box was, as Mason suggests, one of the first serious dramatic inquiries into the (then changing) force of the Catholic Church in Irish society.[26] The special position of the church (enshrined in the 1937 Constitution) had come under pressure in the 1960s and '70s as the country became increasingly modern and international in outlook. The priest figure in *Talbot's Box* acknowledges as much when s/he encourages an imaginary congregation to draw strength from Talbot's simple background as 'the modern attacks upon the Christian family close in upon you, divorce – contraception – abortion – drugs – delinquency – foreign periodicals – everything against our Irish way of life' (p. 38). The board of the 1977 Dublin Theatre Festival initially had some qualms about staging what might be a controversial play – Tom Murphy's *The Sanctuary Lamp* had provoked strong reactions two years earlier – and before *Talbot's Box* opened, there had been rumblings about protests, but the predicted rallies did not materialise; in his review of the play in the *Irish Independent* Desmond Rushe castigated those responsible for suggesting there might be demonstrations 'for giving the public a deplorably dishonest slant on "Talbot's Box"'.[27] Ironically, in fact, the opposite happened; devotees of Talbot made their way to the theatre and held up their rosary beads as they were witnessing the performance, constituting 'perhaps the strangest crowd the Peacock has ever seen'.[28] Kilroy was amused and bemused:

'it went totally against my sense of what should be going on, but it is an acknowledgment of what theatre is capable of'.[29]

Speaking in 2004, Kilroy noted that for him, 'theatre is very physical' and 'all about the human body on a stage' – indeed, that a 'total physical performance' by a great performer is 'the essence of theatre'.[30] More than twenty-five years earlier, however, when he was writing *Talbot's Box*, he was still in the process of developing that aspect of his own drama. As he revealed in an interview with Gerry Dukes, the physical nature of the play only emerged fully during rehearsal, when Kilroy worked closely with the actors and with director Patrick Mason: 'It was Patrick who "discovered" the strong, almost frontal physicality and imagery in the play. I like to think all of that was there in the text but Patrick was wonderful in bringing it out and showing the possibilities.'[31] Nevertheless, it was Kilroy himself who had 'conceived of the play as happening within a particular, free-flowing, theatrical style' at a time when he had become 'more attracted to pure theatrical playfulness, playing with different elements of the stage'.[32] His adoption of this style owed much to the work of Peter Brook at the Royal Court, particularly his production of Peter Weiss' *Marat/Sade* which Kilroy had seen in 1964, and to the 'total theatre' of Maurice Béjart which he had encountered in Paris.

Kilroy has frequently acknowledged that the stage adaptation of Gustave Flaubert's *La Tentation de Saint Antoine* he saw in 1967 had a great deal to do with the development of his sense of theatricality. It was performed by the Renaud-Barrault Company at the Théâtre de France-Odéon in a choreography by Béjart, with Jean-Louis Barrault in the title role. Barrault was the founder of the Théâtre des Nations which he envisioned as 'a meeting-place where the traditions of the Far East – Bunraku, Kabuki, Nōh – could cross-fertilize with modern experiments by the Living Theatre, Grotowski . . . or Eugenio Barba'.[33] Kilroy himself, of course, would later combine the methods of Kabuki and Bunraku with modernist techniques in *The Secret Fall of Constance Wilde*. Béjart was one of the first to explore the idea of dance theatre in France, and his 'hallucinatory staging' of St Anthony's temptation had a huge effect on Kilroy's 'sense of what stage choreography could be'.[34] It was, as Kilroy remembers it, 'an extraordinary production, a kind of total theatre in its day. . . . Coming from Dublin theatre and seeing this kind of work in the sixties was just mind-blowing.' Kilroy also saw, around the same time, 'a Polish ... mime company', which had an equally strong impact on him.[35]

A year earlier, in June 1966, Barrault had managed to bring Jerzy Grotowski's Theatre Laboratory of Wrocław to the Festival du Théâtre des Nations to present its version of Calderón's *The Constant Prince*.[36] Loosely based on Juliusz Słowacki's 1874 Polish translation-adaptation, it featured Ryszard Ciéslak, one of the Laboratory's founding members, in the title role. Kilroy says he did not see the performance, and is not generally drawn to Grotowski's method; any affinity with Grotowski's work in the case of *Talbot's Box* should be seen as a 'one-off' in his oeuvre, and parallels between John Molloy's interpretation of Matt Talbot in the Abbey production and Ciéslak's Don Fernando were serendipitous rather than intended.[37] Nevertheless, various archived materials, which Kilroy himself labelled 'Important Background to go in *Talbot's Box* Collection',[38] relate to the production of *The Constant Prince*. These include published materials on Grotowski's methods and objectives as well as documentation (in French) about the production, including several black and white photographs, which indicate that Kilroy was aware of its particular aesthetic and certainly of Grotowski's imaginative use of space in the creation of what Kilroy, in a note on one of the documents, summarises as 'A theatre of ritual: a theatre of mystery'.[39]

Both Barrault and Brook were strongly influenced by Antonin Artaud. In his day, Barrault was 'one of the contemporary theatre's most dynamic actors and one of its most creative and imaginative directors', and the basis of his aesthetic was 'his sense of the relationship of actor and audience as a kind of communion, a communion which is achieved in ecstasy'.[40] Something of this sentiment is echoed in Kilroy's own theatrical philosophy. Béjart's version of Flaubert's drama was a baroque spectacle of dazzling movement, fantastic costumes and grotesque masks. In a 1967 French television interview, Barrault said he loved playing the role of the hermit saint, who is tempted by many dream-characters personifying doubt, the desire for riches, sex and death, while holding fast to the belief that his faith is best practised – and tested – in isolation from the world.[41] Kilroy remembered the details of the Paris production, some of which reverberate in his own oeuvre:

> Béjart built a long gangway, like an oversized model's catwalk, from the back of the auditorium down through the audience to the centre of the stage. Barrault, as the mystic saint, writhed in a sand pit on stage in his desert, pouring out the rich orientalism of Flaubert's language. Down the walkway, to heavy percussion, paraded the nightmarish figures of the mystic in elaborate costumes and masks. It was a parade of oriental monsters not unlike the strut of the lead actor across the stage-bridge in Japanese Kabuki, weighed down, too, with voluminous costume and painted with similar, garish make-up.

It was, Kilroy recalls, 'a highly dramatic way of exteriorizing the monstrous visions of a man in religious delirium', and he himself has also been drawn throughout his career 'to figures like these who have put themselves beyond the pale with a demented belief in their own exceptionalism'.[42]

The spectacle in Béjart's production around the figure of St Anthony, whose temptations Talbot likens several times to his own in *Talbot's Box*, inspired the way Kilroy dramatised his own character's being in the world. The moment in Act I when Talbot kneels in prayer, for example, echoes the sound and costuming of the Paris performance:

> (*The sound of a thumping heartbeat begins, at first low, then amplified to fill the theatre.* TALBOT *becomes frightened by it. The* PRIEST FIGURE *appears.* TALBOT *is aware of the presence but as if in his mind*) Father – Father – can ya tell me? There's something in me that isn't natural. Can ya tell me what it is, Father? Can ya tell me? (PRIEST FIGURE *disrobes to a bright leotard.* TALBOT *screams and bows his head. A church bell in the distance. He rises*) Hafta go to Mass. Mass! (p. 24)

In Kilroy's play, Talbot tells the priest figure that Anthony, in his cave, did not see demons but 'the rest o' the world dressed up for a circus. Aye. All the helter-skelter for what it was' (p. 55). Talbot too, in the words of Declan Hughes, 'is set down to walk among a carnival of earthly distractions – priests, politicians, businessmen and family members – all demanding a piece of him',[43] while he endeavours to inhabit only the quietness within himself.

According to Innes, the principles of avant-garde theatre in the broadest sense of the word are shared by its adherents 'quite independent of direct influence. For example, there are striking similarities between the work of Antonin Artaud in the 1930s and of Jerzy Grotowski in the 1960s, even though Grotowski knew nothing of the "theatre of cruelty" when he developed his concept of "poor theatre".'[44] In this way, too, *Talbot's Box* may have elements in common with the work of Grotowski that were not deliberately intended but rather the consequence of their similar subject matter. *The Constant Prince* was developed by Grotowski between 1965 and 1968 and went through three different versions. Calderón's seventeenth-century drama focuses on Prince Fernando's almost masochistic fortitude during captivity in the face of degradation and torture, and is in its essence 'a study of how man achieves sainthood'.[45] In adapting Słowacki's Polish language version, Grotowski cut down the text to almost a third and reduced the fourteen major parts to seven, which were played by six actors. With the historical specifics removed, the action came to represent 'an archetypal conflict of an individual versus a sadistic, spiritually castrating society'.[46]

Donald R. Larson points out that, throughout his career, 'Grotowski was concerned with the figure of the outsider, the individual who, through whatever concatenation of circumstances, finds himself placed in the midst of hostile and uncomprehending outside forces'.[47] There is certainly an analogy here with Kilroy's focus, in much of his oeuvre, on uniquely gifted individuals whose self-absorption conflicts with the demands placed on them by their surrounding communities. On the surface, the subject matter of *The Temptation of Saint Anthony* and *The Constant Prince* has much in common with that of *Talbot's Box*. All three plays deal with the connection between suffering and saintliness, with the violent conflict between body and spirit, and between society and the individual who has separated himself from the world for reasons incomprehensible to it. Like Talbot, St Anthony in his desert cave battles physical and mental demons who seek to tempt him away from his spiritual devotions and draw him back into the world. Much in the way that Talbot's spirituality transcends both the praise and blame of those who seek to appropriate him as a positive or negative example, the imprisoned Prince Fernando responds to his tormentors, whose aim is to make him a docile and cooperative pawn in their system, with a passivity that puts him spiritually beyond their reach, something they find both baffling and fascinating, and which leads them first to torture him to death, and then to elevate him as a martyr.

Grotowski's production of *The Constant Prince* included elements from the liturgy at key points in the performance. Traditional images of the stations of the cross were evoked by Don Fernando's attire – a white loincloth – as well as certain of his poses and the marks of physical distress on his body such as sweating and reddening of skin caused by whippings with a red cloth. Although, as Innes suggests, there may have been an element of critique in Grotowski's conflation of the Prince's self-absorbed martyrdom with Christ's sacrifice on the cross, the impact of that critique was diminished by the 'emotional power in the truth and intimacy of the actor's self-revelation'[48] – that is, by the lack of distance between the performer and the part performed.

Talbot's Box uses some of the same iconic imagery and elements of physicality, but Kilroy's association of Talbot with the figure of Christ is more overtly ironic. In the opening scene of *Talbot's Box* the protagonist is lying on a trolley when the other actors knowingly set the play in motion:

> FIRST MAN: Right! What've we got here on this fine Sunday morning back in 1925 in the morgue of Jervis Street Hospital in the city of Dublin?
>
> *He strips the sheet off the trolley. The body is that of a frail old man, bald, with a white moustache. A white towel is about the waist but otherwise it is naked with the torso, arms, shoulders and legs painted garishly with stripes of red and blue.* (p. 11)

The faintly ridiculous towel and the obviously fake welts and bruises caricature the iconic image of Christ's sacrificial body, something blasphemously reinforced by the morgue attendant's exclamations of 'Christ Almighty!' (p. 11), 'God Almighty!' (p. 12), 'Begod' (pp. 12, 13, 14), 'For Christ's sake' (p. 13) and 'Jaysus' (p. 16) throughout the subsequent dialogue. The irony, however, is less a means of questioning Talbot's sincerity than it is to suggest the manipulation by others of his public image after his death. This

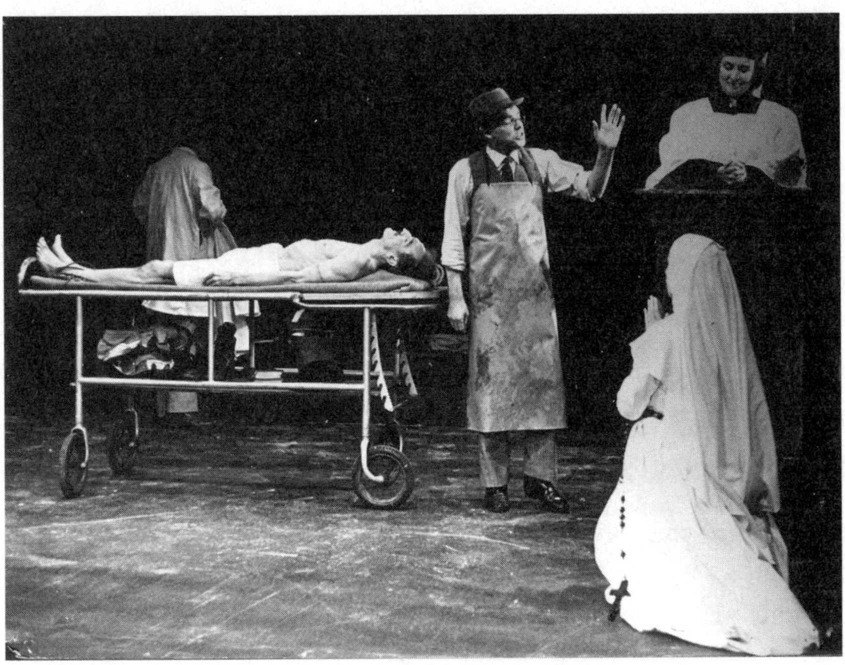

Stephen Brennan, John Molloy, Clive Geraghty, Ingrid Craigie and Eileen Colgan in *Talbot's Box*, Peacock Theatre, 1977. Directed by Patrick Mason. Photograph: Fergus Bourke. Courtesy Abbey Theatre.

theme is verbalised by the morgue attendants who discuss what is to be done with the corpse: 'Where's the instructions? . . . If we don't have instructions we can't put a label on him like a normal corpse. If we can't put a label on him we can't shove him in wan of the drawers' (p. 12). As in *The Constant Prince*, society is intolerant of the extremist and the outsider when he is alive, and eager to incorporate and integrate him into the existing structures once he is safely dead, but unlike Grotowski's Fernando, there is no sense that Talbot is revelling in the performance of his own martyrdom. In his review of the 1977 production, Frank Marcus characterised John Molloy's 'stooped, ragged, emaciated' Talbot as 'the personification of holy simplicity'.[49] Rushe recognised a 'remarkable tenderness and sensitivity' in Molloy's performance, as well as 'a strong, endearing human element' and 'an evident and touching sincerity'.[50]

John Molloy was an inspired choice to play Talbot as a seriocomic Christ figure. As Kilroy describes him, it is clear why he was perfect for the part:

> John Molloy was a stand-up comic, and had a very bizarre presence on the Irish theatrical scene. He played very little straight theatre. He was a wonderful mimic and comic. He came to Paris and studied mime, so that he was part of that whole Barrault tradition of theatre, but in the service of comedy, white-faced comedy, almost. He was cast in this part, in a stroke of genius by Patrick Mason, who felt that this would be a conjunction . . . – maybe a violent conjunction – of two different things.[51]

According to Honor Molloy, however, her father 'was a fabulist, which is a nice way of saying that the truth never stopped him from telling a good story'.[52] Molloy's contention that he had studied under Marcel Marceau in Paris was apparently one of his inventions.[53] Mason describes Molloy as a 'particular kind of Dublin working class figure' and 'a very charismatic performer'. His background brought authenticity to the play's Dublin idiom, which Kilroy wrote as almost mock O'Casey, to fit in with the ironic tone of the work. Molloy was also a drinker and a reprobate, a very difficult man to work with, but 'all that fed into the characterization of Matt Talbot and his struggle with alcohol'.[54] Kilroy recalls how Molloy 'became totally self-identified with the mystical person. To the degree that he was going around like a saint. It was bizarre, it was very funny.'[55]

In his production of *The Constant Prince*, Grotowski foregrounded both the torment and humiliation undergone by Don Fernando, and the erotic attraction between the vain and inconstant Princess Fénix and the captive Prince, thereby underlining the pornographic aspect of physical torture and the double nature of the Prince's 'passion'. Kilroy translates similar gestures of abuse and attraction into stylised expressions of the appropriation of Talbot's image for political and religious ends. As Talbot lies inert on the trolley, the First Man approaches him in the guise of 'an existentialist' and 'slaps the face of Talbot several times, sharply. Then stands, weeping'. The Second Man exclaims, 'Stop hittin' the corpse. Ya can't be hittin' the corpse' (p. 13). In similar mock-ritual fashion the Woman then comes forward as a religious fanatic carrying chains and cords; she compares Talbot's 'incredible exercises of penance' to those of Saint Anthony, 'who wrestled for twenty years in the desert with a nightmare circus of demons', and Saint Catherine of Siena, 'whose self-flagellations astounded Satan', before she 'throws herself upon the trolley and kisses the figure of Talbot, passionately', as the Second Man calls out again, 'Hey! Stoppit! Ya can't be kissin' the corpse!' (p. 15). His argument that Talbot is dead and that 'Yis have no claim on him, anymore', is summarily dismissed by the others before the holy man is theatrically resurrected and presented to the world as a spectacle that will at different times take the form of 'a sorta trial', 'an entertainment', a 'kind of temptation of the saint', or a 'sorta quiz show' (p. 11): 'Ladies and Gentlemen! We give you – Matt Talbot! Servant of God!' (p. 17).

On this cue Talbot rises on his trolley and binds himself with the cords and chains. Then, suddenly, he

> flings both arms out in the shape of crucifixion. As he does so, blinding beams of light shoot through the walls of the box, pooling about him and leaving the rest of the stage in darkness. The other four figures cringe back, the women screaming. A high-pitched wailing cry rises, scarcely human but representing human beings in great agony. As it reaches its crescendo it is of physical discomfort to the audience. The four figures race about, hands aloft, to block the lights. (p. 17)

Recalling Molloy's remarkable performance as Talbot, John Devitt commented on 'how strange and uncanny he was in the resurrection scene'.[56] For this brief but unsustainable moment the audience share something of the agony and ecstasy experienced by Talbot when he enters into what Kilroy in his notes for the play calls his 'very immediate relation' with the 'Absolute',[57] while the four figures cannot bear the light and do their best to separate Talbot from his inner illumination. The moment over, Talbot dresses in trousers, boots, an old shirt, frock-coat and derby hat, and is ready to be put through scenes from his life.

Kilroy's working notes for the play suggest that he started *Talbot's Box* with the idea of 'an enactment within an enclosed space',[58] a concept that was utilised in much theatre of the period. Among other background materials for the play he consulted André Acquart and Michel Raffaelli's *Contemporary Theatre Design* (1970), which features many settings that involve movable screens, panels, platforms, and walls,[59] including the design for the

1967 Paris production of *Marat/Sade* by Peter Weiss at the Théâtre Sarah Bernhardt. Grotowski's version of *The Constant Prince* was performed on a small stage surrounded by wooden barricades: 'approximately thirty members of the public were seated on benches around three sides of the playing area, but at a higher elevation, so that they were separated from, but still close to, the actors'.[60] Innes suggests that the associations evoked for the audience were 'simultaneously those of voyeurs . . . , of spectators at the barbaric ritual of a bullfight . . . , and of "witnesses" in a religious sense'.[61] In *The Secret Fall of Constance Wilde* Kilroy employed the white circle as a 'stage within a stage' to achieve similar effects. In *Talbot's Box*, Kilroy conceptualised the enclosed stage as, literally, a large box containing the action of the play, described by Anthony Roche as a 'flexible metaphor' open to a variety of interpretations.[62] According to Kilroy's notes, it was meant to represent both the world made by man, particularly his institutions, and the body, the prison of the flesh. The worldly aspect could be suggested through hints of red brick and graffiti ('daubed signs') on the inside walls. The box itself should be made of timber, whose rough, natural appearance should contrast with the 'glittering metal' (p. 9) of the hospital trolley contained within it (as an object representing one of society's establishments).

The material of the box – rough wood – is as significant as its function; throughout the play, carpentry associates Talbot with Jesus, and in that way timber connects his worldly life to his inner mysticism. In 1913, at the time of the lockout, Talbot worked in the timber yard at T. & C. Martin. Kilroy represents his labour in this 'big tomb of a place' (p. 25) by having him walk around in a circle with the Second Man while shouldering a plank. Throughout the scene, the First Man, in the role of the foreman, keeps up a diatribe in which he praises Matt's saintliness, cautions the men not to pay heed to agitators, and extols the virtues of piety and obedience: 'Christ carried timber, men. Not a chip on his shoulder' (p. 27). Talbot staggers, falls to one knee and gets up again, only to fall flat moments later before rising and struggling on. Eventually he collapses into a kneeling position, the plank falling between the two men. Talbot's movements here echo the three times Christ falls while carrying the cross to Golgotha, but for the Dublin labourer there is no Simon of Cyrene to help him carry his burden. The other men wait impassively for him to get up after he falls the second time, and leave him on his knees the third time while they argue at length over his head as to whether Talbot was 'a model of all Christian workers' or a strike breaker and scab. The words with which the Second Man closes the scene – 'Jaysus, the way they ignore ya!' (p. 30) – convey the labourer's frustration with the boss's attitude but also reflect ironically on Talbot's position as an isolated and neglected Christ figure.

Kilroy's intention to depict the unknowable quality of Talbot's faith is captured in his two compulsions of work and prayer. 'I hafta go to work' (p. 20), he tells his down-to-earth but worried sister Susan, just as he later insists, 'Hafta go to Mass' (p. 24). These occupations express the paradox of his conviction: that the happiness of God can only be known through physical labour and suffering. 'Blessed be the body / For its pain is the message of the spirit' (p. 36), he says at the end of Act I; but earlier he had mused, 'Isn't it a quare thing the way the body does stand in the way of Eternity?' (p. 24). The chains he wears are the way for him to know the darkness of his own body so that he may overcome it. Suffering for Talbot is connected with desire: it emanates from, as he puts it in his Dublin vernacular, 'the terrible hunger for what oders might have, instead of lettin' them be, 'n turnin' to wha's missin' inside hisself' (p. 50). Darkness (desire, lack), he says, is 'in every man, woman 'n child born inta the world' (pp. 46–47), and if, as Talbot also claims, 'the darkness is Gawd' (p. 47), it is so both in the sense that God can only be approximated through that which separates man from Him (the 'darkness' of pain and envy), and in the sense that He is beyond cognition (in the dark, so to speak). This is the paradox Talbot struggles to express when he says, 'There be nuthin' to see when Gawd comes 'cause . . . yerself is wan with what ya see so ya see nuthin' 'cause ya can only see what's separate than yerself' (p. 58). In other words, the fulfilment of Talbot's own desire to be with God, to be whole, would mean a loss of differentiation and the surrendering of subjectivity; the very condition, therefore, that would make knowing the desired object impossible.

Within the play, the timber box that literally frames the action is echoed by the boxy room in which Matt Talbot lives. There, visions come to him of a world made whole: 'Nothing twisted 'n broken as it is in this world. Everything straight as a piece of good timber, without warp' (p. 23). The room constitutes a symbolic locale of containment that allows its occupant to dream perfection into being. Within a broader context it serves as an analogy to Éamon de Valera's vision of an isolationist Irish state – 'the ideal Ireland that we would have, the Ireland that we dreamed of' – with as its cornerstone the 'happy, vigorous, spiritual' nuclear family;[63] it was a utopian vision he sought to implement in his 1937 Constitution. In practice, attempts by church and state to force purity into existence through the legislation of morality are inevitably doomed to become oppressive, as Kilroy's *Christ, Deliver Us!* documents in the case of mid-century Ireland. For Talbot, too, the wholeness he sees in his visions is always elusive in the world outside his room, something brought home to him most bitterly and profoundly in his futile quest for the street musician whose fiddle he had stolen during his drinking days: 'I searched for twenty years round all the shelters of the city. . . . Sure, I knew he was long dead 'n buried. . . . An' what would I've said to him if I'd found him? I couldn't give back to him what we'd stolen offa him' (p. 41). If the vision of wholeness and integrity can come to Talbot only in his little room, it is also because the small space evokes both the womb and the grave, the condition before and after desire: 'I've measured it,' Talbot says of the box-like space; 'The length and the breadth of it. I fit into it' (p. 51). Talbot's search for transcendence in the isolation of his room may be a quest for the divine and the absolute, but this embrace of 'one purpose alone', as Yeats described another kind of fanatical devotion in his poem 'Easter, 1916', also amounts to a denial of life's imperfection and a refusal to engage with the 'living stream' of the world where everything changes 'minute by minute'.[64]

Talbot expresses his attraction to the eternal when he tells the Priest Figure towards the end of the play: 'I never wanted anything but to work wid timber', because 'timber never dies when 'tis cut, only changin' with age' (p. 58). Patrick Mason explained at the time of the play's first production that the Priest Figure was acted by a woman 'both as a visual pun on "Mother Church" and to express the deeper point that religious emotion is a maternal attraction'.[65] Behind the slumping figure of Talbot, the actress 'disrobes to an old woman, long dress, long grey hair', and places her hands on his shoulders, 'gently rocking him from side to side. Talbot closes his eyes and rocks silently for a little while. The sound of a thumping heartbeat begins again.' In agony and ecstasy he exclaims, 'Oh, Mother! Mother! Oh, Mother of God!' (pp. 58–59). If the box represents the prison of the world and the flesh, the heartbeat suggests his own living body, the maternal womb, and the pulse of his faith. The tableau created on stage, of Talbot cradled in the old woman's arms, evokes the iconic image of the Pietà, although some distance is maintained by the fact that Talbot is an old man dressed in his labourer's clothes and boots. The effect is both reminiscent of and very different from a similar moment in Grotowski's version of *The Constant Prince*, when Don Fernando falls physically exhausted but spiritually uplifted into the arms of Taroudant, who is also played by a woman. At the end of *Talbot's Box*, after Talbot has fallen to his knees for the last time, the old woman appears again behind him, but this time as a figure of death, 'a grotesque old crone, attending but rigid' (p. 63). The female figure in these pivotal moments again embodies the womb and the grave, to the exclusion of the living world – a world where things change minute by minute – that lies between the beginning and the end.

Analogous to Christ who, before his crucifixion, experienced a sleepless night of anguish in Gethsemane, Talbot in his final moments expresses doubts about the visions that came to him in his room, and admits to fearing death: 'Oh, Gawd, will it ever change in this world? (*Cry*) Christ let out! Haven't I been yer auld fool long enough? (*Change*) God forgive me! It's afraid o' the last darkness I am. When I should see it as the start of Eternal Light' (p. 62). In his closing reverie, however, Talbot – who, as his sister points out, was always a loner, '[e]ven when we was all small' (p. 21) – becomes childlike in his acceptance of the end as he identifies with the boy Jesus, the carpenter's apprentice, who also left home to set out alone towards his inevitable destination:

> The old man worked at the bench, shavin' the yella timbers in the sunlight. An' the boy used help him. They worked together. They niver spoke. No need for words. Nuthin' was heard but the sound of timber. Then wan day – wan day, the boy left. He put down the tools outta his hands. Again, nare a word. The old man came to the door with him. They kissed wan another. Then the mother came like a shadda from the house 'n she kissed the boy too. Then the boy walked down the road in the dust 'n the

> hot sun. An' way in the far distance of the city he could hear them, the sound of the hammers 'n they batin' the timbers inta the shape o' the cross. (p. 63)

Through this visionary narrative, the elements of Talbot's own broken background – the roaring, alcoholic, wife-beating father who forced drink upon his sons, the appalling poverty of the Dublin slums, the back-breaking labour – are made 'straight as a piece of good timber, without warp' (p. 23). But Jesus in Matt Talbot's story walks away from his harmonious family towards certain suffering and death inflicted with the means and tools of his own trade. In the Christian narrative that Talbot follows in his own life, the opposites of wholeness and brokenness inescapably lead into each other with the logic of a Moebius strip.

What his death means for Talbot only he can know, even if he cannot articulate it; in the play's final moment, the great doors of the box are closed by the two Men and the Woman, leaving Talbot and the old crone inside. The figures left outside stand 'looking in through cracks in the walls from which bright light comes which illuminates their faces' (p. 63). Talbot had said earlier that 'There be nuthin' to see when Gawd comes 'cause . . . ya can only see what's separate than yerself'. The architecture of the timber box renders that paradox visible. Talbot inside the box cannot convey the experience of leaving behind worldly temptation and desire, whether it means becoming one with God or dissolving into the void; those outside the box can only know what it means still to want the fulfilment that is promised inside. Early in the play, the First Man, as the doctor who examined Talbot's corpse, expressed regret that he was not allowed to carry out an autopsy: 'I should have discovered all, if they had allowed me to open the heart!' (p. 18). Such a tangible means of approximating knowledge about Talbot's inner mystery – a posthumous examination of his physical life and deeds – in the end is shown to be inadequate or even counterproductive, except insofar as the play's ending has shifted the focus of characters and audience alike from trying to define Matt Talbot – as 'a scab!', 'irrelevant!', or 'a saint!' (p. 35) – to an awareness of what lies beyond comprehension and representation. Theatre, Kilroy has said, has to do with 'artifice at the level of revelation and concealment, with illusion'. Thematically, this statement applies to *Talbot's Box*, whose central metaphor of opening and closing the box fulfils precisely this purpose, and whose mystical protagonist remains enigmatic even after endless scrutiny. On a more subtly personal level, however, Kilroy also calls theatre and playwriting 'ways of, inevitably, giving public exposure to privacies'.[66] That observation is more immediately relevant for those works that examine the psychological travails of creative artists: sculptor Nell Jeffrey in *The Shape of Metal*, and poet-engraver William Blake in *Blake*.

9

The Art of Imperfection: *The Shape of Metal*

The Shape of Metal brings together several thematic strands Kilroy also addresses, separately or together, in his other plays: the quest for perfection in art and life, the sublime artist as reprehensible human being, mental illness and psychological breakdown, the Protestant Anglo-Irish versus the Catholic Irish sensibility, the fluidity of gender, and the Second World War as eye-opener about the perils of fanatical extremism. In *The Secret Fall of Constance Wilde* and in *Blake*, Kilroy filters these questions through the lens of historical figures, while *Tea and Sex and Shakespeare* and *The Shape of Metal* investigate them by using fictitious characters. These latter two plays, though otherwise very different, both engage with creative breakdown and familial crisis, each involving connections between an artist's inability to perform and the figure of a lost or absent child. While Brien, the writer in *Tea and Sex and Shakespeare*, is mentally fragile and struggles to find a way into starting his play, eighty-two-year-old sculptor Nell Jeffrey in *The Shape of Metal* is a domineering woman, filled with a sense of entitlement by virtue of her Anglo-Irish heritage, who finds it impossible to complete her final work. Nell is a great artist, but her daughter Judith also calls her a 'monstrous person' for the role she played, long ago, in driving away her older daughter Grace, who suffered from mental illness.[1]

While it is clear that Nell has had a successful artistic career, the play's focus is on her inability to deal with failure. Even as the art museum in Kilmainham (a barely veiled version of Dublin's IMMA) is in the process of dedicating a room to her work, there is one sculpture she has been struggling with for decades but has been unable to complete. In her black-and-white view, its unfinished state renders the piece invalid as a work of art: '*Woman Rising from Water*. That's its title. I've spent a lifetime trying to create finished objects. There is no meaning if it isn't finished' (p. 15). The other, related 'unfinished business' in Nell's life is the disappearance of her daughter Grace, who left home around the time her mother was first working on the sculpture, thirty years earlier. The lost child is the pivot in the play around which personal and artistic success and failure revolve. Grace's absence signifies both the human cost of the artist's single-minded concentration on the expression of her vision, and the ultimate impossibility of the quest to translate that vision of perfection into the materiality of art; also, in the final analysis, the absent figure acts as a metaphor for the loneliness of the artist, which in turn is a device for exploring the loneliness of the human condition.

In works from *Tea and Sex and Shakespeare* to *The Secret Fall of Constance Wilde*, Kilroy's tendency to 'produce a binary opposition between (male) creativity and (female) reality, (male) invention and (female) responsibility',[2] has left him open to the charge that, for all the attention his plays pay to performativity and the destabilisation of identity, their representations of gender tend to follow conventional patterns. In this regard, *The Shape of Metal* is a new departure in that it moves away from the gendered division between male (artistic) and female (biological) creativity and responsibility in its portrayal of a female artist who is also a parent. Kilroy himself has talked about the use of a female protagonist less in terms of overcoming this division and more as a liberating strategy for himself, one he also employed two decades earlier in his unpublished novel 'Angela': 'there's a freeing up, certainly of treating the whole subject of sexuality'.[3] Indeed, he suggests that his original plan for *The Shape of Metal*, 'to write the story about a male artist', would not work.[4] The reverse had been the case in his early play *The Death and Resurrection of Mr Roche*, which would only allow itself to be written when Kilroy had replaced the female character he had originally envisaged with the eponymous Mr Roche. In *The Secret Fall of Constance Wilde*, Kilroy attempted to bridge the gendered divide between the demands of life (represented by Constance) and art (Oscar's concern) via the figure of the Androgyne. In *The Shape of Metal*, Nell Jeffrey and her daughters Grace and Judith embody similarly conflicting forces, but because they are all women, though with different sexual personalities – Nell aggressively devours men, Judith is a lesbian, Grace chooses an unremarkable boyfriend because he makes her feel 'normal' (p. 37) – the split between life's exigencies and the demands of art is here no longer played out along such starkly demarcated gendered lines.

The opening and closing sections of *The Shape of Metal* are set in 2002, while the action in the central part of the play takes place thirty years earlier, in 1972. Nell is unmarried but has two daughters from different relationships in her bohemian past. The oldest, Grace, left home when she was in her mid-twenties, shortly after the events depicted in the play's middle part, when Nell forced her to break off her relationship with a Catholic, working-class village boy called Shay whom she considered an unsuitable companion for her daughter. Grace ended up in London's Notting Hill – at that time an ungentrified area of slum rentals and counter-cultural squats – from where she disappeared without a trace in 1975. In the course of the play the youngest daughter, Judith, now forty-seven, is prompted by the death of her father, Eddie, to confront Nell about her sister's fate, forcing her mother to revisit the events that led up to Grace's departure and face up to her role in her older daughter's disappearance. Kilroy had explored a similar theme in his half-hour television drama *Gold in the Streets*, first broadcast by RTÉ in November 1993. In that work, an Irish farmer travels to London to find his daughter living in a derelict squat of Georgian vintage. The two exchange 'sometimes angry, sometimes poignant' words but the father is unable to persuade his daughter to return to Ireland and to her mother, 'a dark and crippling person, a character seething with envy and hatred' who has 'driven the girl – and her three other daughters – away'. After the father leaves, the girl puts on a sari to go out and meet her Indian boyfriend, with whom she is going to live; when the father returns later 'with a heater to keep her warm in the old squat', she is gone.[5] Unlike the girl in this drama, who clearly knows what she wants and who – at least according to her father – is as stubborn as her mother, Grace Jeffrey in *The Shape of Metal* is confused, impressionable and lacking in self-esteem. She also often feels that she 'couldn't possibly be' Nell's daughter (p. 36). In both plays, however, the separation that occurs between child and parent is presented as final and irreversible.

The Shape of Metal premiered at the Abbey Theatre on 29 September 2003 as part of the Dublin Theatre Festival, with the English actor Sara Kestelman as Nell, Justine Mitchell as Grace, and Eleanor Methven as Judith. The Abbey's artistic director at the time was Ben Barnes. In 2000, when he was appointed to the position, he had been excited by Kilroy's plans for an Irish version of Wedekind's *Spring Awakening*. However, when the script of that adaptation, *Christ, Deliver Us!*, arrived on his desk in 2001 it disappointed him, and he eventually turned down the play, which would consequently not see a production until 2010. With that rejection still fresh in his mind in 2003, Barnes was worried when the completed draft of *The Shape of Metal* struck him as 'less than overwhelming'.[6] He sent Kilroy a set of 'detailed notes' on the script,[7] which the latter, although irked by the fourteen pages of questions 'for the sake of questioning',[8] proceeded to address, in a spirit of cooperation. Kilroy also had misgivings about Barnes' choice of Lynne Parker to direct the work, feeling she might not be right for the play. The production nevertheless went ahead as planned, but Barnes remained negative once the play had opened. In his diary entry for 12 October 2003 he called *The Shape of Metal* 'a rather old fashioned play'; he also felt (ironically, given Kilroy's intuitions) that it was not helped by Parker's 'heavy production which only occasionally sparks into life' or by 'the leaden set' designed by Alan Farquharson.[9]

In her review of the production in the *Sunday Independent*, Emer O'Kelly's reaction to *The Shape of Metal* was almost the exact opposite of Barnes'. 'Nothing is resolved in this play,' she wrote, 'the audience is left to answer for itself the ethical questions that society asks artists and vice versa. It's fascinating, stimulating, and disturbing. And it is, of course, beautifully constructed.' She also praised the work of the actors in 'an extraordinary set and lighting plan that give detailed voice and vision to Lynne Parker's delicate direction'.[10] Fintan O'Toole, likewise, understood exactly what Kilroy was about: 'The shape that emerges . . . is not a patent heroic sculpture, but a more abstract, suggestive and incomplete work', which 'acknowledges its own inadequacies with the acute intelligence and unflinching integrity that have always marked Kilroy's theatre'.[11] For Karina Buckley in *The Sunday Times*, it was the subtlety of the script that stood out: 'Rich, thoughtful and achingly human, this is another gem in Kilroy's portfolio.'[12] Surprised to hear that the reviews of the play had been generally favourable, Barnes wrote in his diary that the discrepancy between the positive notices and his own negative response only went to prove that 'we hold ourselves to a higher standard than the media who sit in judgment over what we do'.[13]

For *The Shape of Metal*, Kilroy took the core ideas he wanted to express from the book *Henry Moore on Sculpture*, in which the great British sculptor wrote: 'One must try to find a synthesis, to come to terms with opposite qualities. Art and life are made up of conflicts.'[14] The tension between the impossible purity of the ideal and the inevitable imperfection of life had, of course, begun to fascinate Kilroy long before he started work on *The Shape of Metal*. The relationship between the two very different plays produced by Field Day, for example, *Double Cross* and *The Madame MacAdam Travelling Theatre*, hinges on the contrast between the former's focus on its characters' certainty and extremism and the latter's foregrounding of human frailty. In *The Shape of Metal*, the tension between the ideal and the actual is presented in the conflict between Nell as artist and as mother, and in questions raised in the play about the human as well as artistic desire to strive for absolute perfection and the need to come to terms with fallibility. In great art, Moore wrote, 'this conflict is hidden, it is unsolved. Great art is not *perfect*. Take the *Rondanini Pietà*, one of the greatest works of Michelangelo. It is not a perfect work of art. . . . All that is bursting with energy is disturbing – not perfect. It is the quality of life. The other is the quality of the ideal.'[15] The *Pietà* presents Moore with an important question: why should he and sculptors of his acquaintance like Giacometti and Marini 'find this work one of the most moving and greatest works we know of when it's a work that has such disunity in it?'[16] In *The Shape of Metal*, Kilroy addresses these very questions of life, art and (im)perfection through Nell's observations about the *Pietà*, as well as her assessment of Giacometti's art and that of his friend Samuel Beckett, both of whom she knew in Paris in the 1930s.

To represent Nell's work as a sculptor convincingly, Kilroy turned to the career of Barbara Hepworth (1903–75), a friend of Henry Moore's, who was considered 'the world's greatest woman sculptor' by the end of her life.[17] A stage direction in *The Shape of Metal* describes the signature of the middle period of Nell's work, some pieces of which are on display in the 1972 version of her studio, as 'the circle, versions of the circle in coiled springs of metal, cones, undulating ribbons of metal, vortices, gyres, ovoid-shaped balls, perhaps a few large industrial springs' (p. 27). Her unfinished piece 'Woman Rising from Water' is described as a 'powerful female face emerging from the stone', deriving its inspiration from works by Michelangelo and Constantin Brancusi. Like her contemporary Brancusi, Hepworth extrapolated totally abstract sculpture from human and organic forms and 'developed a repertory of very simple abstract shapes with titles such as "Single Form", "Two Forms", "Pierced Hemisphere", "Helicoids in Sphere", "Conoid, Sphere and Hollow"'.[18] 'Form' – shape – is the operative word, too, in *The Shape of Metal*: 'Form – question at heart of play,' Kilroy wrote in a note to himself on a typescript of his work in progress.[19] Hepworth sometimes worked in bronze, as does Nell in Kilroy's play, and later introduced a figurative aspect into her work, as in the blue marble 'Cosdon Head' or her sculptures on the theme of the mother and child. Both the head and the mother and child are thematically important elements in *The Shape of Metal*.

To create Nell Jeffrey as a person, Kilroy drew on the traits of a group of Anglo-Irish women – writers and theatre makers – he had met at the beginning of his career. To Brian Friel, who had wondered whether *The Shape of Metal* owed something to Mary Lavin and her daughters,[20] Kilroy explained:

> Nell has been with me a long time. She comes out of the Molly Manning – Sheila Richards world [Molly Keane, Mary Manning, Shelagh Richards] and that coven of blue-tongued, 'artistic'/posh ladies I met with them all those years ago. I suppose it's a case of: Imagine what would happen if there were a lone remnant of that world still around! Besides, the A[nglo]-Irish distancing from myself allowed me to write a highly personal play with my usual obsessions. What you said about Lavin bothers me in that, yes, the car trips, must have come from there. . . . [21]

In a note to the director of the New York production of *The Shape of Metal*, which opened in September 2007, Kilroy mentioned that Mary Manning 'was a lover of Beckett and I heard a hell of a lot about him' – that he had a ferocious temper, for example, particularly with drink taken.[22] Nell dines out on similar stories about the Beckett she knew when she was young.

Kilroy based some of Nell's vocal tics on the speech mannerisms of the writer Molly Keane, which are captured in an interview she granted the *New Yorker* magazine in 1986, when she was eighty-two – the same age Kilroy makes the older Nell in *The Shape of Metal*. Nell has a habit of summing up information in the form of a two-point list, just as Keane does in her conversation with the *New Yorker*'s Mary Kierstead. Kierstead relates that Molly Skrine and Bobbie Keane, who was four years her junior, were lovers for five years before they married in 1938: 'she wanted to be sure he'd made up his mind – "and, B, I wasn't about to do any cradle snatching"'.[23] In *The Shape of Metal*, Nell expresses herself similarly: 'Can't be bothered with niceties, never had much time for good manners and all that tommyrot. . . . Engage, that's all that matters. Besides, B, I'm dying' (p. 23). Some details about Molly Keane's sister Susan related in the *New Yorker* profile may also have made their way into the plot of Kilroy's play. Keane believed her sister was 'destroyed' by her mother's neglect of her when she was growing up, while Susan's only love affair was 'nipped in the bud' by her parents, 'because they didn't think he was socially right'. When Susan had a breakdown late in life the doctor '"put her into the bin and, B, gave her electric-shock treatment, aged seventy-six!"'.[24] In *The Shape of Metal*, Nell also thwarts the budding romance between a village boy and her daughter Grace, who is a 'manic depressive with schizoid tendencies' (p. 26). Kilroy corresponded with the well-known Irish psychiatrist Dr Anthony Clare about the appropriate depiction of her mental illness in the play.

The questions Kilroy asks in his plays about artists are pared down to the fundamentals in *The Shape of Metal*: why is the artist compelled to create art, and how should that art embody the answer to that question? One answer is that creative activity is a persistent but futile effort to overcome death. Towards the end of the play, Judith expresses sadness in the face of 'all that human effort in the world to – make things' (p. 46), given that those 'things' are in the final instance ephemeral and transitory, as evidenced throughout the play. Nell's studio, which appears pristine and in working order in 1972 in the central part of the play, is cleared out and 'like a tomb' in the first and third sections, set in 2002. The adjacent garden, in the flashback section, is 'splendid' (p. 27), while in the final part we see that it 'has been neglected in recent years' (p. 57). The 'slim blond boy' Grace loved in 1972 has become, when Judith seeks him out in 2002, '[t]his heap with his guts spilling out over the old jeans', his garage 'sinking, roof with holes, so much rusted junk' (p. 46). The place reminds Judith of Nell's studio, to which it seems 'somehow – connected' (p. 46). Nell, too, is deteriorating, no longer able to work with her hands, and prone to moments of forgetfulness, although her mind is still creative. Her frustration at this deterioration translates itself into rudeness and aggression, which mask her real fear: 'I don't want to die, that's all, I don't want to die!' (p. 14). That is why she has 'spent a lifetime trying to create finished objects', while around her 'the bloody place is disintegrating' (p. 15). Yet the conundrum Nell wrestles with throughout the play is that, while life is defined precisely by its protean and transitory nature, art, in its unchanging finality, seems to stand for death: 'I suppose that's what death is. The end of all response. No further answers. Or questions' (p. 50). Even though she calls the piece of art she is unable to finish a 'failure', subconsciously her inability to complete it is a way of refusing the finality of death.

Nell Jeffrey's artistic personality is made up of conflicting creative and destructive impulses that feed on each other. If there are times when she feels she could kill herself, these are counteracted when 'all that energy starts pouring through everything again' and she knows she 'can't die!' (p. 18). Her attitude to the men she has known in her life is equally ambivalent, even paradoxical. Eddie, Judith's father, 'had an immense sense of life', which is what Nell 'loved about him' (p. 46); he also 'carried this tremendous failure around with him', which is why she had to 'throw him out in the end' (p. 16). About Herbert, Grace's father, she remembers that he had a 'foul mouth' but 'beautiful hands' (p. 24). She might be talking about herself. The same tension informs her attitude towards Shay, 'that boy in the garage' (p. 36), whom Grace had been meeting against her mother's will in 'the field behind the RC Church in the village' (p. 38), something Nell deduces from a bunch of wildflowers Grace has brought back to give to her. Kilroy himself commented in a note: 'that Grace is betrayed through a bunch of innocent wild flowers which she has picked because of their beauty . . . is a motif which echoes the theme of art in the play, the fault-line through a thing of beauty'.[25] Nell feels about Shay much as she does about cars, which she condemns for polluting the atmosphere, but also loves because of 'all that concealed power under the whatchamacallit' (p. 13). On the one hand, Shay represents, to Nell's Anglo-Irish sensibility, the reprehensible way of life of 'them' – '[n]ot our kind of person' – from which she is attempting to 'save' her daughter (p. 25). On the other, she is unable to resist her own animalistic urges – the 'living pulse' – as she is driven to seduce the boy while he is posing for her to 'shape' his 'statue'. She tells Judith: 'I was unable to stop myself. It's true! I seized him. Yes. In this chair. A monster? Possibly. But there was more. I also knew I was trying to show what he was really like. For Grace' (p. 48). Nell's contradictory statements are made quite categorically, but Kilroy notes in an interview that such pronouncements by his characters are 'a way of . . . alerting the audience to an issue', and are therefore to be taken as 'provisional'.[26] In *The Shape of Metal*, opposites turn out to be two sides of the same coin.

While Nell's artwork is being installed in the Nell Jeffrey Room at the gallery, there is one piece left behind in the studio because it is unfinished, a 'failure'. In the opening and closing parts of the play, the piece is 'covered completely in sacking or cloth' (p. 11), but in the flashback section, it is uncovered:

> A marble piece entitled *Woman Rising from Water*. The shape is ovoid, beautifully carved and polished to a high finish. One side is as if it had been attacked and out of the rubble, this powerful, female face emerging from the stone. This piece was inspired by Michelangelo's *Rondanini Pietà*. See, also, Brancusi's *Sleep*, although NELL's head is far less benign, more witch-like with wild hair. (p. 27)

Director Lynne Parker noted that the presence on stage of the artwork created a practical conundrum: 'you are asking people who are prop makers and set designers suddenly to be great artists. And when they are great artists, there's always the question of who's to decide what a great piece of sculpture should look like.'[27] This is one instance (the transformation of Oscar into the Androgyne at the end of *The Secret Fall* being another) where the burden of

Kilroy's uncompromising theatrical vision falls onto the shoulders of the director and designer. It should also be remembered, however, that the piece in this case is unfinished and – at least in Nell's final assessment – a failure. Nell's reaction when she remembers Grace asking, during a visit to Milan, why the figures in the Pietà were 'only half there', indicates that, to her, art is a striving for perfection, an attempt to overcome the human condition: 'Indeed! That's what makes the piece so unbearably – human, the failed touch, the unfinished carving, something which could never, ever be completed successfully' (p. 16). This, of course, also becomes a reflection on her own unfinished piece, and on her inability to accept the humanity of her own failed touch. Stone, she argues, 'is pure before we touch it . . . I think we're trying to blend into that purity' (p. 23). Given her quest for inhuman perfection in art, it is no surprise that the dominant image of the work we see displayed in her 1972 studio is the circle.

The unfinished sculpture's two names – Nell's official title, 'Woman Rising from Water', and Grace's nickname, 'Egg Woman' – are indicative of the different ways mother and daughter see themselves and each other reflected in the carved woman's face. 'Egg Woman' suggests that the figure is being born from the egg, but has not fully emerged into life – like Grace herself, who is described by Nell as weak and immature. Perhaps the woman is trapped in the egg, having 'never been born entirely'; the phrase was used by Carl Jung, at the end of his 1935 lecture on dreams and the unconscious at London's Tavistock Clinic, to describe the condition of a young girl who was experiencing 'mythological dreams'.[28] The image of an incomplete birth made such a lasting impression on Samuel Beckett that he referenced the notion in a number of his works. In Kilroy's play, Beckett is the writer who introduced Nell to the sculptor Giacometti in Paris in 1938, at least one of whose works also resonates with Nell's unfinished piece. 'Is the *Petit buste* being submerged or emerging?', Timothy Mathews asks: 'That indeterminacy, her own incompletion, is the material of her grace made static, untouchable, barely there.'[29]

Grace's recitation to the Egg Woman, however, also associates the figure with the water of her official name, 'Woman Rising from Water':

Oh, Egg-woman, Egg-woman, where have you been?
I've been to the bottom of the ice-cold sea.
Oh, Egg-woman, Egg-woman, what have you seen?
I've seen all the monsters
That are there to be seen.
But now I've come back to Judy and Grace.
Feel my cold forehead,
Feel my cold face – (p. 34)

As an image of Nell, the woman/artist rising to the surface has faced the 'monstrous' depths of the subconscious but returned less than human, 'cold' as marble in the presence of her children. For Grace, the monsters at the bottom of the sea are also the demons of her manic depression, of which she is never free and by which she will always be damaged no matter how '[t]errifically restored' the doctor declares she is (p. 21). The layers of the subconscious that feed Nell's art form a source of anxiety for her daughter. In that regard, the artist-parent and the troubled child resemble the writer James Joyce and his daughter Lucia, another mentally unstable young woman. The shadowy presence of Joyce *père et fille* in *The Shape of Metal* is brought into focus by Kilroy's choice of Lucia as the protagonist of his 2009 radio drama *In the Garden of the Asylum*.[30] While Joyce could see that his daughter's behaviour was erratic, he was initially reluctant to seek medical intervention and inclined to interpret her psychological condition as something akin to his own genius. Carl Jung observed about father and daughter that they were 'like two people going to the bottom of a river, one falling and the other diving'.[31] Lucia eventually entered St Andrew's psychiatric hospital in Northampton, England; Raymond Douglas, the son born in 1902 from the marriage between Lord Alfred Douglas and Olive Custance, was also a patient there. Kilroy examined the causes of Douglas' mental illness in the one-act play *My Scandalous Life*; in his radio drama, Kilroy imagines that Lucia and Raymond encounter each other in the hospital garden and strike up a friendship of sorts, which comes to an end when their conversations about their (in)famous fathers inevitably lead to a dramatic crisis.

In *The Shape of Metal*, Nell's sculpture of the woman rising from water represents her younger daughter Judith in the sense that the latter accuses herself of being self-absorbed, of being '[h]alf present, half absent, all my life' (p. 28). As a character in the play, Judith is also only 'half there', in that practically nothing is revealed about her present life. Parker found Judith the most difficult character to represent because of this absence of background information, and noted that it was particularly hard for Eleanor Methven to get to grips with her inner motivation because she is such a 'cipher'.[32] Looking back on the production eight years later, Parker stated that, were she to direct the play again, she would reinforce the fact that Judith is gay to indicate her 'dislocation' from the Anglo-Irish establishment.[33] Judith's name evokes the biblical beheader of Holofernes, a comparison that plays out in the aggressive way she pursues her mother about the past until she makes her 'face' herself and the way she tends to wipe others, including Grace, 'off the face of the earth' (pp. 48–49). In that sense, Judith will have Nell's head. Back in 1972, when her sister was falling to pieces, Judith's own head was elsewhere, stuck in a book while she was sitting in the studio watching her mother work on the sculpture, which she loved because it was 'so – complete, somehow' (p. 29). Judith's memory of reading about Virginia Woolf's suicide, 'stones in her pocket, entering the water for the last time' (pp. 27–28), is a reminder that the artist, too, is not always immune to the power of subconscious monsters, and sometimes fails to rise again from the watery depths.

In the play's opening scene, and again towards the end, Nell is haunted by suppressed fears and desires connected with the memory of her lost daughter. Grace twice appears to her in a dream, expressionistically represented on stage by a surreal, speaking head. As a stage device, this recalls the talking heads in works by Beckett such as *Endgame* (Nagg and Nell), *Play* (M, W1, W2), and *Happy Days* (Winnie), where the characters' buried or entombed bodies signify their existential paralysis and impotence while memory persists in the repeated patterns of words spilling from their immobilised heads. In both instances when Grace's head appears to Nell, the daughter speaks of her mother's promise to sculpt her head, but while the first dream suggests that Nell thinks of the artistic project as benevolent, the second implies a more sinister motive.

In the opening scene, as Nell sits dozing in her chair, Grace's face appears suddenly through the wall of the studio; the effect is of 'a mounted head, speaking' (p. 11). Emmaleene O'Brien argues that, when it appears through what Kilroy's stage direction suggests is an 'elasticated or other opening' in the back wall of the set (p. 11), Grace is 'symbolically depicted as frozen in the process of birth, and still part of her mother's body'.[34] Nell's kneading fingers, the head says, will transform material into 'Grace finally at peace, head still and quiet', because 'Mummy stop everything, head on pedestal, absolutely still. Grace inside the silence. Safe' (p. 11). Csilla Bertha remarks that 'Mummy kneading the head' (p. 11) can also be heard as 'Mummy "needing" Grace's head for her creation just as she is "kneading", that is, massaging the head to heal her in life'.[35] But Grace's almost immediate outburst of distress – 'Don't be cross, Mumsie. Won't let you down this time' – suggests that Nell's 'shaping' is also a controlling act, a symbolic representation of her desire to 'stop' her daughter from going 'off on one of her walkabouts' to places beyond her control – 'who's she meeting, the little tramp, in pubs, casual pick-ups!' (p. 12) – even when Nell's own diaries suggest that she herself had been much given to drinking in pubs and picking up casual lovers in her earlier days.

Before the second dream scene, we see mother and daughter interacting in the central part of the play set in 1972. Grace is caught impossibly between her wish to be soothed and stilled by her mother and her resistance to being shaped and smothered. As Nell massages her head, kneading and caressing the parts of her face, Grace has 'gone limp, drawn into her mother's body for support and the two of them sway together. Almost in dance', until she suddenly breaks free, 'wild and struggling, someone escaping immense danger, flailing about', and accuses Nell of trying to kill her (p. 31). Grace's illness is making her behave erratically, but her accusation comes to haunt Nell towards the end of her life, as the latter is beginning to understand the damage that has been done by her quest for control and perfection in her life as well as her art.

At the end of the play, Grace's head appears again behind the sleeping Nell, 'this time a bronze death head on a plinth . . . which speaks, the mouth moving but the eyes closed over, metallic' (p. 51). Earlier, Nell had quoted Giacometti as saying that a sculpture must 'embody its own particular failure' (p. 44). The single problem to be solved by Giacometti and other contemporary sculptors was, according to Jean-Paul Sartre, 'how to mold a man in stone without petrifying him'.[36] Nell's act of immortalising Grace in bronze has indeed had the effect of 'petrifying' her, as the act of kneading her head in life, symbolic of the attempt to form her life into a desired shape, had likewise 'petrified' her with fear and anxiety. Perhaps, as the metal death head implies, it killed her: 'Silence. All finished. Nothingness. No feel, no fear, no sight, no sound, no touch, no taste. All finished' (p. 51). Waking abruptly from her dream, Nell realises, however imperfectly, that it was her inability to accept her daughter for who she was, her insistence that Grace was not mentally ill but 'terribly immature' and 'utterly unaware, fragile, weak' (pp. 25–26), that resulted in her loss: 'You see, to be human you have to live with failure' (p. 52), she acknowledges. Her inability to do so has made her, in Judith's accusatory words, 'capable of monstrous things' (p. 45).

The insight Nell gains from Grace's talking dream-head – that she has failed 'because [she] evaded failure' (p. 52), both as a human being and an artist – leads her to attack the covered, unfinished sculpture of the face of the 'Woman Rising from Water' with a sledgehammer, in an expression of her anger and frustration at herself, at Grace, and at the nature of her art. The ambiguity of her explanation of the destructive act, however, is indicative of the complex motivation behind it, for she paradoxically expresses her acknowledgement of the necessity of failure, of imperfection, in the language of completion: 'I want to *finish* – all this. All finished. That's what Gracie said. All finished. *Finish* it!' (p. 53, my emphasis). Yet in almost the same breath she goes on to diagnose the impossibility of any kind of finality: 'I have spent a lifetime trying to create perfect form. The *finished*, rounded, perfect form. Mistake. No, take that back. Colossal fucking blunder. And, B, I knew it. All along I knew this. Knew what I was doing. Knew it was an illusion. And still persisted' (p. 53, my emphasis).

Kilroy captures the courage, tragedy and futility of Nell's act by not showing the theatre audience what it is she has attacked, thereby holding us suspended in the doubleness of her deed of 'finishing' her sculpture. For what has she smashed? The sculpture of the Egg Woman that stands exposed to the eyes of the audience in the central part of the play set in 1972 is 'covered completely in sacking or cloth' (p. 11) in the opening and closing sections taking place in 2002. While mounting the 2003 production, set designer John Comiskey worried about 'the covering breaking down on the sculpture' during the attack, but Kilroy insisted that the piece 'really *has to be* covered'.[37] Nell tells us that the work in question is unfinished, but we do not know what that means: has it remained untouched since 1972, or has Nell worked on it since? When we see it uncovered in 1972, one side of the beautifully polished ovoid piece already looks 'as if it had been attacked', and, like the unfinished Rondanini Pietà, the piece therefore perfectly expresses the 'unbearably – human . . . failed touch' (p. 16) which Nell recognises as being the antithesis to the 'colossal blunder' of her own attempts at perfection. If this is the version Nell smashes in 2002, its destruction is yet another tragic refusal on her part to come to terms with the necessity of open endings. If, on the other hand, she had been trying to perfect the piece since 1972, it now will look again, as it did at that time, 'as if it had been attacked'. Either way, Nell can only achieve different, if perhaps better, degrees of failure. The impossible dilemma of the artist's quest (both to achieve perfection and to acknowledge failure) is also captured in Judith's question, as she 'touch[es] the damaged piece of sculpture through its covering': 'Can this *(sculpture)* be – fixed?' (p. 53). To 'fix' can either mean 'repair' (change) or 'immobilise' (leave as is), and choosing between these options is also the 'fix' we are in as spectators, the dilemma we are left with, depending on what we imagine lies beneath the cloth.

Nell's smashing of the sculpture is followed by her telling Judith 'what really happened' on the day in 1938, 'before the Hitler war' (pp. 15, 44), when she and her friend Betty visited Giacometti and Beckett in Paris. Judith has heard the story of the visit many times before, to the point where she knows it by heart and can repeat it verbatim, but in this latest version, Nell deflates the importance of the two men by switching her focus from the greatness of their art to their fallibility as human beings, and from the head to the feet, relating how, as the afternoon progressed into the evening, they got steadily drunk, argued about their 'midnight walks through the city . . . punctuated by their encounters with whores' (p. 54), and then quarrelled about the act of walking itself, Giacometti 'prancing about with his walking cane' and marvelling at the way the foot touches the ground, Beckett 'emphasizing the importance of sturdy footwear' and pulling off his boots in order to praise their ability to 'carry us everywhere' (pp. 55–56).

Judith interprets this version of the story from a feminist perspective, arguing that 'what was really going on' was that here were two young women hoping to be artists, 'bowing the knee before the two great male artists – how predictable!' (p. 56). Nell sees in the argument a lesson that 'everything comes down to the ordinary . . . Down, down further, down to the common animal – . . . . Snuffling and scratching and guzzling and breaking wind, that's the base! On which everything is constructed! Then you build and build!' (p. 56). This sounds more like late Yeats than Beckett: 'Those masterful images because complete / Grew in pure mind, but out of what began? / A mound of refuse or the sweepings of a street, / Old kettles, old bottles, and a broken can.'[38] If these are the lines being echoed, Nell is still holding on to the idea that the images the artist strives to build, eventually, out of the banal, are 'masterful' and 'complete'. In *The Madame MacAdam Travelling Theatre* Kilroy had also played with the shift from 'McMaster' to 'MacAdam' to signal his protagonist's embrace of human fallibility and resilience, focused in the resolve to 'begin again' after each inevitable failure. As both that play and its predecessor *Double Cross* imply, quests for mastery and perfection, whether on a global, national, or familial scale, always end in destruction: the 'Hitler war' that involved a fascist effort to create the perfect race; the Anglo-Irish endeavour to keep class and faith pure against the 'deplorable' and 'thuggish' Catholic Irish (p. 25); or Nell's attempt to 'save' her daughter Grace from a life of 'squalor' with Shay (p. 25).

Nell's greatest failure is that she only partly sees the connection between the subject matter of Giacometti and Beckett's drunken quarrel in 1938 'about the relevance or irrelevance of footwear' (p. 56) and the art they produced from it in the post-war years. As James Olney points out, 'Giacometti spoke always of "work in progress", Beckett of "going on"'; in resisting the expression of mastery and completeness, their oeuvre embodies the very notion of achievement in failure.[39] Nell's conclusion that Beckett and Giacometti 'have little to offer us anymore', because '[t]hey're dead. We're alive. What we know now comes to us from the future' (pp. 56–57), is another categorical pronouncement begging to be questioned. Nell's statement that 'the future is rushing towards us with immense speed' (p. 57) recalls a phrase from Walter Benjamin's much-quoted essay, 'Theses on the Philosophy of History', on which he was working between 1937 and 1940 while he, too, was exiled in Paris. In the ninth thesis, Benjamin writes about Paul Klee's painting 'Angelus Novus':

> His face is turned toward the past. Where we perceive a chain of events, he sees one single catastrophe which keeps piling wreckage upon wreckage and hurls it in front of his feet. The angel would like to stay, awaken the dead, and make whole what has been smashed. But a storm is blowing from Paradise; it has got caught in his wings with such violence that the angel can no longer close them. The storm irresistibly propels him into the future to which his back is turned, while the pile of debris before him grows skyward. This storm is what we call progress.[40]

Benjamin's Angel, Mathews suggests, 'is of the most human kind – he cannot stay, he will die, he cannot redeem himself or others, he saves only the idea of saving with which he comes to us'.[41] Profoundly affected by the Second World War, Beckett and Giacometti, in their post-war art, sought forms that could express something along these same lines; they found them 'in uncertainties about place, about emerging and being submerged, about standing or walking, beginning to walk or ceasing to, about arriving at a point of view or departing from one, about the absence of a frame or its ever-present invisibility and potency'.[42]

Nell laughs at the memory of Giacometti prancing about, but fails to note that in his immediate post-war art, the figure of the walking man became the embodiment of 'going on' in the face of the storm. Such figures are always 'already walking, for in a still sculpture can we tell the difference between walking and being about to walk, standing and being about to walk, walking and standing? Staying and leaving? Changing and repeating?'[43] Nell ridicules Beckett's infatuation with 'a pair of prized Austrian or Swiss walking-boots' (p. 55), but boots are among the 'essential accessories' of the protagonists in many of Beckett's works, and in *Waiting for Godot* become central signifying objects; indeed, as Beckett told Roger Blin, Godot's name 'was suggested by *godillots* and *godasses*, French slang for boots'.[44] Much like Giacometti's walking figures, Beckett's tramp-like characters are caught in the moment between staying and leaving, changing and repeating, going on and not going on. There is no conclusion to plays like *Waiting for Godot* and *Endgame*: their characters are put on hold; their action is suspended; but they do not 'end'. Giacometti's method is similar: 'When he lets a sculpture leave the studio, it is because of an arbitrary, insignificant decision. He does not stop, he interrupts the work in progress.'[45] In this moment the shape of metal, of art, takes on the shape of mettle – of courage and endurance in the face of inevitable failure.

Like Benjamin's Angel, Nell is powerless in her own life to 'awaken the dead, and make whole what has been smashed', a fallibility represented by the unfinished carving of the Egg Woman, now itself smashed. But Nell is herself a female character in a work of the ephemeral art of the stage created by Kilroy, and recreated in each theatrical performance: 'The woman, the artist's creation and her metaphorical self-portrait, rises from the rubble again and again, to give hope and healing and to be destroyed again. The art of failure, in the last analysis, does not become the failure of art.'[46] Yet the relationship between creation, destruction, resurrection, and art has been on Nell's mind, too, all along. She finds it amusing that her own sculptures are housed in the museum in Kilmainham, a former military hospital. Nell thinks of the future as female-dominated, but not necessarily different from the past. Early in the play she wonders how women will fight in war – for 'fight they will!' – when they 'take over the mess' (p. 15). At the end of the play, when she muses that the human race has already created the conditions for both its own extinction and recreation, she can only wonder what kind of art the woman of the future will create after that holocaust, what kind of forms she will come up with to accommodate that 'mess'. That woman of the future would have to be, like Beckett and Giacometti, an artist of 'achievement in failure', a quality Nell herself has only belatedly, and imperfectly, grasped at.

At the end of *The Shape of Metal*, Nell expresses the urgent need to go outside. Although she is 'quite feeble', she verbally declines Judith's help, but accepts her arm when it is offered, and although she asserts that she is fine 'on [her] own', she asks Judith to stay the night (p. 57). Mother and daughter bicker about the extent to which Judith is like Nell, and they argue about Grace, the symbol of failure, absence, and lack of closure in their lives. When Judith asserts with 'realistic' finality that Grace 'is not out there', and 'hasn't been out there for a very long time', it is Nell who refuses closure, wanting to believe that Grace is 'out there somewhere', needing 'to – dream' (p. 58). Judith had earlier reminded her mother that all love 'has to be earned!' (p. 43), but their acknowledgement of Grace, the absent other, the lost one who could not be saved, evokes the idea of grace, the gift of undeserved love and mercy. Nell exhorts Judith to '[k]eep moving, darling, just keep moving!' (p. 58). In this ending that is no ending, Kilroy gives us a female combination of Giacometti's walking figures and Beckett's 'pseudo-couple',[47] two characters suggesting 'solitude as plural':[48]

> NELL: . . . I am going into the garden.
>
> *They walk out together through the open doorway, into the gathering darkness, and the play ends.* (p. 58)

As the play 'ends' in a kind of limbo, its characters walking together-apart into the neglected garden, the flawed paradise, it accomplishes what Nell understands rationally but cannot quite accept in her own art: it embraces the lack of finality. Salman Rushdie, speaking in relation to Beckett, suggests that all literature is 'an interim report from the consciousness of the artist, and so it can never be "finished" or "perfect"'.[49] Kilroy, similarly, has said that what is represented in his plays on stage is 'provisional, it's an attempt at something', and that his work 'embodies this process, including the failure of so much human endeavor'.[50] His fallible, human characters in *The Shape of Metal* can only 'go on' and 'keep moving', in each other's precarious company, acknowledging Grace who is not there, invoking the possibility of grace.

When *The Shape of Metal* premiered in 2003 Fintan O'Toole noted that Kilroy's theme – 'the Yeatsian question of whether it is better to perfect the life or the work' – was also present in Brian Friel's one-act play *Performances*, which was staged at the Gate Theatre around the same time his friend's work opened at the Abbey. For O'Toole, both these works signalled a kind of sea-change in the relationship between Irish theatre and Irish society: 'In a different way, both Friel's *Performances* and Kilroy's *The Shape of Metal* had decidedly valedictory tones. Neither had much relationship to Ireland now, or indeed to Ireland at all.' To O'Toole, both works suggested 'a conscious turning away from the notion that a play could itself be an intervention in life, an engagement with the messy development of a society'.[51] The inward turn, however, did not set the beginning of a trend. In his final original play, *The Home Place* (2005), Friel went on to engage full-on with the colonial history out of which contemporary Irish society emerged. Set on an Anglo-Irish estate in 1878, the play employs the pseudo-science of phrenology as a metaphor for the unsuccessful English attempt to 'get the measure' of the Irish, against a backdrop of social and political unrest. Friel's main intervention in his version of Ibsen's *Hedda Gabler* (2008), which turned out to be his swan song, was to add flashes of ironic humour and to infuse the heroine's gradual mental disintegration with greater psychological realism. When *The Shape of Metal* was staged, Kilroy was already working on two new plays: a free interpretation of *Spring Awakening* and an original drama based on a nebulous period in the life of the English poet and engraver William Blake. By moving Wedekind's material to 1950s Ireland and taking on those aspects of the nation's culture that had enabled the various abuse scandals of the past several decades, Kilroy certainly chose to engage with the very 'messiest' of social issues. In *Blake*, by contrast, he once more narrowly focused the spotlight on the figure of the uncompromising, psychologically tormented artist, as he had first done in *Tea and Sex and Shakespeare*. This time, however, the journey leads the protagonist through a dark tunnel of mental breakdown and creative stagnation into an unprecedented state of equilibrium and productivity.

10

A Time of Joy and Love: *Blake*

Kilroy had been intrigued by William Blake's life and work ever since he read his poetry as a student in the 1950s, but it was not until 2001 that he completed a script in which he depicts the eighteenth-century visionary artist undergoing a personal and creative crisis. *Blake* therefore reprises a theme Kilroy had also explored in other works such as *Tea and Sex and Shakespeare* and *The Shape of Metal*; but unlike Brien and Nell in those plays, whose personal and artistic recovery is tentative, Blake emerges from his breakdown a changed man filled with creative energy and new-found tolerance, in no small measure due to the intervention of his wife Catherine. 'I think I've been moving towards this play all my life,' Kilroy told Christopher Innes in 2002.[1] In an interview with Anthony Roche, he characterised *Blake* as 'a kind of summation':

> It's very obviously related to something like *Talbot's Box*, which also tried to deal with the eccentric or exceptional or unusual kind of individual who is a mystic. It is a play that tries to explore the burden of that kind of a vision and of testing that kind of a vision against grosser daily reality. But I think it may be the end of that kind of exploration.[2]

Kilroy would revisit the theme, however, in his 2016 *Signatories* monologue for Pádraig Pearse, discussed in the coda following this chapter, where he concentrates on the revolutionary's unflinching visionary quality as well as the personal cost of that singularity of purpose.

Given the play's focus on an English subject, Kilroy believed from the outset that *Blake* should be premiered in England. Negotiations with the National Theatre were unsuccessful, however, and Kilroy soon conceded that it would be no easy task to get the play staged at all, even in Britain; *Blake*, he suggested, is 'so ambitious that it invites failure'.[3] In 2006 he approached the Abbey Theatre about the possibility of having the work produced in Dublin, but Fiach Mac Conghail decided against it 'for reasons relating to its subject, or that is, the possibly remote relationship between Blake and an Irish audience',[4] thereby confirming what Kilroy had already anticipated when he originally concluded the play would have to be done by 'a London company'.[5] Although it still awaits a full production, *Blake* was performed in a staged reading on 30 April 2011 at TCD's Samuel Beckett Theatre, where it formed the final event of a two-day symposium celebrating Kilroy's career. Produced in association with the Abbey and directed by Patrick Mason, the reading featured a noted cast including Jim Norton, Barbara Brennan and Cathy Belton.

For Kilroy, the urge to write imaginatively about historical figures leads him invariably to 'silences and disappearances' in the historical record that may be filled by the playwright with 'imaginative reconstructions' of how the lives of the historical personages might have been.[6] In *Blake*, Kilroy imagines that, sometime during the years of his life about which little is known, the poet was locked up in Finchley Grange lunatic asylum. According to Arthur Symons, next to nothing is known of Blake's life between 1809, when he mounted an unsuccessful exhibition of his work in his brother's shop, and 1818, but '[e]verything leads us to believe that those nine years were years of poverty and neglect'.[7] In his 'Author's Note' introducing the text of *Blake*, Kilroy states: 'From about 1806 to about 1815 Blake and his wife Catherine withdrew into isolation ("I am hid") and the play is set towards the latter part of that period of withdrawal.'[8] Blake wrote the phrase 'I am hid' in the margins of *Discourses on Art* by Sir Joshua Reynolds, whose work and that of other Augustans he hated for dominating the English art world at the expense of artists like himself: 'Fuseli, Indignant, almost hid himself. I am hid.'[9] Blake seems to have meant that his creative work was largely ignored, but Kilroy interprets the three last words literally when he suggests that the poet and his wife withdrew from public life and shrouded themselves from the world. Innes interprets Blake's words as meaning that the artist considered himself marginalised in the world of the arts; he suggests that Kilroy, too, 'has taken the position of an outsider in Irish theatre' or perhaps has been placed in that position, and as such, like Blake, 'might be seen as "hid"'. The focus in *Blake* on a writer-artist underlines that self-reflexive quality by highlighting, also in relation to Kilroy himself, 'the question of creative imagination – which is literally dramatized in this script'.[10]

Kilroy has acknowledged that the 'free-flowing style' of both *Talbot's Box* and *Blake* was inspired in no small measure by the early work of Peter Brook, particularly his hugely influential 1964 production of *Marat/Sade*. Innes argues that, as the most 'Artaudian' of Kilroy's plays, '*Blake* calls for the type of non-representational performance where eurythmics, visual display, and music . . . all coalesce into a "concrete" theatricality', but also points out that, unlike *Talbot's Box*, the play has no meta-theatrical moments when the actors step out of their role or the fourth wall is breached. Instead, the stage becomes a space where Blake's private life, his politics, his psyche and his artistic vision are seamlessly integrated with each other and with many of the themes that have preoccupied Kilroy himself throughout his career as a dramatist, including mental illness, the performance of gender, marital strife, absent children and social fragmentation. *Blake* is thus, as Innes points out, personal and subjective as well as 'a statement of artistic intent'.[11]

The echoes in *Blake* of *Marat/Sade* are evident in the asylum setting, the use of hospital patients as singers, and the behaviour of some of the inmates. The affliction of both the Catatonic and the Silent Woman in Kilroy's play resembles that of Charlotte Corday in Weiss' drama, who 'moves like a somnambulist',[12] while Kilroy's Frenetic shares his sexual obsession with the erotomaniac Duparret in *Marat/Sade*. The patient in Weiss' play who claims to be 'a thousand years old and in my time / I've helped commit a million murders',[13] resembles the Murderer in *Blake*, who contends at one point that he is not in his cell but 'in the streets . . . in the palace . . . in my lady's chamber', which Blake acknowledges is true because 'Murder is everywhere' (p. 60). One of the characteristics of *Marat/Sade* that may have made the work attractive to Kilroy is that Weiss attempted 'to write a "thinking" play to be performed in a "feeling" way'.[14] Brook likewise believed that the separation between intellect and emotion in the theatre is artificial, that theatre 'is made up of the unbroken conflict between impressions and judgments – illusion and disillusion cohabit painfully and are inseparable'.[15] Kilroy echoes this view almost verbatim: 'For me, the distinction between the intellectual and emotional life is spurious. They are of a piece. I have ideas with feeling, feelings with ideas. They are inextricable.'[16] Brook's production of *Marat/Sade* employed both Artaudian shocks to the system and Brechtian exposition and commentary. In Kilroy's case, Brechtian techniques are more prominent in *Talbot's Box*; *Blake* is, as Innes suggests, more Artaudian in its approach.

The fine line between madness and reason is central to both *Talbot's Box* and *Blake*. Both Talbot and Blake are characterised by Kilroy as eccentric individuals who are also visionaries, and whose extreme individualism is tested against the demands and pressures of family and society; but there are as many differences between the two figures as there are broad similarities. Talbot fits squarely into the notion of Christian mysticism, which 'is based upon a mortification of the body so absolute that it attains a condition of ecstasy'. The mystic 'lives only for the journey of the soul that will take him away, upward to God. What would be physical pain to others, to him is purgation'.[17] While Blake has 'the mystic's tormented sense of the doubleness of life between reality and the ideal', he 'tries to resolve it on earth, in the living person of man'; he is 'against everything that submits, mortifies, constricts and denies', including 'all accepted Christianity' and 'the churches'.[18] Although Kilroy's Blake is a visionary and shares some of Talbot's single-minded obsessiveness, the latter divested himself of all emotional human connections, whereas at the centre of *Blake* is what Kilroy has called 'a love story between Blake and Catherine Boucher'.[19] The importance of the artist's relationship with his wife also connects *Blake* thematically with *The Secret Fall of Constance Wilde*, where Constance's practical concerns about her children serve as a corrective to Oscar's 'dream of perfection' – of 'Paradise restored'.[20] One of the historical Mrs Blake's few complaints about her husband was that he 'was incessantly away "in Paradise"'.[21] In Kilroy's play it is Catherine Blake who ultimately helps her husband plant his feet on solid ground.

Division is the central concept of *Jerusalem*, the great poem on which Blake was working during the period considered in Kilroy's play, although its trajectory is towards eventual reconciliation. *Blake* is divided into two parts, and Kilroy envisions a performance space that is likewise 'split in two'. Upstage is a raised area above a wall that can open in various ways, 'making up cells and entrance gates to the asylum' (p. 11), while the main acting area is located downstage at the lower level. Reminiscent of the box that contains the action of *Talbot's Box*, the whole stage in *Blake* is, as Kilroy himself suggests, a 'box of tricks, of various shutters and things opening and so on'.[22] The upper stage functions in part as the asylum's panopticon that allows Dr Hibbel and his distinguished visitors, Sir James and Lady Fetchcroft, to observe the inmates without being seen themselves; but Kilroy also uses the device to draw attention, as he did with the enclosed space in *Talbot's Box* and the circle in *The Secret Fall of Constance Wilde*, to 'the voyeurism of theatre itself and the voyeuristic gaze on art'.[23]

Blake is an attempt at 'total theatre', as was *Talbot's Box*; but compared to the earlier work, Kilroy sees *Blake* as more ambitious, 'almost operatic in its use of choral singing', with large scenic effects.[24] In his 'Author's Note', Kilroy acknowledges that the choral passages 'will undergo transformations when a composer is in place', but specifies that the singing 'should be unaccompanied', so that the emphasis falls on the singer's voice. Song is used at three key moments in the play, in each instance using Blake's lyrics. In Part One, the music illustrates Catherine's contention that her husband 'dreams, constantly, of children singing – ' (p. 29). Before the play proper begins, with the theatre still in darkness, 'a single adolescent voice sings in the distance' the familiar verses of the poem 'Jerusalem' – 'And did those feet in ancient time . . . ' – to which Blake stands listening, head to one side, in a spot of light (p. 11). Scene Four opens in a similar fashion with Blake in the asylum exercise yard, listening intently to a distant boy soprano, then a chorus of children, singing the verses of 'The Echoing Green'. In *Blake*, children represent innocence, the artist's wish for a son, and perhaps his sense that, without his wife, he is 'but a child' (p. 33). In that regard, it is significant that in the final scene, after William and Catherine have found their freedom and reconciled their differences, the solo voice is that of a male, and the children's choir has been replaced with an adult chorus. As Blake matures psychologically over the course of the play, so too do the manifestations of his visions.

Kilroy stresses in his note for the play that 'Finchley Grange Asylum never existed. However, Blake was widely regarded as mad (but harmless) by friend and enemy alike.' Indeed, even the first editor of Blake's collected poems noted '"something in his mind not exactly sane"'.[25] Robert Hunt, reviewing 'Mr. Blake's Exhibition' in the *Examiner* of 17 September 1809, famously referred to the artist as 'an unfortunate lunatic, whose personal inoffensiveness secures him from confinement', and to his work as 'the wild effusions of a distempered brain'.[26] The poet himself was well aware of how he was perceived, but surmised that 'there are probably men shut up as mad in Bedlam, who are not so: that possibly the madmen outside have shut up the sane people'.[27] Six years after the poet's death in 1827, an unsigned article published in the *Revue Britannique* – apparently translated into French from a source in English – presented as fact Blake's presence as a patient in London's hospital for the insane. The unidentified writer of the piece describes in detail his visit to 'Bethlem, espèce d'hôpital de fous, institution bizarre', and his encounter with some of the asylum's inmates.[28] In *William Blake and His World*, Harold Bruce summarises the gist of the account: 'The author of the article said that "a few years before" he had visited Bedlam Hospital and had called on Blake in a cell there. He found him "a large pale man, an eloquent talker", very ready to discuss his visions.'[29] Few who knew Blake took the report seriously, and the records of Bedlam show no evidence that the poet was ever there. For Kilroy, nevertheless, the idea of Blake in Bedlam offered a creative opportunity that also established an imaginative connection with Weiss' *Marat/Sade*, a play he had long admired, which takes place during the same historical period in the lunatic asylum at Charenton. There, the inmates perform the assassination of Jean-Paul Marat under the direction of the Marquis de Sade, who was a patient in the institution from 1803 until his death in 1814.

Kilroy's frequent concern with the fragmented nature of society and with what *The Madame MacAdam Travelling Theatre* calls the 'crack down the middle of the human specimen' is mirrored by Blake's focus in his visionary poetry on Man's state of disunity. The central theme of *Jerusalem*, the long poem Blake was engaged in composing between 1804 and 1820, is Man's fall into division, most elementally the separation of Man (Albion) from his Emanation or Spiritual Self (Jerusalem). When the male Spectre (the reasoning power or Selfhood) and the female Emanation (the emotional and imaginative life) are parted, 'Man is in a fallen state, and can only be redeemed by their reconciliation'.[30] Man is a union of four elements –

the four Zoas – which are also associated with the four points of the compass; these were plotted geographically onto the four continents, the four regions of Britain, but most specifically onto the city of London: Norwood in the south, Blackheath in the east, Hounslow in the west, and Finchley in the north.[31] Urizen ('your reason', air, the south) stands for the intellect; Luvah ('love', fire, the east) for the emotional life; Tharmas ('Thames', water, the west) for the senses; and Urthona ('earth', the north) for the instinct. Blake implies that Man falls into division when hard rationality comes to dominate emotional life, restricting the place of the imagination, until the eventual resurrection into unity restores the Divine Imagination.

Parallel with the myth of Albion and Jerusalem runs the myth of Los and his separation from his Emanation, Enitharmon. Joseph Wicksteed suggests that, in *Jerusalem*, Blake is represented as Los and his wife Catherine as Enitharmon, and that in the poem, 'Blake goes out of his way to express remorselessly . . . his own domestic difficulties', but on his journey discovers something in his wife 'that only appeared in its full beauty and significance as he reached the end of his story'.[32] Kilroy's Blake follows this trajectory during his incarceration in Finchley Grange Asylum, where he has to confront not only his psychological and artistic demons but also his relationship with Kate, whom he comes to value and recognise as a person in her own right even as she remains completely dedicated to his well-being and the expression of his artistic vision. Wicksteed says of Male and Female in *Jerusalem* that, while Los-Blake 'is forever holding open the Gates of Paradise', Enitharmon-Catherine 'is forever enduring the pains of Purgatory'.[33] In Kilroy's play, Blake sees visions; Kate, who has walked to the asylum to secure her husband's release, suffers perpetually from painful feet.

When Blake is taken from his home by the asylum keepers, he immediately recognises Dr Hibbel from Finchley as Urizen (Reason), 'with his compass, his measurements, his shackles, out of the North come to halt my labours at the anvil – our labours, Kate!' (pp. 14–15). In *Jerusalem*, however, Finchley, as the north, is equated not with Urizen but with Urthona, 'known in its highest form as Inspiration and in its lowest as Instinct', whose 'vehicular form' (the vehicle of inspiration or spirit of Prophecy) was Los.[34] Finchley Grange, then, the asylum where Blake is confined, is as much connected with his own creative ability as with the constrictive forces of Reason, which are associated with the south. Dr Hibbel, the asylum director, is therefore only an external inhibitor of Blake's artistic endeavours; the artist's creative process is blocked in equal if not greater measure by forces within himself. It is in this context that the male hospital inmates – the Murderer, the Catatonic, and the Frenetic – must also be regarded as aspects of Blake's psyche, to be confronted by him, or acknowledged, or denied, while the female threesome of Lady Fetchcroft, the Silent Woman, and Catherine brings him face to face with his most stubborn blind spots and prejudices. The lunatic asylum in which the poet is locked up or 'hid' therefore represents societal restraints upon his imagination but perhaps especially the personal and artistic limitations the artist must overcome within himself before he can continue his creative work towards completion. In *Blake* Kilroy revisits the issues he first attempted to address in *Tea and Sex and Shakespeare*, where the 'white room' to which the blocked writer Brien imagines himself confined serves a psychological purpose not unlike that of the asylum in *Blake*. Much like Brien, Blake finds himself in a creative impasse caused by his lack of communication with his wife about their childlessness, but whereas in *Tea and Sex and Shakespeare* Kilroy struggled to pull together the various strands of his material, his approach in *Blake* is sure-footed and the play's conclusion more robustly optimistic.

The 'gender dichotomy' with which the characters struggle in a play like *The Secret Fall of Constance Wilde* also emerges in *Blake*, where, to quote Innes, '[t]he self-immolating drive to spiritual apotheosis is a specifically male quality; humanity and the demands of social responsibility are feminine'.[35] Of Catherine Blake, Kazin writes: 'She was the ideal wife of his artistic and intellectual alienation; she was the perfect helpmeet in his social and economic desperation', her only fault being, apparently, 'that she was not a person in her own right. The fault was most assuredly not in her but in Blake's annihilating need of her.'[36] For Kilroy, who says that he is 'imaginatively drawn to matters that challenge [him] intellectually', Catherine was a way into the figure of the artist:

> Blake resisted me, I found it extremely difficult to imagine such a man. I think this was due to the sheer difficulty of the poetry. But when I began to imagine the Blakes together, when I began

> to see Blake in an intimate relationship, then it became possible to write a play about him, to hear him speak, as it were.[37]

In *Blake* Kate has a forceful personality and a sense of initiative; it is she who rescues her husband from his uncomprehending adversaries, and from himself. Nevertheless, the play stops short of revising received critical opinion about Catherine and depicts her throughout as a woman entirely devoted to and protective of Blake and his art.

Blake's apprehension by the keepers of Dr Hibbel's hospital on behalf of certain 'concerned bodies' (in the event, Blake's own brother and sister), and his committal to Finchley Grange 'until such time as . . . he be restored to an equilibrium' (p. 16), concretely represent the attempt of the forces of convention to bring the dissident to heel; but the incarceration also acts as a metaphor for the artist's internal struggle with his own paralysing demons. For Kilroy's Blake, the period confined in the asylum embodies the way the artist is locked in self-righteous anger and bitterness against those he feels stand in the way of his visions, a counter-productive state of mind that blocks his creative abilities. Elements from *Jerusalem* feed into the play's representation of the lunatic asylum and its inmates, creating 'an interior psychological realm peopled by creatures who beneath their nineteenth-century costumes approximate to Blake's mystical visions'.[38] Blake himself recognises early on in the play that he is in Finchley Grange because he must 'pass through Evil and out the other side' (p. 26); this is a thought that also preoccupies Matt Talbot when he says that he must pass through the darkness within himself until he emerges 'inta some kinda light'. But whereas Talbot thinks that 'the darkness is Gawd',[39] in that he equates the physical pain caused by the chains that bind him with Christ's suffering and redemption, Blake never wavers in his belief that chains are evil, and that the darkness represents Satan.

Kilroy's interest in – and wariness of – official institutions that seek to regulate the behaviour of individuals is pervasive. In *Christ, Deliver Us!*, for example, he examines what James M. Smith has dubbed Ireland's 'architecture of containment': the systematic way in which the authorities of state and church sought to incarcerate and conceal transgressors of the moral norm in establishments such as industrial schools and Magdalen laundries. Women who persisted in expressing their sexuality outside the confines of marriage were particularly prone to being removed from society, since they were perceived as potential sources of moral contamination.[40] While in mid-twentieth-century Ireland such offenders were essentially 'disappeared', in early-nineteenth-century Europe it was common for institutionalised violators of normative behaviour to be displayed to the public, to set a deterrent example. Foucault states that in London, 'the hospital of Bethlehem exhibited lunatics for a penny, every Sunday', while in Paris at Bicêtre, '[o]ne went to see the keeper display the madmen the way the trainer at the Fair of Saint-Germain put the monkeys through their tricks'.[41] Both *Marat/Sade* and *Blake* exploit this historical reality. Weiss' play puts the asylum director's wife and daughter on stage as an audience for the inmates' performance; in Kilroy's drama, Lady Fetchcroft insists on observing the patients as a 'scientist'. The ideal hospital, according to Foucault, was 'an asylum where unreason would be entirely contained and offered as a spectacle, without threatening the spectators; where it would have all the powers of example and none of the risks of contagion'. Yet the transgressions of normative behaviour that were on display 'also exercised an irresistible attraction. Such nights were peopled with inaccessible pleasures; such corrupt and ravaged faces became masks of voluptuousness; against these dark landscapes appeared forms – pains and delights – which echoed Hieronymus Bosch and his delirious gardens.'[42]

In *Blake*, Sir James Fetchcroft, the police magistrate, suspects his wife of having other than scientific motives for seeking the proximity of madmen. Indeed, Lady Fetchcroft succumbs to the attraction posed by the excesses of madness and bribes the asylum keepers to allow her access to the Frenetic so that he may satisfy her lust. In an early version of the script, Kilroy made the sexual encounter between Lady Fetchcroft and the madman shockingly explicit,[43] perhaps to put the audience in the position of voyeurs and to express upon the stage 'actions and images that violate the ordinary tenor of life'.[44] The revised text leaves more to the imagination by only showing the audience Blake's reactions as he observes the hidden action through the peephole of the cell; the scene, after all, is mainly intended to reveal something about the protagonist's state of mind. Blake's inability to turn away exposes his private attraction to the dark corruption represented by the lurid 'vision' behind the cell door; it is this prurience that also causes him to stray beyond the bounds of marriage. Afterwards, he attempts to deflect his own guilt by condemning Lady Fetchcroft in the moralistic language and imagery of his poetry: 'Out of my sight, harlot, Whore of Babylon!' (p. 47). Before he can be released from the asylum, Blake must shed this hypocritical mindset that blames women for men's imperfections, and shine light on the darker side of his sexuality, which is one of the 'hidden' places in his psyche.

It is the three women in the play who, one after the other, lead Blake to liberation from his mental prison. Lady Fetchcroft's request for his help after her encounter with the Frenetic confronts Blake with the reality of his own lust: '[you] watched and that is why you alone can forgive me!' Erupting in fury and calling her a 'whore', Blake fumes that he 'cannot forgive! Cannot!' (pp. 46–47). In an earlier conversation with the Silent Woman, that psychological barrier had begun to emerge as one of the causes of his writer's block:

> *(Anguished)* I'm unable to forgive, you see. It's as if I am frozen within or maybe consumed with a great fire. Jesus my Saviour tells me to forgive. How to forgive even he who would destroy you. *(Shift. Conversational)* Do you know the worst thing about this place? No? They do not allow me to work. No paper. No colours. No anvil for Los to hammer out thunder of thought and flame of fierce desire. (p. 23)

It is only when Blake is able to express the need to be with his wife and face the flaws in his own psyche as embodied by the other male inmates that his creativity begins to return: 'Oh, dear sweet Jesus, send Catherine to me! Else I will go mad, mad! *(To keepers)* In the name of our Saviour, let me have a little paper and a pencil' (p. 32). Blake recognises the Catatonic (the 'frozen' and unresponsive man), who is Black, as 'my brother!', and suggests that, if he is a slave, 'we must free him. I will draw his picture!' (p. 33). The Murderer (the man 'consumed with a great fire' of rage), who is alternately pathetic and menacing, fails to stir Blake to anger or fear, arousing instead his pity. At that moment, 'A keeper comes in with paper and pencils for Blake who grabs them eagerly. He turns his back on the Murderer and begins to sketch the Catatonic' (p. 34). For the time being, the Murderer is ignored because his face 'does not respond to the discriminating pencil'; the distinguishing 'hard and wiry line' central to Blake's aesthetic has trouble containing the face of anger and chaos (p. 35).

In his 'Introduction' to Blake's *Jerusalem*, Kazin writes that the inner thread in the Prophetic Books is Blake's guilt-ridden 'lament against his own "selfhood" and the appeal against the Accuser':

> The 'Accuser' is Satan, who rules this world . . . The 'Accuser' is the age in which Blake lived and it is the false god whose spectre mocks our thirst for life. It is that spirit, to Blake, of all that limits man, shames man, and drives him in fear. The Accuser is the spirit of the machine, which leads man himself into 'machination'. He is jealousy, unbelief, and cynicism. But his dominion is only in you; and he is only a specter.[45]

Kazin suggests that Blake fought the Accuser so bitterly that he ignored the spectre's dominion within himself, a paradox that caused him, at the end, to long for 'forgiveness', without specifying the nature of his sin: 'What was it he had to be "forgiven" for?'[46]

Kilroy's Blake feels he cannot be forgiven because he is himself 'unable to forgive'. His 'guilt' concerns his 'selfhood' – what Catherine, in Kilroy's play, calls her husband's self-righteousness, which prevents him from relating to other human beings: 'Head in the heavens and tripping over stones, you are' (p. 42). The artist's typical reaction is to close his ears to his wife's words – which are, she tells him, spoken 'out of love for you' – and to push her away. She will not relent: 'You must listen! . . . The demon is not in others. It is in ourselves! Look to yourself, William Blake!' (pp. 43–44). As the action develops, Kilroy's Blake comes face to face with each of his demons (the machine, lust, fear of failure, anger, lack of compassion and closed-mindedness) to learn that the blinding absolutism of his visions has prevented him from seeing the limitations within himself, and the potential in others.

This mental process is evident in Blake's interactions with his fellow asylum inmates. Blake's focus on the Catatonic is a means of distracting himself from the volatile Murderer, who has killed his wife and son, and who claims that he and Blake are one, a notion Blake dismisses by saying he does not have a son, although he would have liked to have one. Ignoring the pathetic ravings of the killer is Blake's way of denying his own aggression and its causes, which include a deeply repressed sense of failure and guilt about his inability to father a child. This is a conflict Kilroy also explored in *Tea and Sex and Shakespeare*, where the artist's writer's block and the strains in his marriage similarly emanate from the absence of a child. When Catherine is asked by Dr Hibbel about the cause of their childlessness, she refuses to discuss the matter out of loyalty to her husband, but agrees with the physician that Blake 'dreams, constantly, of children singing' (p. 29); she also reveals that William has a wandering eye for young girls, which causes friction in their marriage. When Dr Hibbel wants Blake to acknowledge that he is insane, Catherine, in her practical way, proposes to her husband that he 'confess to madness' by telling 'the foolish little man what he wants to hear' so they can go home (p. 42). Blake accuses her of betrayal and of not following him 'without question', but she will not be silenced:

> CATHERINE: . . . You put me aside like this once before. Remember? When we were unable to conceive a child.
> BLAKE: *(Hands to ears)* Stop it! Stop stop stop!
> CATHERINE: As always I took the blame. I was trying to protect you from yourself. What a fool I was. . . . The truth was that you were unable to give me a child.
> BLAKE: I will not listen to you! I'm not listening, woman! (p. 43)

After his wife is taken away, a 'loud, thumping noise' is heard, reminiscent of the 'thumping heartbeat' towards the end of *Talbot's Box*, suggesting a focus on the interiority and intensity of Blake's experience in the scenes that follow. Left in distress, Blake tries in vain to convince himself: 'Children? I don't need children! I have my own children. They come from my head' (p. 44). Part One of the play ends at this psychological crossroads. It is not until after the long dark night of the soul that follows in Part Two, when Blake reluctantly but inexorably comes to acknowledge his own flawed humanity, that he can open himself to his wife's words and emerge into a new dawn.

After Blake's denial of Lady Fetchcroft's request for forgiveness, and therefore of his own culpability, 'a wall opens' before him as if 'one door has closed in his mind and another opens'. He sees the naked Murderer, the symbol of his destructive anger, chained to a wall; in a momentary stage effect the inmate resembles, as in a flash from the poet's mind, the 'one-man *tableau vivant*' of Blake's Plate No. 26 from *Jerusalem*: 'the naked cruciform figure of Hand/Satan splayed in rising flames'. This is the culmination of Evil in Blake's eyes: 'Satan is risen, the Beast stirs and the Whore of Babylon is crowned in dominion over the world of Nature!' (p. 47). In this moment of despair Blake comes to realise that the figure before him is not Satan but an asylum patient being hosed down and beaten by attendants: 'At first I thought I saw Antichrist splayed against the wall there but it was only this poor madman. It is a lesson' (p. 48). He has sunk to the nadir: '"I see the New Jerusalem descending – " Not true. I see nothing! Nothing anymore! My visions have abandoned me. I am broken! I have nothing left, nothing!' (p. 49). As Madame MacAdam might have reminded him, however, the point of deepest failure is also the moment to begin anew.

When the Abbey turned down the script of *Blake*, Aideen Howard, the theatre's literary director, suggested to Kilroy that what the play perhaps lacked at its 'dramatic heart' was a head-to-head confrontation between Blake and Dr Hibbel; despite their adversarial relationship, she argued, 'these two men might still have the most revealing conversation about madness and sanity'.[47] Such intellectual conversations are certainly present in the play, but seeing them as central to Blake's predicament and recovery is to miss the point. The asylum director argues that madness 'is like a curtain. Once we draw it aside . . . we may then see where Reason has been damaged and a cure may begin.' The police magistrate strongly disagrees: 'There is no cure, sir! Your madman is a defect in Nature to be put out of sight! This is why we build walls and erect doors' (p. 19). When Blake first arrives in Finchley Grange, Dr Hibbel discusses his new patient with Lady Fetchcroft:

> LADY FETCHCROFT: Now, this Blake, Dr Hibbel? You speak of him as if he had some secret powers –
> DR HIBBEL: Powers, perhaps, Lady Fetchcroft, secret, no. I never admit the secret in my practice of lunacy. Get it out in the open, I say. Out! Out! (p. 18)

It is therefore ironic that it is the revelation of the scandalous secret within the walls of Finchley Grange that leads both to Blake's 'cure' and Dr Hibbel's professional downfall. When the asylum director once more asks Catherine to cooperate in her husband's treatment by signing papers declaring that he is insane, she refuses to betray Blake and simultaneously professes her central role in his creativity: 'He says he'd never be able to write another word if he couldn't read it to me first' (p. 52). At that very moment Sir James bursts into the room, having just discovered that the asylum director's regime has allowed Lady Fetchcroft to cuckold him with a lunatic; he has sent his wife to prison and proceeds to dismiss Dr Hibbel from his position by announcing the closure of Finchley Grange.

As embodiments of Reason and Authority, Hibbel and Fetchcroft can only turn on themselves and on each other. Their (self-)destructive, male absolutism is irrelevant to the restoration of Blake's equilibrium, which requires him to acknowledge the necessity of a female counterbalance. The play's final scene opens with Blake listening to the sound of an unaccompanied male voice arising out of the darkness, singing verses from his poem *America*: 'Let the inchained soul, shut up in darkness and in sighing, / Rise and look out; his chains are loose, his dungeon doors are open – ' (p. 55). Catherine comes to meet him and he speaks to her of his ordeal, which echoes the imagery of the visionary poetry: 'Oh Kate, I have been to the bottom of the pit where the eternal fire burns. I have been enveloped in the flame and now I see myself as never before.' He has learned that he can 'master Satan on the page but not when he taps me on the shoulder in the light of day . . . '; that '[e]verything begins with failure'; and that he is blessed to have his wife (pp. 56–57).

The 'dungeon doors' of Finchley Grange are about to be opened by the keys of the Silent Woman. This civilised, educated, but dumb character has intrigued, and at times infuriated, Blake throughout his stay in the asylum. As a kind of Emanation she can be regarded as a counterpart to Catherine and a projection of Blake's mind, his idea of Woman as an unquestioning follower, who turns out to be indispensable in securing the release of his 'inchained soul'. Although she does not speak – whether by choice, or because she has been robbed of her voice – she expresses herself intellectually and creatively by making small, intricate devices she carries around on a tray. When Blake first meets her shortly after his arrival in the asylum he fulminates against her for giving herself to 'the machine, the furnace, sword and smoking ruins!' (p. 23), although during a later meeting, when she has put away 'her infernal machines', he insists to his sceptical wife that the woman is 'a messenger from beyond the Mundane Shell' who has 'come from Eternity' (p. 37). It is not until Blake has been to 'the bottom of the pit' and is reunited with Kate that husband and wife together recognise the spiritual and practical value of the Silent Woman. Blake kneels in front of her and begs forgiveness, so that he may be able to forgive her, while Kate is impatient to point out that the woman – 'our angel . . . a messenger of the future' (p. 58) – has used her tools to fabricate a set of keys that will unlock the doors of the asylum. Blake's former anger at the machine is replaced by wonderment as it strikes him that technology may not be all evil: 'Do you think the machine is the future? Sometimes I think that and then I tremble' (p. 58). This revisionist interpretation of the historical Blake owes a good deal to Kilroy's own appreciation of scientific advancement, and to the belief that 'some of the most exciting things that are happening imaginatively at the moment are happening in science, through the scientist. The scientist is very often fulfilling the role traditionally held by art, and that is imaginatively reconstructing reality.'[48] That creative (hence 'female'?) side of science is liberating and mind-expanding, as opposed to the kind of 'enlightened' science practised by Dr Hibbel, who seeks to reduce everything to 'orderly thought' and 'straight lines' (p. 49).

Dr Hibbel's scientific project throughout is to understand madness: 'That which resists understanding has to be hunted down and brought into control. Otherwise there is chaos!' (p. 52). On the surface, Blake's aesthetic seems to be motivated by a similar desire, since his obsession with the line, the 'Golden rule of art and life' (p. 34) is also an effort to resist chaos:

> The line is our containment of love. Oh, Kate! What is it that builds a house and plants a garden but the line? What is it that distinguishes honesty from knavery but the hard and wiry line? Remove it and all is chaos and the Almighty must draw his hand once more across the void! (p. 35)

For the eighteenth-century poet, however, chaos did not equate to madness, and the opposite of chaos was not reason: 'Nature has no outline,' he contended, 'but Imagination has.'[49] That bounding line was an expression both of containment and of relation. As Morris Eaves puts it:

> Minimally, making a line draws a boundary, and the result is a merciful 'limit'. Mediately, making a line expresses identity, and the result is identical form, activating the image with inward life. Ultimately, making a line signals readiness for relation, and the result is the opening of a line of communication.[50]

In Kilroy's play, Dr Hibbel's straight lines are the ultimate application of reason, and a way of creating division; this rigidity becomes his undoing as he tries to use Catherine against William, and unwittingly provides the stage for the unravelling of the already frayed marriage of Sir James and Lady Fetchcroft. Kilroy's Blake has learned the hard way that he is most true to himself and his visions when he relates most fully to his wife, and understands and accepts his own passions and desires. Commenting on his painting *A Vision of the Last Judgment*, Blake wrote: 'Men are admitted into Heaven not because they have curbed & govern'd their Passions, or have No Passions, but because they have Cultivated their Understandings.'[51] This sentiment is not so far removed from Kilroy's contention that, in his art, passionate feeling is inextricably connected with intellectual understanding.

In *Blake*, the unlocking of the asylum doors by the Silent Woman's keys also represents the liberation of the Divine Imagination, now that Blake has faced and overcome the demons of anger, lust, lack of compassion, self-righteousness and closed-mindedness. The brother and sister who had him locked up can be forgiven, and William is able to acknowledge that it was he rather than Kate who 'failed' in the couple's wish to have a child. His wife presents a different view: 'That is not to fail, William. God thought otherwise', to which he agrees with, 'Amen' (p. 63). While the Blakes have reached a new level of harmony during their ordeal in Finchley Grange, Dr Hibbel has gone mad, unable to comprehend how the Blakes were able to walk free from his hospital, and with his bastion of Reason under threat of closure by the forces of law and order. Urizen has been defeated: 'Reason is no more,' Dr Hibbel cries, 'all is chaos and the void has opened beneath our feet!' (p. 63). He throws open the doors of the asylum and the inmates walk free.

William Blake, *Jerusalem: The Emanation of the Giant Albion*, Plate 100.
Yale Center for British Art, Paul Mellon Collection.

Kilroy's final scene has William and Kate back in their home in South Molton Street, 'both working furiously, she printing, he etching. The effect is of two people familiar with a tiny work-space, knowing what to do and how not to get in the way of the other' (p. 64). Wicksteed describes the union of Los and Enitharmon at the end of *Jerusalem* as a complementary partnership of male and female, time and space:

> Without the Woman this inner sanctuary [the House and the household] may become a place of desecration or blank desolation. Without the Man, or the Man's contribution, Time is no more than a tale of the nearer and ever nearer approach of Death. But the Woman, working with the Man, may make the Home their Paradise and their days into still accumulating moments of the Vision Eternal.[52]

At the end of *Blake*, selected plates from *Jerusalem* are projected onto a white sheet lowered from above the stage as husband and wife work at their etching, the desired effect being 'of sheets rising into the atmosphere' (p. 64). These ten images represent, in visual and visionary terms, the journey William and Catherine have accomplished in the course of the play. Wicksteed's commentary on *Jerusalem* is helpful for understanding what the images signify within Blake's mythology. Plate 1, Los the London Watchman, shows the craftsman stepping forward 'in a manner that suggests the undertaking of a dread adventure'.[53] Plate 2 is the Frontispiece of *Jerusalem*. Plate 6 depicts Los in his Forge, 'ever haunted there by his own Selfhood or Spectre',[54] which will enslave him forever unless he master it. In Plate 25, The Torture of Albion, 'Humanity . . . represents the essentially masculine universe controlled . . . by a feminine Nature, from which it can only be redeemed by the gentle feminine Soul of man – Jerusalem'.[55] Plate 26, The Crucifixion of Hand, shows 'the artist . . . bedevilled by false reasoning',[56] mistaking 'the spiritual message of Jerusalem for sanction of his own raging warfare'.[57] Plate 28, The Lovers on the Lily Pad, depicts male and female as distinct individuals in an embrace, suggesting 'perfect accord between the sexes . . . in imaginative sympathy'.[58] In Plate 76, Albion before Crucified Jesus 'wakes from his dreams of "Eternal Death"' to behold the break of dawn.[59] Plate 78, The Birdman, shows the sunrise, watched by a man with the beak of an Eagle and the comb of a Cock, probably Los 'in a mood of profoundly conflicting emotions' of Fear and Hope.[60] In Plate 99, Jehovah Embraces the Androgyne, the Deity descends into the Abyss to find himself received into the arms of the restored Jerusalem – the gentle Spirit who has 'tasted Experience in all its bitterness without being herself embittered' – and who is ultimately a portrait of Blake's 'own faithful Kate'.[61] In Plate 100, The Final Plate, 'Los and Enitharmon-Jerusalem gaze at one another . . . their task accomplished',[62] as 'one sees them for ever bound in love, in need, in sorrow and in joy'.[63]

A theatre audience's understanding of these plates is bound to be impressionistic, but it is Kilroy's aim in the play's final scene to create an apotheosis in which the combined impact of sound, vision and language adds up to more than the sum of its parts and makes for a 'total' theatrical experience involving all the senses, as well as a level of understanding of what has been achieved. As William and Catherine Blake appear in their small work room suspended above the stage, the freed lunatics, dropping their white shifts, become a golden-robed choir. A single male voice singing the lyrics of Blake's poem, 'England! awake! awake! awake!' is joined by the chorus of lunatics (whose voices, Kilroy suggests, 'should be supplemented' to create 'the effect of a huge massed choir') singing the words from the opening of *Jerusalem*: 'Awake! awake O Sleeper of the land of shadows, wake! Expand! / I am in you and you in me, mutual in love divine' (p. 65). The lyrics herald the return of 'a time of joy and love', when 'the Night of Death is past and the Eternal Day / Appears upon our hills' (p. 65). The final sound of the singers' voices 'coincides with the final plate' of Los and Enitharmon gazing at one another (p. 66). The lights go down and the play ends. If *Blake* represents, as Kilroy has suggested, the end of a seam of writing in his work, it is an end that heralds a personal and creative rebirth and a new dawn. No other Kilroy play ends on quite such an affirmative note.

Coda

The work of the artist, Nell Jeffrey reminds us in *The Shape of Metal*, can never be 'finished'. Kilroy's plays likewise resist closure: they often end on a note of ambiguity and inconclusiveness, or with a character's resolve to try again, begin once more, or at least keep going. Given this emphasis in Kilroy's oeuvre on process and continuity, and the 'unfinished' status of his own theatrical work-in-progress, it would be inappropriate to end this study with a formal conclusion. Rather, this coda will put into perspective the thematic strands Kilroy has developed in his stage plays over the past five decades by considering his most recent theatrical venture, a dramatisation of the final thoughts and sentiments of Pádraig Pearse. The Pearse monologue is Kilroy's contribution to *Signatories*, a work commissioned by University College Dublin and performed in 2016 as part of the commemorative celebrations marking the centenary of the 1916 Easter Rising. First performed in Kilmainham Gaol, where the leaders of the rebellion were imprisoned and executed, *Signatories* comprises eight monologues composed by eight different writers, spoken by or about eight prominent figures who took part in the Rising. Patrick Mason, who directed the production, emphasises that the portraits 'are not historical documents. Neither are they acts of national piety. They are acts of theatre – imagined, artistic responses to people and events of the past.'[1] This approach perfectly suits Kilroy's penchant for tweaking the historical record.

Eight pages long in print, about ten minutes in performance, Kilroy's Pearse monologue is an original, moving and fitting tribute to a complex man that also forges connections with several of the major personal and societal issues that have preoccupied the playwright throughout the course of his theatrical career. Pearse's unbending focus on his written legacy, for example, has a counterpart in the ruthless artistry of a character like Nell in *The Shape of Metal*, while the anxiety he displays about his masculinity echoes a similar concern expressed by Kelly in *The Death and Resurrection of Mr Roche*. The 'split' in his personality emanating from the different 'traditions' (English and Irish) to which his parents belonged recalls the divided cultural affiliations of the protagonist in *The O'Neill*. Kilroy's depiction of Pearse's relationship with his father, a looming figure in the son's imagination, reverberates with a strand in his work that includes the 'monstrous' fathers of the Wilde plays and Brendan Bracken's psychologically abusive father in *Double Cross*, all of whom left such a deep and devastating imprint on their children. Pearse's absolute dedication to the national cause and the 'suicidal element' of his extremism further link him to Bracken as well as to William Joyce in *Double Cross*, while his visionary quality connects him to the likes of Matt Talbot and William Blake. Kilroy acknowledges that some of these characters, and the people on whom they are based, 'are exceptionally unattractive creatures' who are 'straining to escape the limits of humanity'. His task, in the *Signatories* monologue as well as in these other plays, is to 'find the human quality' in the fanatic, which is often discovered in a deep-seated psychological trauma blocked out by the character's single-minded focus on an absolutist ideal.[2]

Kilroy depicts Pearse in his Kilmainham Gaol cell shortly before his execution, seated at a table on which lie writing materials, a blindfold and a crucifix. These objects symbolise three aspects of the condemned man's character Kilroy sets out to examine. For the playwright, depicting Pearse's obsession with composing his manifesto was crucial: 'nothing was real unless it was down on paper . . . He was a writer and you must never forget that about Pearse.'[3] The crucifix represents Pearse's self-willed martyrdom and his essentially spiritual nature; Kilroy's character is a loner, the antithesis of the 'materialist' James Connolly who, even in the GPO, is constantly surrounded by 'acolytes' and 'comrades'.[4] The blindfold, which signals the imminence of the firing squad, also indicates the deeprootedness of Pearse's sacrificial self-denial in his refusal to 'see' or acknowledge the entirety of who he is, by disavowing what he calls the 'pathetic otherness' of the 'weakling half' of himself (p. 19).

Pearse's father, James, was an Englishman who, in the 1860s, had moved with his first wife to Dublin, where he worked as a stonemason. Widowed in 1876, he married Margaret Brady the following year; Patrick was the second of the couple's four children. Kilroy's portrayal of his subject as a split personality has its origins in Pearse's autobiographical writings, where he mused that, when his parents married, 'there came together two very widely remote traditions – English and Puritan and mechanic on the one hand, Gaelic and Catholic and peasant on the other'; the fusion of these two streams, he claimed, 'made me the strange thing I am'.[5] In his *Signatories* monologue, Kilroy uses 'Pádraig Pearse', a hybrid form of his subject's name (which is properly rendered in English as Patrick Pearse, in Irish as Pádraig Mac Piarais) to capture that identity dilemma. The same mixed heritage caused Pearse to write elsewhere about himself:

> I don't know if I like you or not, Pearse. I don't know if anyone does like you. I know full many who hate you . . . Pearse you are too dark in yourself. You don't make friends with Gaels. You avoid their company. When you come among them you bring a dark cloud with you that lies heavily on them . . . Is it your English blood that is the cause of this I wonder . . . I suppose there are two Pearses, the sombre and taciturn Pearse and the gay and sunny Pearse.[6]

The Pearse of *Signatories* is also a split personality, but in Kilroy's imaginative recreation one part of Pearse seeks to eliminate the other, not because the *alter ego* is 'sombre and taciturn', but because he may be 'gay' in a different, contemporary sense of the word:

> I don't like you, Pearse. You know that? Never have. My pathetic otherness, my weakling half . . . Actually, I don't think that anyone likes you. That look of – distaste. Get me away from this – creature!
>
> . . .
>
> No. Never liked you. Never! Change that. That's the wrong word, liked! I hate you, Pearse! Hate! Hate! Namby pamby, weakling, no spunk, pasty-faced, pudgy slob, dribbling drawers, afraid of your own shadow – but I'm rising above you, you hear . . . (p. 19)

In her *Irish Times* review of Elaine Sisson's book *Pearse's Patriots: St Enda's and the Cult of Boyhood* (2004), historian Ruth Dudley

Edwards recalls that some people were offended when, in her own 1979 biography of Pearse, she pointed out 'the bleeding obvious', namely that he, 'although almost certainly chaste, was turned on exclusively by young male beauty'. If, she suggests, he was 'a wonderful teacher', this was 'not least because . . . he was in love with his boys. Emotionally and sexually stunted, he wanted to be a boy.'[7] Moving a great deal more subtly along a similar trajectory, Kilroy allows Pearse's sublimated sexuality to resonate increasingly strongly with his contemporary audience as the drama unfolds.

As he has often done in relation to other characters in his work, Kilroy locates the source of Pearse's schizophrenia in his relationship with his father, whose Englishness and overbearing masculinity are mirrored in the patriarchal power of the British colonial administration in Ireland. Pearse's declaration of independence from English rule, then, is also a defiance of his English father and an affirmation of the Irishness he inherited from his mother. Yet Kilroy depicts Pearse's participation in the 1916 Rising not only as an act of rebellion against English power, but also as a bid for paternal validation. As he is sitting in his cell awaiting his execution, he wonders, 'What would he say about me now, if he were here? That's the question. My father, the crude Englishman?' (p. 22). Kilroy's protagonist is a man who still seeks to live up to his father's expectations even as he is about to be killed for violently taking a stand against the English presence in Ireland that he experiences as oppressive.

Kilroy expresses the love-hate relationship between father and son in the way Patrick remembers Pearse senior as always either too distant or too hands-on. The mason would sometimes emerge ominously and silently from his basement workshop, a 'huge figure, shrouded in the white dust of the chiselled stone', a 'giant risen from his den'. At other times he would grasp his children closely to his chest: 'Didn't like that bit,' Pearse confesses, 'I was frightened by it . . . He often hurt me with his clasp, although I knew he didn't mean to' (p. 21). Pearse recalls his father as a man whose own overbearing manliness made it hard for him to understand or tolerate his son's very different personality: 'Stubble on the chin, rasping against my cheek, the whispers: "Is our Pat a Molly boy? Is he? Ha? How are we going to make a man of him, our Paddy?"' (p. 21). These private words, spoken *about* rather than *to* the

Peter Gaynor as Pádraig Pearse in *Signatories*, Kilmainham Gaol, 2016. Commissioned by UCD and produced by Verdant Productions. Directed by Patrick Mason. Photograph: Ros Kavanagh.

disappointing child by his intimate tormentor, carry more than a whiff of the cultural argument about Anglo-Saxon masculinity and Celtic femininity that nineteenth-century theorists like Matthew Arnold employed to justify the subordination of the Irish within the Union. Both the personal and political implications of his father's words determine Pearse's future course of action. When, in the final moments of the monologue, he faces the English firing squad that is about to send him into history as a heroic martyr for the cause of Irish freedom, he does so standing up, blindfolded against his 'weakling' self, and holding up the crucifix. In the manifesto Pearse leaves behind so that he may 'be understood' by posterity, he writes about his fellow commanders, and implicitly about himself: 'If they do not win they will at least have deserved to win. But win it they will although they win it in death' (p. 25). Through the figure of Pearse, Kilroy's contribution to *Signatories* counts the public and private – and human – cost of such a victory.

According to Kilroy, the Pearse monologue 'wrote itself very quickly' once he had found a fictional element, in the shape of a boy in his late teens, to insert into the historical setting.[8] The fair-haired youngster who is hauled up in front of his commander in the GPO comes to embody for Pearse the half of himself he seeks to disavow but also wishes, deep down, to embrace. Denying the accusation that he is a deserter who is trying to run away, the boy instead claims to want to go on living so that he can 'fight in the future' (p. 23). Studying the boy closely, Pearse notes 'the fine down on his cheek and the rivulets of sweat on his skin' (p. 22), a physicality to which his own body responds but by which he cannot allow himself to be stirred: 'He flexed like an athlete about to run a race and my heart beat, painfully. He was exercising his arms and legs and I had this tremendous need to protect his body but I could not move' (p. 24). By dispatching the boy to the Four Courts as his messenger, past the British machine-gun emplacement, Pearse sends him to his certain death, and along with him kills part of his own humanity. 'I didn't want him to go!' he claims. 'But equally I knew he had to' (p. 24). Only by metaphorically killing off his inner 'Molly boy' can Pearse become the sanctioned figure who is remembered in the official historical narrative: the 'incarnation, icon, and public image' of the Easter Rising.[9]

In Pearse's recollection, the running boy moves 'beyond geography' (p. 20), out of history and into myth, where he becomes indistinguishable from Pearse himself:

> Somewhere in the dim past an old man stood in a Grecian field, holding the wreath of olive in his hands to reward the victor. All that mattered now was to reach the finishing line, to break the tape, chest out, hands up, all go to the very end, the final gasp of breath. He was like a white light just before it was extinguished. He was perfection just a moment before he ceased to be. (pp. 24–25)

In his cell, hearing the approach of marching feet, Pearse remembers his English father's 'heavy footsteps on the stairs': 'He has shaped me into the image of the Angel of Death. I am the messenger, the harbinger of the future. I am no longer matter. My useless body has melted away. I am now air and light' (p. 26). Yet at the very moment when he himself faces the firing squad it is the boy's physical presence that comes into sharp focus in his mind's eye: 'The young man is crouched at the starting line once more, about to run his race.

Yet again! And again! And again! . . . As he crouches on the line I brush against his tense, white body as it springs into release' (p. 26). Pearse cannot love and acknowledge the boy, who is also himself, except in the moment of releasing him into death. Sacrificed and resurrected over and over again, the messenger boy of *Signatories* will fail, and fail again, on his way to a future where he, or his likes, will eventually arrive victorious, liberated from self-hate, and made whole. 'Run! Run!' Pearse tells the boy, seconds before the shots ring out (p. 27). The play ends there, with its messenger arriving in the future which is now in a free Irish Republic that guarantees, at least in principle, equal rights and opportunities to all its citizens, and where all the children of the nation, including Molly boys, are cherished equally.[10]

On the occasion of the performance of *Signatories* in Dublin's National Concert Hall on 5 May 2016, Kilroy was presented with the Ulysses Medal, the highest honour awarded by UCD, his alma mater. Inaugurated in 2005 as part of the university's sesquicentennial celebrations to highlight the 'creative brilliance' of UCD alumnus James Joyce, the award is given to individuals whose work has made an outstanding global contribution. That the works Kilroy has written for the theatre in the past half century are indeed creatively brilliant has been witnessed globally, by audiences all over the island of Ireland as well as in England, Scotland, several other European countries, Australia, and various locations in the United States. His original plays and radical adaptations of European classics take us out of our comfort zone and explain us to ourselves; they connect the past to the present, the world to the Irish stage, and Irish theatre to the world.

In his drama, Thomas Kilroy has always challenged absolutes, in both form and content. Committed to theatre as a collaborative, inclusive project, he has consistently refused to take absolute control of his plays, valuing the contributions of directors, designers and actors as essential parts of the whole, and acknowledging the power and validity of sometimes widely diverging interpretations of his work, as well as the possibility of failure. If his characters are often absolutists and extremists – nationalists, fascists, religious zealots, self-absorbed visionaries – it is precisely this quality of certainty and single-mindedness that places them beyond humanity, rendering them capable of great things but also making them 'monstrous' and destructive of both self and others. Yet by exposing the tragic consequences of their quest for an absolute ideal, Kilroy simultaneously portrays these characters as all too human. By resisting finality and refusing simple binary choices and false certainties, his plays urge instead a continual process of questioning and testing of what passes for the 'truth'. His art embraces life's vicissitudes and inconstancies, and celebrates the intellect and the imagination in equal measure. In its very theatricality, Kilroy's theatre embodies the creative possibilities and the transformative potential inherent in human beings, suggesting that all the world's a stage, and that, in the end – to quote from a work still in progress – 'whatever monstrous things may happen there is always the promise of salvation at the final curtain'.[11]

Notes

Introduction

1 Thomas Kilroy, 'From Page to Stage', in Jacqueline Genet and Wynne Hellegouarc'h (eds), *Irish Writers and Their Creative Process* (Gerrards Cross: Colin Smythe, 1996), p. 61.
2 Brian Friel, letter to Thomas Kilroy, 10 September 1990, NUIG P103/538(20).
3 Sara Keating, 'Hearing Voices', *Irish Times*, 2 February 2008, p. 7.
4 'Thomas Kilroy', in Daniel Murphy (ed.), *Education and the Arts: The Educational Autobiographies of Contemporary Irish Poets, Novelists, Dramatists, Musicians, Painters and Sculptors* (Dublin: Trinity College Department of Higher Education, 1987), p. 197.
5 Thomas Kilroy, 'Groundwork for an Irish Theatre', *Studies*, vol. 48, no. 190 (1959), p. 192.
6 Ibid., p. 195.
7 Jonathan Mullin, interview with Thomas Kilroy, *Connaught Telegraph*, 28 January 1998, p. 7.
8 Paul Brennan and Thierry Dubost, 'An Interview with Thomas Kilroy, 2001', in Dubost, *The Plays of Thomas Kilroy: A Critical Study* (Jefferson, NC, and London: McFarland, 2007), p. 126.
9 Michael York, letter to Alan Brodie, 5 July 2001, NUIG, P103/264(3).
10 Fiona Shaw, letter to Thomas Kilroy, 11 December 2001, NUIG, P103/264(5).
11 Kilroy, 'Groundwork', p. 195.
12 See James M. Smith, *Ireland's Magdalen Laundries and the Nation's Architecture of Containment* (Notre Dame, IN: University of Notre Dame Press, 2007).
13 Kilroy, 'Groundwork', p. 198.
14 Aodhan Madden, 'They Don't "Buy" Irish . . . Says Thomas Kilroy' [*Evening Press*, July 1969], newspaper cutting, NUIG, P103/61(43).
15 Christopher Murray, 'Thomas Kilroy's World Elsewhere', in Genet and Hellegouarc'h (eds), op. cit., p. 77.
16 Thomas Kilroy, 'The Irish Writer: Self and Society, 1950–80', in Peter Connolly (ed.), *Literature and the Changing Ireland* (Gerrards Cross: Colin Smythe, 1982), pp. 180–81.
17 Ibid., pp. 180–82.
18 Salman Rushdie, 'Is Nothing Sacred?', *Granta*, no. 31 (spring 1990), pp. 104–105.
19 Kilroy, 'From Page to Stage', p. 58.
20 Thomas Kilroy, 'A Personal View of Theater', *Princeton University Library Chronicle*, vol. 68, no. 1/2 (2007), p. 607.
21 Thomas Kilroy, 'Adaptation: A Privileged Conversation with a Dead Author', *Irish Times*, 13 February 2010, p. 47.

22 For a discussion of Kilroy's version of this play, see José Lanters, 'Groping towards Morality: Feminism, AIDS, and the Spectre of Article 41 in Thomas Kilroy's *Ghosts*', *Estudios Irlandeses*, vol. 13, no. 2 (2018), www.estudiosirlandeses.org.
23 Kilroy, 'A Personal View', pp. 599–600.
24 Thomas Kilroy, 'Playing the Monster on Stage', *Irish University Review*, vol. 45, no. 1 (2015), p. 87.
25 Clyde Haberman, 'He's a Creep, but Wow, What an Artist!', *New York Times*, 14 November 2017, https://nyti.ms/2hA1PX8.
26 Claire Dederer, 'What Do We Do with the Art of Monstrous Men?', *The Paris Review*, 20 November 2017, https://www.theparisreview.org/blog2017/11/20/art-monstrous-men/.
27 Kilroy, 'Playing the Monster', pp. 81–82.
28 Ibid., p. 89.
29 The script of 'The Door' (initially titled 'Say Hello to Johnny') won the 1967 BBC Northern Ireland Drama Competition. On 13 January 1968, the play was broadcast on BBC Radio 4. Thomas Kilroy, 'The Door', typescript, NUIG, P103/324.
30 Thomas Kilroy, 'Secularized Ireland', in Edna Longley (ed.), *Culture in Ireland: Division or Diversity?* (Belfast: Institute of Irish Studies, QUB, 1991), p. 135.
31 Thomas Kilroy, 'The Writers' Group in Galway', *Irish Times*, 8 April 1976, p. 10.
32 Fintan O'Toole, 'Incomplete Ideas', *Sunday Tribune*, 16 February 1986, reprinted in O'Toole, *Critical Moments*, ed. Julia Furey and Redmond O'Hanlon (Dublin: Carysfort Press, 2003), p. 50.
33 'Tradition of Irish Drama Discussed: Thomas Davis Lecture', *Irish Times*, 27 October 1969, p. 14.
34 Quoted in Phil Dunne, 'An Uncluttered Window on Irish Life: The Work of Thomas Kilroy', *Studies*, vol. 89, no. 354 (2000), p. 144.
35 Keating, 'Hearing Voices', p. 7.
36 Ian Kilroy, 'Master of the Pen', *Irish Examiner*, 1 February 2008, p. 18.

1. Divided Loyalties: *The O'Neill*

1 Thomas Kilroy, 'Groundwork for an Irish Theatre', *Studies*, vol. 48, no. 190 (1959), pp. 194–95.
2 Ibid., p. 198.
3 Gabriel Fallon, 'All This and the Abbey Too', *Studies*, vol. 48, no. 192 (1959), p. 441.
4 Thomas Kilroy, 'Dispatches from the Theatrical Front: A Look behind the Abbey's Boardroom Scenes, from 1904 to 1939', *Irish Times*, 26 December 2015, web edition, http://www.irishtimes.com.
5 Seán O'Faolain, *The Great O'Neill: A Biography of Hugh O'Neill, Earl of Tyrone, 1550–1616* (New York: Duell, Sloan and Pearce; London: Longmans, Green, 1942), p. v.
6 'Thomas Kilroy', in Daniel Murphy (ed.), *Education and the Arts: The Educational Autobiographies of Contemporary Irish Poets, Novelists, Dramatists, Musicians, Painters and Sculptors* (Dublin: Trinity College Department of Higher Education, 1987), p. 197.

7 Seamus O'Neill, 'The Great O'Neill', review of Thomas Kilroy's *The O'Neill*, Peacock Theatre, 1969, *Irish Press*, 5 June 1969, p. 11.
8 Anne Fogarty, 'The Romance of History: Renegotiating the Past in Thomas Kilroy's *The O'Neill* and Brian Friel's *Making History*', *Irish University Review*, vol. 32, no. 1 (2002), p. 19.
9 Ibid., p. 24.
10 Ciaran Carty, 'Kilroy Was Here', *Sunday Tribune*, 20 April 1986, p. 18.
11 Mária Kurdi, '"The Whole Idea of Writing Historical Fiction Is Paradoxical": Talk with Irish Playwright Thomas Kilroy', *Hungarian Journal of English and American Studies*, vol. 8, no. 1 (2002), p. 262.
12 'Tom Kilroy in Conversation with Gerry Dukes' in Lilian Chambers, Ger FitzGibbon and Eamonn Jordan (eds), *Theatre Talk: Voices of Irish Theatre Practitioners* (Dublin: Carysfort Press, 2001), p. 240.
13 Gerald Dawe, 'An Interview with Thomas Kilroy', in Gerald Dawe and Jonathan Williams (eds), *Krino 1986–1996: An Anthology of Modern Irish Writing* (Dublin: Gill & Macmillan, 1996), p. 230.
14 O'Faolain, op. cit., p. 95.
15 Ibid., p. 146.
16 Hiram Morgan, *Tyrone's Rebellion: The Outbreak of the Nine Years War in Tudor Ireland* (London: The Boydell Press, 1993), p. 161.
17 Ibid., p. 167.
18 Ibid., p. 165.
19 O'Faolain, op. cit, p. 283.
20 Ibid., p. 285.
21 Ibid., p. 301.
22 Ibid., p. 358.
23 Hilton Edwards, letter to Thomas Kilroy, 13 June 1964, NUIG, P103/ 43(1).
24 Kurdi, '"The Whole Idea"', p. 262.
25 Ernest Blythe, letter to Thomas Kilroy, 24 May 1966, NUIG, P103/47(2).
26 Thomas Mac Anna, letter to Thomas Kilroy, 30 December 1966, NUIG, P103/47(5–6).
27 Tomás Mac Anna, letter to Thomas Kilroy, 22 February [1967], NUIG, P103/57(1). Mac Anna sometimes used the Irish version of his name.
28 Thomas Mac Anna, letter to Thomas Kilroy, 4 December 1967, NUIG, P103/47(7–9).
29 Kilroy, 'A Playwright's Festival', in Nicholas Grene and Patrick Lonergan (eds), *Interactions: Dublin Theatre Festival 1957–2007* (Dublin: Carysfort Press, 2008), p. 19.
30 Ibid., p. 15.
31 Desmond Rushe, 'Excellent Staging of "The O'Neill"', *Irish Independent*, 31 May 1969, p. 5.
32 Thomas Kilroy, *The O'Neill* (Oldcastle: Gallery Press, 1995), p. 11. All subsequent references to the play are to this edition.
33 Bernard Share, review of *The O'Neill*, Peacock Theatre, 1969, newspaper cutting, NUIG, P103/47(30).
34 Rushe, 'Excellent Staging', p. 5.
35 John Arden, 'General Notes', *Armstrong's Last Goodnight: An Exercise in Diplomacy* (London: Methuen, 1965), p. 7.
36 Arden, *Armstrong's Last Goodnight*, p. 20.

37 Ibid., p. 20.
38 Arden, 'General Notes', p. 8.
39 This is true in the published text of the play. In the script of the 1969 production held in the Abbey Theatre Digital Archive at NUIG (4030_S_0001), the two opening scenes are identical and both include the same battle imagery.
40 Fogarty, 'The Romance', p. 19.
41 O'Faolain, op. cit., p. 155.
42 James Clarence Mangan, 'Dark Rosaleen', in *James Clarence Mangan: His Selected Poems*, ed. Louise Imogen Guiney (London: John Lane; Boston and New York: Lamson, Wolffe & Co., 1897), p. 115.
43 Tom Peete Cross and Clark Harris Slover (eds), *Ancient Irish Tales* (New York: Barnes & Noble, 1969), p. 242.
44 O'Faolain, op. cit., p. 150.
45 The frosty setting and the green cloak also echo a story from Kilroy's childhood in Callan ('A Family of Memories', Drama on One, RTÉ Radio 1, 1 March 2015). When Taoiseach Éamon de Valera campaigned in the town during the severe winter of 1948, the children were told he had been led to the town hall 'on a white horse with a green cloak around his shoulders', in 'imitation of the triumphal parade of an ancient Gaelic chieftain'.
46 O'Faolain, op. cit., pp. 232–33.
47 John Jordan, 'Art of History', review of *The O'Neill*, Peacock Theatre, 1969, newspaper cutting, NUIG, P103/47(29).
48 Thomas Kilroy, notes for *The O'Neill*, NUIG, P103/33(2).
49 Aodhan Madden, 'They Don't "Buy" Irish . . . Says Thomas Kilroy' [*Evening Press*, July 1969], newspaper cutting, NUIG, P103/61(43).
50 Des Hickey and Gus Smith, *A Paler Shade of Green* (London: Leslie Frewin, 1972), p. 224.
51 Madden, 'They Don't "Buy" Irish'.
52 Christopher Murray, 'Thomas Kilroy's World Elsewhere', in Jacqueline Genet and Wynne Hellegouarc'h (eds), *Irish Writers and Their Creative Process* (Gerrards Cross: Colin Smythe, 1996), p. 72.
53 Kurdi, '"The Whole Idea"', pp. 262–63.
54 Carolyn Farrar, 'Kilroy Play Opens Earagail Arts Festival', *Derry Journal*, 5 July 2007, p. 17a.
55 Terence Brown, *Ireland: A Social and Cultural History, 1922 to the Present* (Ithaca and London: Cornell University Press, 1981, 1985), pp. 205–06.
56 Ibid., p. 214.
57 Murray, 'Thomas Kilroy's World Elsewhere,' pp. 73–74.
58 'Thomas Kilroy', in Murphy (ed.), op. cit., p. 191.
59 Thomas Kilroy, 'The Irish Writer: Self and Society, 1950–1980', in Peter Connolly (ed.), *Literature and the Changing Ireland* (Gerrards Cross: Colin Smythe; Totowa, NJ: Barnes & Noble, 1982), p. 181.
60 'Talking with Tom Kilroy', *AIB News*, May 1972, p.1, magazine cutting, NUIG, P103/625(5).
61 Paul Bew, Peter Gibbon, and Henry Patterson, *The State in Northern Ireland 1921–1972: Political Forces and Social Classes* (Manchester: Manchester University Press, 1979), p. 193.
62 Thierry Dubost, *The Plays of Thomas Kilroy: A Critical Study* (Jefferson, NC and London: McFarland, 2007), p. 16.

63 Share, review of *The O'Neill.*
64 According to Kilroy, the play received another amateur production in 2000 (see Farrar, 'Kilroy Play Opens', p. 17a).
65 David Grant, personal communication with the present author, 7 January 2014.

2. Deformities of Nationalism: *Double Cross*

1 Thomas Kilroy, *The Big Chapel* (London: Faber & Faber, 1971).
2 Elgy Gillespie, interview with Thomas Kilroy, *Irish Times*, 26 April 1972, p. 12.
3 Thomas Kilroy, 'Introduction', *Double Cross* (Oldcastle: Gallery Press, 1994), p. 13.
4 Ibid., p. 11.
5 Ibid., p. 11.
6 Thomas Kilroy, 'Ireland's Pseudo-Englishman', *Magill*, vol. 11, no. 5 (1988), p. 54.
7 Charles Lysaght, 'Churchill's Faithful Chela', *History Today*, vol. 52, no. 2 (2002), http://www.historytoday.com/print/13435.
8 Kilroy, 'Introduction', p. 11.
9 Kilroy, 'Ireland's Pseudo-Englishman', pp. 53–54.
10 Fintan O'Toole, 'Incomplete Ideas', *Sunday Tribune*, 16 February 1986, rpt in O'Toole, *Critical Moments*, ed. Julia Furay and Redmond O'Hanlon (Dublin: Carysfort Press, 2003), p. 52.
11 Ibid., p. 52.
12 Stephen Rea, letter to Thomas Kilroy, 8 June 1986, NUIG, P103/509(1).
13 Carmen Szabó, 'Doublings: Problematic Identities in Thomas Kilroy's *Double Cross* and *The Madame MacAdam Travelling Theatre*', in Richard Cave and Ben Levitas (eds), *Irish Theatre in England* (Dublin: Carysfort Press, 2007), p. 172.
14 Mary Trotter, '"Double-Crossing" Irish Borders: The Field Day Production of Tom Kilroy's *Double Cross*', *New Hibernia Review*, vol. 1, no. 1 (1997), pp. 36–37.
15 Thomas Kilroy, letter to Robert Cooper, drama producer, BBC Northern Ireland, 23 June 1982, NUIG, P103/340(1).
16 Marilynn J. Richtarik, *Acting between the Lines: The Field Day Theatre Company and Irish Cultural Politics 1980–1984* (1995; Washington DC: The Catholic University of America Press, 2001), p. 7.
17 Ibid., pp. 239–40.
18 Colm Tóibín, 'Parading the Psyche', *Sunday Independent*, 26 April 1986, p. 15.
19 Seamus Deane, letter to Thomas Kilroy, 14 December 1985, NUIG, P103/423(27).
20 Seamus Deane, letter to Thomas Kilroy, 29 January 1985, NUIG, P103/423(26).
21 As suggested by Fintan O'Toole in 'Incomplete Ideas', pp. 51–52.
22 Kilroy, 'Ireland's Pseudo-Englishman', p. 54.
23 NUIG, P103/329(1).
24 Thomas Kilroy, *Double Cross* (Oldcastle: Gallery Press, 1994), pp. 38–39. All references to the play in the text are to this edition.

25 NUIG, P103/329(1).
26 Trotter, '"Double-Crossing" Irish Borders', p. 40.
27 Kilroy, 'Introduction', p. 14.
28 Ibid., p. 13.
29 Kilroy, 'Ireland's Pseudo-Englishman', p. 53.
30 Ruth Sherry, 'Personal Plays on Pieces of History', *Fortnight*, September 1987, p. 25.
31 Clair Wills, *That Neutral Island: A Cultural History of Ireland during the Second World War* (London: Faber & Faber, 2007), p. 207.
32 Ibid., p. 221.
33 Kilroy, 'Ireland's Pseudo-Englishman', p. 54.
34 Anthony Roche, 'An Interview with Thomas Kilroy', *Irish University Review*, vol. 32, no. 1 (2002), p. 157.
35 O'Toole, 'Incomplete Ideas', p. 50.
36 Seamus Deane, *Celtic Revivals* (London: Faber & Faber, 1985), p. 22.
37 Terry Eagleton, *Heathcliff and the Great Hunger* (London: Verso, 1995), p. 43.
38 Tóibín, 'Parading the Psyche', p. 15.
39 Edmund Burke, 'An Appeal from the New to the Old Whigs', in *The Portable Edmund Burke*, ed. Isaac Kramnick (Harmondsworth: Penguin, 1999), p. 496.
40 Ibid., p. 495.
41 Eagleton, op. cit., p. 36.
42 Thomas Kilroy, 'Playing the Monster on Stage', *Irish University Review*, vol. 45, no. 1 (2015), p. 88.
43 Kilroy, 'Introduction', pp. 11–12.
44 Deane, letter to Kilroy, 29 January 1985.
45 Gerald Dawe, 'A Life of Our Own: *Double Cross* by Thomas Kilroy', *Theatre Ireland*, no. 15 (May/August 1988), p. 25.
46 Rebecca West, *The Meaning of Treason* (New York: Viking, 1947), p. 6.
47 Kilroy, 'Ireland's Pseudo-Englishman', p. 54.
48 Dawe, 'A Life of Our Own', p. 26.
49 Typescript of 'Double Cross', Field Day Papers, NLI, MS 46,900.
50 West, op. cit., p. 188.
51 Ibid., p. 6.
52 Ibid., p. 32.
53 Ibid., p. 96.
54 Ibid., p. 16.
55 Ibid., p. 17.
56 Ibid., p. 18.
57 Ibid., p. 194.
58 Ciaran Carty, 'Kilroy Was Here', *Sunday Tribune*, 20 April 1986, p. 18.
59 Trotter, '"Double-Crossing" Irish Borders', p. 43.
60 Brian Friel, letter to Thomas Kilroy, 3 March 1986, NUIG, P103/537(18).
61 Helen Dady, 'Double Cross', *City Limits* (London) [May 1986], magazine cutting, NUIG, P103/143(125).
62 John Cunningham, 'Ireland Calling . . . ', *Guardian*, 9 May 1986, p. 12.
63 Timothy O'Grady, review of *Double Cross* by Thomas Kilroy, Field Day, *Evening Press*, 14 February 1986, newspaper cutting, NUIG, P103/ 143(68).

64 Sherry, 'Personal Plays on Pieces of History', p. 25.
65 Review of *Double Cross* by Thomas Kilroy (Oldcastle: Gallery Press, 1994), *Books Ireland*, October 1996, p. 279.
66 https://www.abbeytheatre.ie/whats-on/double-cross/ (14 February 2018).
67 Deane, letter to Kilroy, 14 December 1985.
68 Margaret Ramsay, letter to Thomas Kilroy, 27 May 1986, NUIG, P103/143(20).
69 David Nowlan, review of *Double Cross* by Thomas Kilroy, Field Day, *Irish Times*, 13 February 1986, p. 12.
70 Carty, 'Kilroy Was Here', p. 18.
71 David Wade, 'Arts (Radio): Inventive Species', *The Times*, 21 June 1986. *That Man Bracken* by Thomas Kilroy, dir. Robert Cooper, BBC Radio 3, 20 June 1986.
72 Kilroy, 'Introduction', p. 13.

3. Mum's the Word: *The Madame MacAdam Travelling Theatre*

1 Michael Kennedy, '"Plato's Cave"? Ireland's Wartime Neutrality Reassessed', *History Ireland*, vol. 19, no. 1 (2011), p. 48.
2 Ian Hill, 'Last Fit-Up Tours Land in Search of the Truth', *Sunday Business Post*, 8 September 1991, newspaper cutting, NUIG, P103/199(13).
3 Thomas Kilroy, *The Madame MacAdam Travelling Theatre* (London: Methuen Drama, 1991), p. 2. All references to the play in the text are to this edition.
4 Max Stafford-Clark, letter to Thomas Kilroy, 12 January 1990, NUIG, P103/198(3).
5 John McGahern, letter to Thomas Kilroy, 5 March 1990, NUIG, P103/446(10).
6 Seamus Deane, letter to Thomas Kilroy, 25 May 1990, NUIG, P103/423(36).
7 Christopher Fitz-Simon, letter to Thomas Kilroy, 7 March 1990, NUIG, P103/198(5).
8 Thomas Kilroy, letter to Gary McKeone, 14 November 1990, Field Day Papers, NLI, MS 47,122/2.
9 Field Day Theatre Company, letter to Thomas Kilroy, 9 November 1990, Field Day Papers, NLI, MS 47,122/2.
10 Max Stafford-Clark, letter to Thomas Kilroy, 21 January 1991, NUIG, P103/198(17).
11 Mel Kenyon, letter to Thomas Kilroy, 22 January 1991, NUIG, P103/198(21).
12 Thomas Kilroy, letter to Charlotte Moore, 17 August 1992, NUIG, P103/200(30).
13 Martine Pelletier, '"Against Mindlessness": Thomas Kilroy and Field Day', *Irish University Review*, vol. 32, no. 1 (2002), pp. 119–20.
14 Notes for 'Mrs. MacAdams' Travelling Show', NUIG, P103/177(29).
15 According to Kilroy, his Garda sergeant father engaged in similar activities: 'I witnessed many examinations of greyhounds in our kitchen. And the painting of the greyhound actually happened.' Thomas Kilroy, notes for Declan [Donnellan], [1997], NUIG, P103/204(8).
16 Clair Wills, *That Neutral Island: A Cultural History of Ireland during the Second World War* (London: Faber & Faber, 2007), p. 29.

17 Thomas Kilroy, personal communication with the present author, 26 November 2014.
18 Synopsis of 'Mrs. Macadams Travelling Show', NUIG, P103/177(29).
19 Ibid.
20 Martin Cowley, 'In the World of Travelling Theatre', *Irish Times*, 6 September 1991, p. 6.
21 Christopher Fitz-Simon, 'Master of the Parish Hall', *Irish Times*, 10 December 1991, p. 14.
22 Harold Pinter, *Mac* (London: Emanuel Wax for Pendragon Press, 1968), p. 16.
23 *A Tale of Two Cities*, produced by Hilton Edwards, Gaiety Theatre, Dublin, September 1945. Leslie Staples noted the adaptation was 'very successful but the Irish press thought that *A Tale of Two Cities* was too melodramatic and sentimental for the 1940s'. See Ruth F. Glancy, *A Tale of Two Cities: An Annotated Bibliography* (New York: Garland, 2013), p. 136.
24 Joseph P. Walshe, Memorandum on Irish Neutrality for Éamon de Valera, 25 August 1939, Documents on Irish Foreign Policy No. 350 UCDA P150/2571, http://www.difp.ie/docs/Volume5/1939/2496.htm.
25 Ian Kilroy, 'Master of the Pen', *Irish Examiner*, 1 February 2008, p. 18.
26 Ian Herbert, 'Nationalism on the Agenda Made for a Fiery Weekend', *The Stage*, 13 May 1993, p. 38.
27 Hill, 'Last Fit-Up Tours'.
28 Thomas Kilroy, fax to Declan [Donnellan] and Nick [Chelton] (Channel 4), [December 1996], NUIG, P103/204(4).
29 The nudity was toned down in the actual production. A reviewer commented: 'Rumour had it that there was to be a nude scene and I wonder if the playwright was telling us something when the girl left her slip on, rather incongruously. Another solution to an Irish problem?' Barry White, 'Just Having a Field Day', *Belfast Telegraph*, 12 September 1991, newspaper cutting, NUIG, P103/199(21).
30 Hill, 'Last Fit-Up Tours'.
31 Thomas Kilroy, letter to Max Stafford-Clark, n.d. [c. January 1991], NUIG, P103/198(23).
32 Anthony Roche, 'Thomas Kilroy', in Martin Middeke and Peter Paul Schnierer (eds), *The Methuen Drama Guide to Contemporary Irish Playwrights* (London: Methuen Drama, 2010), p. 155.
33 Kilroy, letter to Moore, 17 August 1992.
34 Thomas Kilroy, letter to Richard Cottrell, 17 November 1994, NUIG, P103/198(35).
35 Thomas Kilroy, notes for Declan [Donnellan], December 1996, NUIG, P103/204(5).
36 Hill, 'Last Fit-Up Tours'.
37 Christopher Murray, 'Thomas Kilroy's World Elsewhere', in Jacqueline Genet and Wynne Hellegouarc'h (eds), *Irish Writers and Their Creative Process* (Gerrards Cross: Colin Smythe, 1996), p. 77.
38 'Travelling Show I'd Love to Follow across the Border', *Ulster Newsletter*, 12 September 1991, newspaper cutting, NUIG, P103/199(20).
39 Joseph Woods, 'The Play of Paradox in a Comic Invasion', *Irish Stage and Screen*, October–November 1991, p. 29.

40 'Tom Kilroy in Conversation with Gerry Dukes', in Lilian Chambers, Ger FitzGibbon, and Eamonn Jordan (eds), *Theatre Talk: Voices of Irish Theatre Practitioners* (Dublin: Carysfort Press, 2001), p. 242.
41 Cowley, 'In the World of Travelling Theatre', p. 6.
42 Thomas Kilroy, notes for Declan [Donnellan], [1997], NUIG, P103/204(8).
43 Field Day Theatre Company, cast and stage managers of *The Madame MacAdam Travelling Theatre* by Thomas Kilroy, letter to Field Day, 9 November 1991, NUIG, P103/199(6).
44 Thomas Kilroy, fax to Field Day, 3 January 1992, Field Day Papers, NLI, MS 46,936.
45 Quoted in Aidan O'Malley, *Field Day and the Translation of Identities: Performing Contradictions* (London: Palgrave Macmillan, 2011), p. 163.
46 Patrick Mason, letter to Thomas Kilroy, 30 April 1992, NUIG, P103/452(1).
47 Kilroy, letter to Moore, 17 August 1992.
48 Thomas Kilroy, letter to Gary McKeone, 21 September 1992, Field Day Papers, NLI, MS 47,122/2.
49 Kilroy, fax to Field Day, 3 January 1992.
50 Gerald Dawe, 'An Interview with Thomas Kilroy', in Gerald Dawe and Jonathan Williams (eds), *Krino 1986–1996: An Anthology of Modern Irish Writing* (Dublin: Gill & Macmillan, 1996), p. 234.
51 Notes for Declan [Donnellan], NUIG, P103/204(8).
52 Anthony Roche, 'An Interview with Thomas Kilroy', *Irish University Review*, vol. 32, no. 1 (2002), p. 158.
53 Thomas Kilroy, 'The Life and Art of Brian', *Irish Times*, 24 April 1999, p. 60.

4. Bachelors Gay: *The Death and Resurrection of Mr Roche*

1 J.J. F[inegan], 'Saturday Night in Dublin . . . ', *Evening Herald*, 8 October 1968, p. 7.
2 As suggested by T.P. McKenna, who directed the play in 1973, in his programme note, 'Tom Kilroy Author', Abbey Theatre, 8 May 1973, NUIG, P103/65(5).
3 The Ryan Report (published in May 2009) investigated all forms of child abuse in Irish institutions for children from 1936 onwards; it was compiled by the Commission to Inquire into Child Abuse, chaired by Mr Justice Seán Ryan. The text of the report is available at www.childabusecommission.ie/rpt/pdfs/. The Murphy Report (officially the Report of the Commission of Investigation into the Catholic Archdiocese of Dublin) was released in July 2009 by Judge Yvonne Murphy. The commission investigated the sexual abuse of children by Catholic clergy in the Dublin Archdiocese. For details of the report, see www.justice.ie/en/JELR/Pages/PB09000504.
4 'Caroline Walsh Talks to Tom Kilroy', *Irish Times*, 25 November 1975, p. 8.
5 Thomas Kilroy, 'A Playwright's Festival', in Nicholas Grene and Patrick Lonergan with Lilian Chambers (eds), *Interactions: Dublin Theatre Festival 1957–2007* (Dublin: Carysfort Press, 2008), p. 13.
6 Ibid., p. 13.
7 NUIG, P103/1(1–17).
8 NUIG, P103/52.
9 '"A Walk on the Water," at the Eblana', *Irish Times*, 20 September 1960, p. 5.

10 Margaret Ramsay, letter to Thomas Kilroy, 23 August 1966, NUIG, P103/58(1).
11 See Joan FitzPatrick Dean, *Riot and Great Anger: Stage Censorship in Twentieth-Century Ireland* (Madison: University of Wisconsin Press, 2004), chapter 8.
12 Tomás Mac Anna, letter to Thomas Kilroy, 30 December 1966, NUIG, P103/47(5–6).
13 Tomás Mac Anna, letter to Thomas Kilroy, 22 February [1967], NUIG, P103/57(1).
14 *Mr Roche* initially had three acts – The Death of Mr Roche, The Disposal of the Body and a Requiem, and The Resurrection of Mr Roche – but Kilroy combined the second and (short) third acts into one after the play's initial festival run, a change easily accommodated by new lighting directions to indicate a brief passage of time at the end of the original Act II. The programme of the 1973 Abbey Theatre production, however, lists the original three acts by their titles, with one interval between the first and second acts. The programme of the 1989 Abbey production mentions two Acts, 'The Death of Mr Roche' and 'The Resurrection'.
15 Kilroy, 'A Playwright's Festival', p. 19.
16 Thomas Kilroy, 'A Personal View of Theater', *Princeton University Library Chronicle*, vol. 68, nos. 1/2 (2007), p. 603.
17 Seamus Kelly, 'No "Idle Tiers" for Plays', *Irish Times*, 5 October 1968, p. 15.
18 'Kilroy in Conversation with Adrian Frazier', in Guy Woodward (ed.), *Across the Boundaries: Talking about Thomas Kilroy* (Dublin: Carysfort Press, 2014), p. 92.
19 Colm Cronin, 'Festival Preview', *Hibernia*, October 1968, p. 21.
20 'His Own Play Disturbs Him', *Irish Press*, 5 October 1968, p. 6.
21 Kelly, 'No "Idle Tiers"', p. 15.
22 Thomas Kilroy, *The Death and Resurrection of Mr Roche* (Oldcastle: Gallery Press, 2002), p. 30. All references to the play in the text are to this edition.
23 Finegan, 'Saturday Night'.
24 'Theatre Festival Reviewed', *Irish Independent*, 9 October 1968, p. 3.
25 Seamus Kelly, 'Record 37,000 Audience', *Irish Times*, 9 October 1968, p. 10.
26 John Higgins, 'Mr Roche', *Financial Times*, 8 July 1969, p. 3.
27 Thomas Kilroy, *The Death and Resurrection of Mr Roche*, Abbey Theatre, 8 May 1973, script, Abbey Theatre Digital Archive at NUI Galway, 4582_S_0004, p. 1.
28 Len Falkenstein, 'Critical Remembering: Reading Nostalgia in Contemporary Irish Drama and Film', *Canadian Journal of Irish Studies*, vol. 25, no. 1/2 (July/December 1999), p. 269.
29 Joseph Valente, 'Self-Queering Ireland?' *Canadian Journal of Irish Studies*, vol. 36, no. 1 (spring 2010), p. 27.
30 Anthony Roche, *Contemporary Irish Drama: from Beckett to McGuinness* (Dublin: Gill & Macmillan, 1994), p. 194.
31 Finegan, 'Saturday Night'.
32 Eve Kosofsky Sedgwick, 'Queer and Now', in Sedgwick, *Tendencies* (Durham, NC: Duke University Press, 1993), p. 9.
33 Fr Lucius McClean OFM, 'The Loneliness of the Homosexual', *Sunday Independent*, 15 October 1967, p. 2.

34 'Your Child and Homosexuality', *Sunday Independent*, 13 April 1969, p. 22.
35 Áine O'Connor, interview with David Norris, *Last House*, RTÉ television, 24 July 1975. www.rte.ie/archives/2014/0212/503805-david-norris-chairman-of-the-gay-rights-movement-1975/
36 The piece was first written by John Henry Titus in 1872 and published in the *New York Dispatch* in 1887 in an adaptation by Hugh Antoine d'Arcy.
37 Roche, *Contemporary Irish Drama*, p. 195.
38 In *Irish Drama, Modernity and the Passion Play* (London: Palgrave Macmillan, 2016), Alexandra Poulain suggests that forcing Mr Roche into the 'holy-hole' acts out 'an unspeakable fantasy of anal penetration' (p. 167).
39 Eve Kosofsky Sedgwick, *Epistemology of the Closet* (Berkeley: University of California Press, 1990), p. 205.
40 Hilton Edwards, letter to Thomas Kilroy, 17 May 1968, NUIG, P103/57(4–5).
41 Fintan O'Toole, 'Mr Roche Earns His Place in the Repertoire', *Irish Times*, 3 June 1989, p. 29.
42 Thomas Kilroy, notes on *The Death and Resurrection of Mr Roche* for the New York production (New Theatre Workshop, March 1971, dir. Mike Kellin), NUIG, P103/68(1).
43 Kilroy, notes for the New York production.
44 O'Toole, 'Mr Roche Earns', p. 29.
45 Kilroy, notes for the New York production.
46 John Devitt with Nicholas Grene and Chris Morash, *Shifting Scenes: Irish Theatre-Going, 1955–1985* (Dublin: Carysfort Press, 2008), pp. 84–85.
47 Christopher O'Rourke, 'Speaking with . . . Tom Kilroy', *InCognito: An Irish Journal of Literary Culture*, vol. 2 (1997), p. 13.
48 Elgy Gillespie, interview with Thomas Kilroy, *Irish Times*, 26 April 1972, p. 12.
49 NUIG, P103/53.
50 Thomas Kilroy, personal communication with the present author, 26 November 2014.
51 David Rudkin, *Afore Night Come* (New York: Grove Press, 1963), p. 2. All references to the play in the text are to this edition.
52 René Girard, *Violence and the Sacred*, trans. Patrick Gregory (Baltimore and London: The Johns Hopkins University Press, 1977), p. 82.
53 David Rudkin, 'Interview: September 2001', p. 3 of 5 pp. http://www.davidrudkin.com/html/commentary/commentary.html
54 Colin Chambers, *Peggy: The Life of Margaret Ramsay, Play Agent* (London: Palgrave Macmillan, 1998), p. 132.
55 Edwards to Kilroy, 17 May 1968.
56 Hilton Edwards, letter to Thomas Kilroy, 29 May 1969, NUIG, P103/43(6).
57 Éibhear Walshe, 'Sodom and Begorrah, or Game to the Last: Inventing Micheál Mac Liammóir', in Walshe (ed.), *Sex, Nation and Dissent in Irish Writing* (Cork: Cork University Press, 1997), p. 159.
58 McClean, 'The Loneliness of the Homosexual', p. 2.
59 Leslie Faughnan, '"Mr Roche" Is Good Company', *Irish Press*, 8 October 1968, p. 11.
60 Kilroy, notes for the New York production.
61 'Kay Kent Talks to Christopher Cazenove', *Irish Times*, 4 October 1973, p. 10.

62 Abbey Theatre, programme, 'Brian Friel: A Birthday Celebration', NUIG, P103/544(29).
63 Shaun Richards, 'Subjects of "the Machinery of Citizenship": *The Death and Resurrection of Mr Roche* and *The Gentle Island* at the Dublin Theatre Festival', in Nicholas Grene and Patrick Lonergan (eds), *Interactions: Dublin Theatre Festival 1957–2007* (Dublin: Carysfort Press, 2008), p. 71.
64 O'Toole, 'Mr Roche Earns', p. 29.
65 'Thomas Kilroy', in Daniel Murphy (ed.), *Education and the Arts: The Educational Autobiographies of Contemporary Irish Poets, Novelists, Dramatists, Musicians, Painters and Sculptors* (Dublin: Trinity College Department of Higher Education, 1987), p. 191.
66 Finegan, 'Saturday Night'.
67 Gus Smith, 'The Abbey Picks Two Losers', *Sunday Independent*, 12 May 1973, p. 15.
68 David Nowlan, review of *The Death and Resurrection of Mr Roche* by Thomas Kilroy, Abbey Theatre, 1989, *Irish Times*, 16 May 1989, p. 12.
69 Emer O'Kelly, 'An Embarrassment of Riches in a Nation of Playwrights', *Sunday Independent*, 24 May 1998, p. 8.
70 Kilroy, notes for the New York production.
71 Ibid.
72 Lord Alfred Douglas in Thomas Kilroy, *My Scandalous Life* (Oldcastle: Gallery Press, 2004), p. 22.

5. Psychological Baggage: *Tea and Sex and Shakespeare*

1 'Curtain Calls', *Evening Herald*, 9 October 1976, p. 7.
2 'Books after Booker', *The Times*, 28 November 1971, newspaper cutting, NUIG, P103/623(5).
3 Elgy Gillespie, interview with Thomas Kilroy, *Irish Times*, 26 April 1972, p. 12.
4 'Tom Kilroy in Conversation with Gerry Dukes', in Lilian Chambers, Ger FitzGibbon and Eamonn Jordan (eds), *Theatre Talk: Voices of Irish Theatre Practitioners* (Dublin: Carysfort Press, 2001), p. 243.
5 Thomas Kilroy, *Farmers*, prod. Michael Garvey, RTÉ Radio 1, 11 January 1979, typescript, NUIG, P103/375(1).
6 Fr Michael Campbell, CC, letter to the editor, *Irish Independent*, 22 February 1979, p. 8.
7 Mária Kurdi, '"The Whole Idea of Writing Historical Fiction Is Paradoxical": Talk with Irish Playwright Thomas Kilroy', *Hungarian Journal of English and American Studies*, vol. 8, no. 1 (2002), p. 266.
8 Thomas Kilroy, *Tea and Sex and Shakespeare* (Oldcastle: Gallery Press, 1998), p. 13. All references to the play in the text are to this edition.
9 'Tom Kilroy in Conversation with Gerry Dukes', p. 243.
10 NUIG, P103/68.
11 NUIG, P103/75(19).
12 NUIG, P103/75(1).
13 Mary Manning, letter to Thomas Kilroy, n.d., NUIG, P103/450(1).
14 Seamus Kelly, 'Kilroy's "Tea and Sex and Shakespeare"', *Irish Times*, 7 October 1976, p. 9.
15 Dublin Theatre Festival retrospective, *Irish Times*, 8 October 1976, p. 11.

16 Elgy Gillespie, interview with Max Stafford-Clark, *Irish Times*, 5 October 1976, p. 8.
17 Thomas Kilroy, letter to Brian Friel, n.d., Brian Friel Papers, NLI, MS 37, 254.
18 Thomas Kilroy, *Tea and Sex and Shakespeare,* Abbey Theatre, 6 October 1976, prompt script, Abbey Theatre Digital Archive at NUI Galway, 2585_PS_0002, p. 108.
19 Thierry Dubost, 'A Telephone Interview with Max Stafford-Clark, June 3, 2004: On *Tea and Sex and Shakespeare* and *The Seagull*', in Dubost, *The Plays of Thomas Kilroy: A Critical Study* (Jefferson, NC and London: McFarland, 2007), p. 162.
20 Ibid., p. 161.
21 Manning to Kilroy, n.d., NUIG, P103/450(1).
22 Thomas Kilroy, letter to Brian Friel, 25 January 1991, Brian Friel Papers, NLI, MS 37, 254.
23 NUIG, P103/75(2).
24 NUIG, P103/75(9).
25 Script of *Tea and Sex and Shakespeare*, Abbey Theatre, 6 October 1976, Abbey Theatre Digital Archive at NUIG, 2585_S_0001, p. 54.
26 NUIG, P103/75(36).
27 Script of *Tea and Sex and Shakespeare*, Abbey Theatre Digital Archive, 2585_S_0001, p. 66.
28 'Caroline Walsh Talks to Tom Kilroy', *Irish Times*, 25 November 1975, p. 8.
29 Thomas Kilroy, 'Her Whiteness Attracts a Blackness', *Irish Press*, 1 February 1980, p. 1.
30 Thomas Kilroy, application for a month-long residence, Bellagio Studio, Lake Como, Italy, 18 April 1985, Brian Friel Papers, NLI, MS 37, 254.
31 Kilroy, 'Her Whiteness', p. 1.
32 'Caroline Walsh Talks to Tom Kilroy', p. 8.
33 Thomas Kilroy, letter to Brian Friel, 21 November [1976], Brian Friel Papers, NLI, MS 37, 254.
34 Declan Hughes, 'Visceral Force and Haunting Lyric Beauty', *Irish Times*, 27 April 2011, p. 14.
35 Charles Hunter, 'Thomas Kilroy: A Private Subversive', *Irish Times*, 2 July 1988, p. A11.
36 'Tom Kilroy in Conversation with Gerry Dukes', p. 243.
37 Ibid., p. 244.
38 Ronan Farren, 'Farce Clouds Tom Kilroy's Portrait of an Artist', *Sunday Independent*, 17 July 1988, p. 17.
39 David Nowlan, '*Tea and Sex and Shakespeare* at the Project', *Irish Times*, 13 July 1988, p. 14.
40 Patrick Burke, 'Thomas Kilroy's Latest and Rough Magic', *Irish Literary Supplement*, vol. 7, no. 2 (1988), p. 15.
41 Fintan O'Toole, 'Second Half Smash', *Sunday Tribune*, 17 July 1988, p. 18.
42 Script of *Tea and Sex and Shakespeare*, Abbey Theatre Digital Archive, 2585_S_0001, p. 62.
43 Jerome L. Singer and Michael V. Barrios, 'Writer's Block and Blocked Writers: Using Natural Imagery to Enhance Creativity', in Scott Barry Kaufman and James C. Kaufman (eds), *The Psychology of Creative Writing* (Cambridge: Cambridge University Press, 2009), pp. 230–31.

44 Joan Acocella, 'Blocked: Why Do Writers Stop Writing?', *New Yorker*, 14 June 2004, http://www.newyorker.com/magazine/2004/06/14/blocked#ixzzo KJfyZx.
45 Script of *Tea and Sex and Shakespeare*, Abbey Theatre Digital Archive, 2585_S_0001, pp. 91–92.
46 Prompt script of *Tea and Sex and Shakespeare*, Abbey Theatre, 6 October 1976, Abbey Theatre Digital Archive at NUIG, 2585_PS_0002, p. 95.
47 Des Hogan, review of *Tea and Sex and Shakespeare* by Thomas Kilroy, *In Dublin*, 16 October 1976, press cutting, Abbey Theatre Digital Archive at NUIG, 2585_PC_0001, p. 26.
48 Prompt script of *Tea and Sex and Shakespeare*, Abbey Theatre Digital Archive, 2585_PS_0002, p. 95, p. 97.
49 Thomas Kilroy, 'From Page to Stage', in Jacqueline Genet and Wynne Hellegouarc'h (eds), *Irish Writers and Their Creative Process* (Gerrards Cross: Colin Smythe, 1996), p. 60.
50 O'Toole, 'Second Half Smash', p. 18.
51 Christopher Murray, 'Thomas Kilroy's World Elsewhere', in Genet and Hellegouarc'h (eds), op. cit., p. 76.
52 Lesley Adamson, 'Matt Talbot is Dublin's Twenties Saint', *Guardian*, 22 November 1977, p. 12.
53 Seamus Kelly, 'Kilroy's "Tea and Sex and Shakespeare"', *Irish Times*, 7 October 1976, p. 9.
54 Desmond Rushe, 'Abbey: Tricks, Gags and Pretensions', *Irish Independent*, 6 October 1976, p. 12.

6. The Wound of Gender: *The Secret Fall of Constance Wilde*

1 Mária Kurdi, '"The Whole Idea of Writing Historical Fiction Is Paradoxical": Talk with Irish Playwright Thomas Kilroy', *Hungarian Journal of English and American Studies*, vol. 8, no. 1 (2002), p. 265.
2 Thomas Kilroy, 'The Wildean Triangle', in Bernhard Reitz and Heiko Stahl (eds), *What Revels Are in Hand? Assessments of Contemporary Drama in English in Honour of Wolfgang Lippke* (Trier: WVT, 2001), p. 49.
3 Ibid., p. 51.
4 Patrick Mason, letter to Thomas Kilroy, 21 February 1994, NUIG, P103/240(8).
5 Thierry Dubost, 'A Telephone Interview with Patrick Mason, September 27, 2004', in Dubost, *The Plays of Thomas Kilroy: A Critical Study* (Jefferson, NC, and London: McFarland, 2007), p. 169.
6 NUIG, P103/228(1).
7 Ibid.
8 NUIG, P103/227.
9 NUIG, P103/228(1).
10 NUIG, P103/233(1).
11 Patrick Mason, letter to Thomas Kilroy, 13 January 1995, NUIG, P103/549(10).
12 Kilroy, 'The Wildean Triangle', p. 47.
13 Eileen Battersby, 'Kilroy Is Here', *Irish Times*, 2 October 1997, p. 13.
14 Dubost, 'A Telephone Interview with Patrick Mason', p. 169.
15 NUIG, P103/236(4).

16 NUIG, P103/232(1).
17 Thomas Kilroy, *The Secret Fall of Constance Wilde* (Oldcastle: Gallery Press, 1997), p. 11. All references to the play in the text are to this edition.
18 NUIG, P103/219(22).
19 The Abbey production travelled to the Melbourne Festival a year later, and was revived at the Barbican Centre, London, where it opened on 27 September 2000, after a brief run-in of sixteen performances at the Abbey.
20 Patrick Mason, 'Acting Out', *Irish University Review*, vol. 32, no. 1 (2002), p. 140.
21 Dalya Alberge, 'Letters Unravel Mystery of the Death of Oscar Wilde's Wife', *Guardian*, 2 January 2015, web edition, http://www.guardian.co.uk.
22 Kilroy, 'The Wildean Triangle', p. 53.
23 Quoted in Anne Clark Amor, *Mrs Oscar Wilde: A Woman of Importance* (London: Sidgwick & Jackson, 1983), p. 15.
24 Quoted in ibid., p. 183.
25 Mason, 'Acting Out', p. 140.
26 Kilroy, 'The Wildean Triangle', p. 53.
27 Christopher O'Rourke, 'Speaking with . . . Tom Kilroy', *InCognito: An Irish Journal of Literary Culture*, no. 2 (1997), p. 14.
28 Olga Taxidou, *Modernism and Performance: Jarry to Brecht* (London: Palgrave Macmillan, 2007), p. 10.
29 Ibid., p. 15.
30 Quoted in Mason, 'Acting Out', p. 141.
31 Paul Brennan and Thierry Dubost, 'An Interview with Thomas Kilroy, 2001', in Dubost, op. cit., p. 129.
32 Barbara Fassler, 'Theories of Homosexuality as Sources of Bloomsbury's Androgyny', *Signs*, vol. 5, no. 2 (1979), p. 250.
33 Lisa Rado, *The Modern Androgyne Imagination: A Failed Sublime* (Charlottesville and London: University Press of Virginia, 2000), p. 12.
34 NUIG, P103/233(1).
35 Catriona MacLeod, *Embodying Ambiguity: Androgyny and Aesthetics from Winckelmann to Keller* (Detroit: Wayne State University Press, 1998), pp. 40–41.
36 Oscar Wilde, letter to Lillie Langtry, *c.* 22 January 1884, in Merlin Holland and Rupert Hart-Davis (eds), *The Complete Letters of Oscar Wilde* (New York: Henry Holt & Company, 2000), p. 224.
37 Frank Harris cited in Richard Ellmann, *Oscar Wilde* (London: Hamish Hamilton, 1987), p. 250.
38 Oscar Wilde to Robert Ross, *c.* May–June 1892, in *The Complete Letters of Oscar Wilde*, p. 526.
39 Oscar Wilde to Lord Alfred Douglas, *c.* January 1893, in ibid., p. 544.
40 MacLeod, op. cit., p. 38.
41 Ibid., p. 31.
42 Ibid., p. 15.
43 Francette Pacteau, 'The Impossible Referent: Representations of the Androgyne', in Victor Burgin, James Donald, and Cora Kaplan (eds), *Formations of Fantasy* (London and New York: Methuen, 1986).
44 Judy Friel, notes on draft of 'The Secret Fall', March 1997, NUIG, P103/240(21).

45 Dubost, 'A Telephone Interview with Patrick Mason', p. 171.
46 Pacteau, 'The Impossible Referent', p. 82.
47 Ibid., p. 63.
48 Dubost, 'A Telephone Interview with Patrick Mason', p. 169.
49 Thomas Kilroy, 'From Page to Stage', in Jacqueline Genet and Wynne Hellegouarc'h (eds), *Irish Writers and Their Creative Process* (Gerrards Cross: Colin Smythe, 1996), pp. 57–58.
50 Tom Kilroy, 'Afterword', in Joe Vaněk, *Irish Theatrescapes: New Irish Plays, Adapted European Plays and Irish Classics* (Kinsale: Gandon Editions, 2015), p. 106. Moving the disk in the way Kilroy had envisaged proved technically impossible within Vaněk's design on the Abbey stage.
51 MacLeod, op. cit., p. 32.
52 Kevin Ohi, *Innocence and Rapture: The Erotic Child in Pater, Wilde, James, and Nabokov* (London: Palgrave Macmillan, 2005), p. 12.
53 Ibid., p. 10.
54 Thomas Kilroy, *My Scandalous Life* (Oldcastle: Gallery Press, 2004), p. 30. The play was first performed in a staged reading at the Peacock Theatre on 3 December 2000, with Mark Lambert as Alfred Douglas.
55 Ohi, op. cit., p. 6.
56 Kilroy, 'From Page to Stage', p. 56.
57 Christopher Murray, 'Worlds Elsewhere: The Plays of Thomas Kilroy', *Eire-Ireland*, vol. 29, no. 2 (1994), p. 132.
58 Ibid., p. 128.
59 MacLeod, op. cit., pp. 180–81.
60 Dubost, 'A Telephone Interview with Patrick Mason', p. 165.
61 Ibid., pp. 172–73.
62 Thierry Dubost, 'An Interview with Thomas Kilroy, 2004', in Dubost, op. cit., p. 151.
63 Dubost, 'A Telephone Interview with Patrick Mason', p. 169.
64 Vaněk, op. cit., p. 104.
65 Hugh Leonard, review of *The Secret Fall of Constance Wilde* by Thomas Kilroy, Abbey Theatre, 1997, *Sunday Independent*, 19 October 1997, p. 35.
66 Dubost, 'A Telephone Interview with Patrick Mason', p. 169.
67 Louise East, 'Abbey Goes Wilde', *Irish Times*, Weekend, 11 October 1997, p. 61.
68 Thomas Kilroy, 'The Intellectual on Stage', *Irish Pages*, vol. 7, no. 2 (2012), p. 100.
69 Dubost, 'A Telephone Interview with Patrick Mason', pp. 169–70.
70 Dubost, 'An Interview with Thomas Kilroy, 2004', pp. 151–52.
71 Joe Dowling, 'A Skillful, Theatrical Irish Writer', programme note, *The Secret Fall of Constance Wilde* by Thomas Kilroy, Guthrie Theater, Minneapolis, 31 May–11 July 2008, p. 6.
72 Dubost, 'A Telephone Interview with Patrick Mason', p. 170.
73 Michael Lupu (ed.), Play Guide for *The Secret Fall of Constance Wilde* by Thomas Kilroy, Guthrie Theater, Minneapolis, MN, p. 37. http://www.guthrietheater.org/sites/default/files/studyguide_SecretFallofConstanceWilde.pdf (8 May 2008).
74 Ibid., p. 35.
75 Ibid., pp. 36–38.
76 Dubost, 'An Interview with Thomas Kilroy, 2004', p. 138.

77 Lupu (ed.), Play Guide, p. 36.
78 Rachel Halliburton, 'Wilde's Bitter Sweet Love', *Evening Standard*, 29 September 2000, p. 62.
79 Kilroy, 'The Intellectual on Stage', p. 98.
80 Ibid., p. 97.

7. No Such Thing as Love: *Christ, Deliver Us!*

1 'Playwrights Speak Out: Round-Table Discussion on Translation and Adaptation with Thomas Kilroy and Michael West', in Ros Dixon and Irina Ruppo (eds), *Ibsen and Chekhov on the Irish Stage* (Dublin: Carysfort Press, 2012), p. 176.
2 Ibid., p. 181.
3 Phyllis Ryan, letter to Thomas Kilroy, 8 November 1988, NUIG, P103/165(17).
4 Elizabeth Boa, *The Sexual Circus: Wedekind's Theatre of Subversion* (Oxford: Blackwell, 1987), p. 1.
5 Anthony Roche, 'An Interview with Thomas Kilroy', *Irish University Review*, vol. 32, no. 1 (2002), p. 155.
6 Thomas Kilroy, letter to Brian Friel, July 1998, Brian Friel Papers, NLI, MS 37,254.
7 Ben Barnes, letter to Thomas Kilroy, 2 December 1999, NUIG, P103/549(16).
8 Victoria White, 'A New Stage for the Abbey', conversation with Ben Barnes, *Irish Times*, 17 February 2000, p. 16.
9 Ben Barnes, letter to Thomas Kilroy, 2 March 2001, NUIG, P103/549(41).
10 Emma Browne, 'Arts Council Decision "Extraordinary"', *Village*, 11–17 January 2007, p. 8.
11 Aedín Gormley, interview with Thomas Kilroy, *Arts News*, RTÉ Lyric FM, 16 February 2010.
12 Thomas Kilroy, 'Secularized Ireland', in Edna Longley (ed.), *Culture in Ireland: Division or Diversity?* (Belfast: Institute of Irish Studies, QUB, 1991), p. 135.
13 J.L. Hibberd, 'Imaginary Numbers and "Humor": on Wedekind's *Frühlings Erwachen*', *Modern Language Review*, vol. 74 (1979), p. 639.
14 Frank Wedekind, 'Was ich mir dabei dachte', *Gesammelte Werke*, vol. 9 (München: Georg Müller Verlag, 1921), p. 424.
15 'Thomas Kilroy', in Daniel Murphy (ed.), *Education and the Arts: The Educational Autobiographies of Contemporary Irish Poets, Novelists, Dramatists, Musicians, Painters and Sculptors* (Dublin: Trinity College Department of Higher Education, 1987), p. 191.
16 Thomas Kilroy, *Christ, Deliver Us!* (Oldcastle: Gallery Press, 2010), p. 51. All references to the play in the text are to this edition.
17 Diarmaid Ferriter quoted in Michael Viney, 'Michael Viney's Ireland: 50 Years a Blow-in', *Irish Times*, 19 March 2016, Weekend Review, p. 1.
18 Rosita Boland, 'If I'd Stayed in Dublin I'd Probably Be Dead', Interview with Michael Viney, *Irish Times*, 10 July 2010, p. 37.
19 Thomas Kilroy, 'Adaptation: A Privileged Conversation with a Dead Author', *Irish Times*, 13 February 2010, p. 47.
20 Judy Murphy, 'Play about Ireland's Past Throws Light on Shape of Country Today', *Connacht Tribune*, 12 February 2010, p. 29.

21 Longman Oz, review of *Christ, Deliver Us!* by Thomas Kilroy, Abbey Theatre, February 2010, http://noordinaryfool.com/2010/02/17/christdeliverus_abbey theatre/ (17 February 2010).
22 Boa, op. cit., p. 26.
23 Ibid., p. 2.
24 Ibid., pp. 22–23.
25 Ibid., p. 26.
26 Anthony Roche, *Contemporary Irish Drama: From Beckett to McGuinness* (Dublin: Gill & Macmillan, 1994), p. 191.
27 Fintan O'Toole, 'We Live in the 19th Century as Well as the 21st', *Irish Times*, 6 March 2010, p. 44.
28 Hibberd, 'Imaginary Numbers', p. 643.
29 Fintan Walsh, review of *Christ, Deliver Us!* by Thomas Kilroy, Abbey Theatre, February 2010, *Irish Theatre Magazine*, 16 February 2010, http://www.irishtheatremagazine.ie (19 February 2010).
30 Peter Crawley, review of *Christ, Deliver Us!* by Thomas Kilroy, Abbey Theatre, February 2010, *Irish Times*, 18 February 2010, p. 18.
31 'Thomas Kilroy', in Murphy, op. cit., p. 191.
32 Frank Wedekind, *The Awakening of Spring: A Tragedy of Childhood*, trans. Francis J. Ziegler (Philadelphia: Brown Brothers, 1910), p. 39. All references to the play in the text are to this edition.
33 Thomas Kilroy, notes on first half draft of 'Christ, Deliver Us!', 27 October 2000, NUIG, P103/301(9).
34 Andy Hinds, notes for 'Christ, Deliver Us!', NUIG, P103/311(1).
35 Emily O'Reilly, 'The Unfinished Business of Anne [*sic*] Lovett and What We Never Managed to Learn', *Sunday Times*, 30 March 2003, web, www.timesonline.co.uk (4 July 2010).
36 Colin Murphy, 'Breaking the Stranglehold of Cultural "Rules"', *Sunday Business Post*, 15 March 2015, www.businesspost.ie. Also see 'Ócáid Chomórtha/A Celebration of Máiréad Ní Ghráda', http://www.irishtheatre institute.com/event.aspx?t=mir%C3%A9ad_n%C3%AD_ghrda&contentid=9289&subpagecontentid=9297 (15 January 2016).
37 Thomas Kilroy, 'The Irish Writer: Self and Society, 1950–80', in Peter Connolly (ed.), *Literature and the Changing Ireland* (Gerrards Cross: Colin Smythe, 1982), p. 181.
38 Oz, review of *Christ, Deliver Us!*
39 Caroline O'Doherty, 'The Virgin Mary and the "Tainted" Teenage Girl Who Came to Her for Sanctuary', *Irish Examiner*, 26 January 2004, p. 11.
40 Edna O'Brien, *Down by the River* (New York: Farrar, Straus & Giroux, 1997).
41 Hibberd, 'Imaginary Numbers', p. 633.
42 Ibid., p. 424.
43 Kilroy, 'Adaptation', p. 47.
44 Liam Murphy, review of *Christ, Deliver Us!* by Thomas Kilroy, Abbey Theatre, February 2010, *Munster Express*, 25 February 2010, www.munster-express.ie (30 June 2010).
45 Mick Heaney, 'The Joylessness of Sex', *Sunday Times*, 21 February 2010, p. 21.
46 Kilroy, 'Secularized Ireland', p. 136.
47 Wedekind, 'Was ich mir dabei dachte', p. 424.

48 Breda O'Brien, response to *Christ, Deliver Us!* by Thomas Kilroy, *Irish Times*, 2 March 2010, p. 19.
49 Emer O'Kelly, 'Scorching Indictment of Sexual Repression', *Irish Independent*, 20 February 2010, p. 36.
50 Oz, review of *Christ, Deliver Us!*

8. Relations with the Absolute: *Talbot's Box*

1 Aodhan Madden, 'They Don't "Buy" Irish . . . Says Thomas Kilroy' [*Evening Press*, July 1969], newspaper cutting, NUIG, P103/61(43).
2 'Matt Talbot: What His Name Means Today', *Kerryman*, 7 January 1977, p. 16.
3 'Matt Talbot "No Strike Breaker"', *Irish Press*, 23 June 1975, p. 4.
4 John Cooney, 'Archbishop Welcomes Prospect that Matt Talbot May Be Ireland's First Lay Saint', *Irish Times*, 4 October 1975, p. 13.
5 J.P. Murphy, letter to the editor, *Irish Times*, 11 October 1975, p. 13.
6 Sé Geraghty, letter to the editor, *Irish Times*, 7 October 1975, p. 9.
7 Kane Archer, '"Talbot's Box" at the Peacock', *Irish Times*, 14 October 1977, p. 11.
8 John Devitt in Conversation with Nicholas Grene and Chris Morash, *Shifting Scenes: Irish Theatre-Going, 1955–1985* (Dublin: Carysfort Press, 2008), p. 85.
9 Declan Hughes, 'Visceral Force and Haunting Lyric Beauty', *Irish Times*, 27 April 2011, p. 14.
10 Mária Kurdi, '"The Whole Idea of Writing Historical Fiction Is Paradoxical": Talk with Irish Playwright Thomas Kilroy', *Hungarian Journal of English and American Studies*, vol. 8, no. 1 (2002), p. 262.
11 Thomas Kilroy, 'Author's Note', in *Talbot's Box* (Oldcastle: Gallery Press, 1997), p. 6.
12 Lesley Adamson, 'Matt Talbot is Dublin's Twenties Saint', *Guardian*, 22 November 1977, p. 12.
13 Thomas Kilroy, review of *Peggy: The Life of Margaret Ramsay, Play Agent*, by Colin Chambers, *Irish Times*, Supplement, 8 July 1997, p. 8.
14 Margaret Ramsay, letter to Thomas Kilroy, 16 July 1974, NUIG, P103/98(58).
15 'Caroline Walsh Talks to Tom Kilroy', *Irish Times*, 25 November 1975, p. 8.
16 Adamson, 'Matt Talbot', p. 12.
17 Thomas Kilroy, *Talbot's Box* (Oldcastle: Gallery Press, 1997), p. 9. All subsequent references to the play in the text are to this edition.
18 Archer, '"Talbot's Box" at the Peacock'.
19 'Caroline Walsh Talks to Tom Kilroy', p. 8.
20 Fintan O'Toole, 'This Red Kettle Puts Matt Talbot to Rights', *Sunday Tribune*, 9 September 1988, newspaper cutting, NUIG, P103/100(14).
21 Diane Chanteau, 'Kilroy's Matt Talbot', *Evening Press*, 8 October 1977, p. 6.
22 Adamson, 'Matt Talbot', p. 12.
23 Chanteau, 'Kilroy's Matt Talbot', p. 6.
24 Fintan O'Toole, 'Double Vision: The Ambivalences of Thomas Kilroy', *Magill*, vol. 11, no. 11 (1988), p. 58.

25 Fintan O'Toole, 'No Resting Place in Kilroy's Plays', *Irish Times*, 10 May 1990, p. 8.
26 Thierry Dubost, 'A Telephone Interview with Patrick Mason, September 27, 2004', in Dubost, *The Plays of Thomas Kilroy: A Critical Study* (Jefferson, NC, and London: McFarland, 2007), p. 165.
27 Desmond Rushe, review of *Talbot's Box* by Thomas Kilroy, Abbey Theatre, 1977, *Irish Independent*, 14 October 1977, p. 9.
28 Rosita Sweetman, 'Talbot's Box: Just Look What's in It!', *Sunday Independent*, 23 October 1977, p. 20.
29 Thierry Dubost, 'An Interview with Thomas Kilroy, 2004', in Dubost, op. cit., p. 153.
30 Ibid., p. 144.
31 'Tom Kilroy in Conversation with Gerry Dukes', in Lilian Chambers, Ger FitzGibbon and Eamonn Jordan (eds), *Theatre Talk: Voices of Irish Theatre Practitioners* (Dublin: Carysfort Press, 2001), p. 244.
32 Kurdi, '"The Whole Idea"', p. 261.
33 Christopher Innes, *Avant Garde Theatre 1892–1992* (London and New York: Routledge, 1993), p. 126.
34 Christopher Innes, 'Immortal Eyes and Fearful Symmetry: Towards a Drama of Vision', *Irish University Review*, vol. 32, no. 1 (2002), p. 173.
35 Paul Brennan and Thierry Dubost, 'An Interview with Thomas Kilroy, 2001', in Dubost, op. cit., p. 128.
36 *El Principe Constante* (1629), by Pedro Calderón de la Barca.
37 Thomas Kilroy, personal communication with the present author, 26 November 2014.
38 NUIG, P103/89.
39 NUIG, P103/89(10).
40 Charles R. Lyons, 'Le Compagnie Madeleine Renaud – Jean-Louis Barrault: The Idea and the Aesthetic', *Educational Theatre Journal*, vol. 19, no. 4 (1967), pp. 416–17.
41 Michel Dumoulin, 'Maurice Béjart: "La Tentation de Saint Antoine"', television documentary, *Panorama*, 17 March 1967, http:// www.ina.fr/art-et-culture/arts-du-spectacle/video/CAF86014586/maurice-bejart-la-tentation-de-saint-antoine.fr.html (23 February 2012).
42 Thomas Kilroy, 'Playing the Monster on Stage', *Irish University Review*, vol. 45, no. 1 (2015), pp. 86–87.
43 Hughes, 'Visceral Force'.
44 Innes, op. cit., p. 2.
45 Ibid., p. 158.
46 Ibid., p. 159.
47 Donald R. Larson, 'Embodying Transcendence: Grotowski's *The Constant Prince*', *Comedia Performance*, vol. 1, no. 1 (2004), p. 39.
48 Innes, op. cit., p. 162.
49 Frank Marcus, 'From Sinner to Saint', *Sunday Telegraph*, 27 November 1977, p. 18.
50 Rushe, review of *Talbot's Box*, p. 9.
51 Dubost, 'An Interview with Thomas Kilroy, 2004', p. 153.
52 Honor Molloy, 'Up the Pillar', http://www.vulgo.ie/features/up-the-pillar-about-nelsons-pillar-and-actor-john-molloy-by-his-daughter-honor-molloy (26 June 2015).

53 'Molloy's "Smarty Girl" Delves into Family's Past', *Irish Echo*, 4 April 2012, http://irishecho.com (15 January 2014).
54 Dubost, 'A Telephone Interview with Patrick Mason', p. 168.
55 Dubost, 'An Interview with Thomas Kilroy, 2004', p. 153.
56 Devitt, op. cit., p. 86.
57 NUIG, P103/90(4).
58 NUIG, P103/91(1).
59 NUIG, P103/89(11).
60 Larson, 'Embodying Transcendence', p. 22.
61 Innes, op. cit., p. 152.
62 Anthony Roche, *Contemporary Irish Drama: From Beckett to McGuinness* (Dublin: Gill & Macmillan, 1994), p. 201.
63 Éamon de Valera, 'On Language and the Irish Nation', radio address, Raidió Éireann, 17 March 1943, http://www.rte.ie/archives/exhibitions/eamon-de-valera/719124-address-by-mr-de-valera/
64 W.B. Yeats, 'Easter, 1916', in *Later Poems* (London: Macmillan, 1926), p. 335.
65 Frances O'Rourke, '"Priest" in Talbot Play is a Woman', *Sunday Press*, 2 October 1977, newspaper cutting, NUIG, P103/98.
66 'Tom Kilroy in Conversation with Gerry Dukes', p. 242.

9. The Art of Imperfection: *The Shape of Metal*

1 Thomas Kilroy, *The Shape of Metal* (Oldcastle: Gallery Press, 2003), p. 47. All references to the play in the text are to this edition.
2 Anna McMullan, 'Masculinity and Masquerade in Thomas Kilroy's *Double Cross* and *The Secret Fall of Constance Wilde*', *Irish University Review*, vol. 32, no. 1 (2002), p. 136.
3 Thierry Dubost, 'An Interview with Thomas Kilroy, 2004', in Dubost, *The Plays of Thomas Kilroy: A Critical Study* (Jefferson, NC, and London: McFarland, 2007), p. 145.
4 Patrick Brennan, 'Kilroy Shows His Metal', *Irish Examiner*, 26 September 2003, p. 14.
5 Eddie Holt, 'Shots of Rough Justice and Dublin 4 Angst', television review, *Irish Independent*, 12 November 1993, p. 31. *Gold in the Streets*, featuring Alan Devlin as the father and Derbhle Crotty as the daughter, was directed by Thaddeus O'Sullivan and first broadcast on RTÉ 1 on 10 November 1993.
6 Ben Barnes, diary entry for 12 October 2003, *Plays and Controversies: Abbey Theatre Diaries 2000–2005* (Dublin: Carysfort Press, 2008), p. 286.
7 Ben Barnes, fax to Thomas Kilroy, 28 January 2003, NUIG, P103/278(12).
8 Thomas Kilroy, response to questions by Ben Barnes about *The Shape of Metal*, NUIG, P103/278(26).
9 Barnes, diary entry for 12 October 2003, op. cit., p. 285.
10 Emer O'Kelly, 'Masters Wreak Fierce Festival Magic', *Sunday Independent*, 4 October 2003, p. 28.
11 Fintan O'Toole, 'Festival Openers Shape Up Well', *Irish Times*, 1 October 2003, p. 14.
12 Karina Buckley, review of *The Shape of Metal*, Abbey Theatre, October 2003, *Sunday Times*, 5 October 2003, p. 35.
13 Barnes, diary entry for 12 October 2003, op. cit., p. 286.

14 Philip James (ed.), *Henry Moore on Sculpture* (London: MacDonald, 1966), p. 93.
15 Ibid., p. 93.
16 Ibid., p. 180.
17 Alan Bowness, 'Barbara Hepworth: Life and Work', p. 3 of 3 pp., http://www.barbarahepworth.org.uk/about-barbara-hepworth/alan-bowness-life-and-work.html (1 August 2013).
18 Ibid., p. 1 of 3 pp.
19 NUIG, P103/271(2).
20 Brian Friel, fax to Thomas Kilroy, 31 January 2003, NUIG, P103/278(17).
21 Thomas Kilroy, letter to Brian Friel, 1 February 2003, NUIG, P103/278(23).
22 Note for the New York production, NUIG, P103/279(29).
23 Mary D. Kierstead, 'Profiles: A Great Old Breakerawayer', *New Yorker*, 13 October 1986, p. 104.
24 Ibid., p. 101.
25 Note for the New York production, NUIG, P103/279(29).
26 Dubost, 'An Interview with Thomas Kilroy, 2004', p. 147.
27 Lynne Parker in 'Panel Discussion 2: Directing Kilroy', in Guy Woodward (ed.), *Across the Boundaries: Talking about Thomas Kilroy* (Dublin: Carysfort Press, 2014), p. 79.
28 Cited in Deirdre Bair, *Samuel Beckett: A Biography* (1978; New York: Summit Books, 1990), p. 209.
29 Timothy Mathews, 'Walking with Angels in Giacometti and Beckett', *L'Esprit Créateur*, vol. 47, no. 3 (2007), p. 39.
30 *In the Garden of the Asylum* was first broadcast in 'Sunday Playhouse', RTÉ Radio 1, on 6 December 2009. http://www.rte.ie/static/drama/radio/player_revisited/player.html?clipId=3033456&imgId=00061b4b.
31 Richard Ellmann, *James Joyce* (Oxford: Oxford University Press, 1982), p. 679.
32 Thierry Dubost, 'An Interview with Lynne Parker, Dublin, October 30, 2003' in Dubost, op. cit., p. 157.
33 Parker in 'Panel Discussion 2', p. 79.
34 Emmaleene O'Brien, 'The Birthing Process in Thomas Kilroy's *The Shape of Metal*', in Cathy McGlynn and Paula Murphy (eds), *New Voices in Irish Literary Criticism: Ireland in Theory* (Lewiston: Edwin Mellen Press, 2007), p. 138.
35 Csilla Bertha, 'Thomas Kilroy's *The Shape of Metal*: "Metal . . . Transformed into Grace" – Grace into Metal', *ABEI Journal*, vol. 9 (2007), p. 86.
36 Laurie Wilson, *Alberto Giacometti: Myth, Magic, and the Man* (New Haven and London: Yale University Press, 2003), p. 243.
37 Thomas Kilroy, note to Lynne Parker, John Comiskey and Alan Farquharson, 19 May 2003, NUIG, P103/278(1).
38 W.B. Yeats, 'The Circus Animals' Desertion', in *Last Poems and Plays* (London: Macmillan & Co., 1940), p. 81.
39 James Olney, *Memory and Narrative: The Weave of Life-Writing* (Chicago: University of Chicago Press, 1998), p. 317.
40 Walter Benjamin, *Illuminations*, ed. Hannah Arendt, trans. Harry Zohn (New York: Schocken, 1969), pp. 257–58.
41 Mathews, 'Walking with Angels', p. 39.

42 Ibid., pp. 34–35.
43 Ibid., p. 41.
44 S.E. Gontarski and Anthony Uhlmann, 'Afterimages: Introducing Beckett's Ghosts', in S.E. Gontarski and Anthony Uhlmann (eds), *Beckett after Beckett* (Gainesville: University Press of Florida, 2006), pp. 70–71.
45 Jacques Dupin, 'Texts for an Approach', in *Giacometti: Three Essays*, trans. John Ashbery and Brian Evenson (New York: Black Square Editions/ Hammer Books, 2003), p. 51.
46 Bertha, 'Thomas Kilroy's *The Shape of Metal*', p. 96.
47 Gontarski and Uhlmann, 'Afterimages', p. 7.
48 Dupin, 'Texts for an Approach', p. 58.
49 Salman Rushdie, 'Is Nothing Sacred?', *Granta*, no. 31 (spring 1990), p. 110.
50 Dubost, 'An Interview with Thomas Kilroy, 2004', p. 154.
51 Fintan O'Toole, 'Irish Theatre's Permeable Borders', *Irish Times*, 15 October 2003, p. 16.

10. A Time of Joy and Love: *Blake*

1 Christopher Innes, 'Immortal Eyes and Fearful Symmetry: Towards a Drama of Vision', *Irish University Review*, vol. 32, no. 1 (2002), p. 174.
2 Anthony Roche, 'An Interview with Thomas Kilroy', *Irish University Review*, vol. 32, no. 1 (2002), p. 156.
3 Michael Ross, 'Try Again, Fail Again, Fail Better', *Sunday Times Magazine* [2002], p. 15, newspaper cutting, NUIG, P103/166(16).
4 Aideen Howard, letter to Thomas Kilroy, 22 March 2006, NUIG, P103/549(55).
5 Paul Brennan and Thierry Dubost, 'An Interview with Thomas Kilroy, 2001', in Dubost, *The Plays of Thomas Kilroy: A Critical Study* (Jefferson, NC, and London: McFarland, 2007), p. 135.
6 Mária Kurdi, '"The Whole Idea of Writing Historical Fiction Is Paradoxical": Talk with Irish Playwright Thomas Kilroy', *Hungarian Journal of English and American Studies*, vol. 8, no. 1 (2002), p. 262.
7 Arthur Symons, *William Blake* (New York: Dutton, 1907), p. 218.
8 Thomas Kilroy, *Blake* (Oldcastle: Gallery Press, 2015), n.p. All references to the play in the text are to this edition.
9 Quoted in Alfred Kazin, 'Introduction', in Kazin (ed.), *The Portable Blake* (New York: Viking, 1946), p. 34.
10 Innes, 'Immortal Eyes', p. 168.
11 Ibid., p. 174.
12 Peter Weiss, *The Persecution and Assassination of Marat as Performed by the Inmates of the Asylum of Charenton under the Direction of the Marquis de Sade*, trans. Geoffrey Skelton and Adrian Mitchell (London: John Calder, 1965), p. 10.
13 Ibid., p. 40.
14 Peter Brook, *A Theatrical Casebook*, compiled by David Williams (London: Methuen, 1988), p. 61.
15 Peter Brook, 'Introduction', in Weiss, *Marat/Sade*, p. 6.
16 Ian Kilroy, 'Master of the Pen', *Irish Examiner*, 1 February 2008, p. 18.
17 Kazin, 'Introduction', p. 9.
18 Ibid., p. 10.

19 Ross, 'Try Again, Fail Again, Fail Better', p. 15.
20 Thomas Kilroy, *The Secret Fall of Constance Wilde* (Oldcastle: Gallery Press, 1997), p. 20.
21 Symons, op. cit., p. 237.
22 Roche, 'Thomas Kilroy: An Interview', p. 156.
23 Ibid., p. 156.
24 Ibid., p. 156.
25 Quoted in Symons, op. cit., p. 11.
26 Quoted in ibid., pp. 199–200.
27 Alexander Gilchrist, *The Life of William Blake*, ed. W. Graham Robertson (London and New York: John Lane, The Bodley Head, 1907), p. 344.
28 Anon., 'Hôpital des Fous à Londres', *Revue Britannique*, July 1833, p. 180.
29 Harold Bruce, *William Blake in This World* (London: Jonathan Cape, 1925), p. 192.
30 E.R.D. MacLagan and A.G.B. Russell (eds), 'Introduction', in *The Prophetic Books of William Blake: Jerusalem* (London: A.H. Bullen, 1904), p. ix.
31 Ibid., p. xiii.
32 Joseph Wicksteed, *William Blake's Jerusalem* (London: Trianon Press, n.d. [1953]), p. 27.
33 Ibid., p. 9.
34 MacLagan and Russell, 'Introduction', p. x.
35 Innes, 'Immortal Eyes', p. 171.
36 Kazin, 'Introduction', pp. 35–36.
37 Kurdi, '"The Whole Idea"', p. 267.
38 Innes, 'Immortal Eyes', p. 169.
39 Thomas Kilroy, *Talbot's Box* (Oldcastle: Gallery Press, 1997), p. 47.
40 James M. Smith, *Ireland's Magdalen Laundries and the Nation's Architecture of Containment* (Notre Dame, IN: University of Notre Dame Press, 2007).
41 Michel Foucault, *Madness and Civilization: A History of Insanity in the Age of Reason*, trans. Richard Howard (New York, Toronto and London: New American Library/Plume, 1971), p. 68.
42 Ibid., pp. 207–08.
43 The text of the scene is quoted in Dubost, op. cit., p. 95.
44 Dubost, 'An Interview with Thomas Kilroy, 2004', p. 150.
45 Kazin, 'Introduction', pp. 53–54.
46 Ibid., p. 54.
47 Aideen Howard, letter to Thomas Kilroy, 22 March 2006, NUIG, P103/549(55).
48 Dubost, 'An Interview with Thomas Kilroy, 2004', p. 148.
49 Quoted in Morris Eaves, *William Blake's Theory of Art* (Princeton, NJ: Princeton University Press, 1982), p. 25.
50 Ibid., pp. 43–44.
51 Quoted in Kazin, op. cit., p. 668.
52 Wicksteed, op. cit., p. 9.
53 Ibid., p. 104.
54 Ibid., p. 93.
55 Ibid., p. 155.
56 Ibid., p. 156.

57 Ibid., p. 94.
58 Ibid., p. 160.
59 Ibid., p. 76.
60 Ibid., p. 226.
61 Ibid., p. 248.
62 Ibid., p. 102.
63 Ibid., p. 251.

Coda

1 Patrick Mason, 'A Director's Note', in *Signatories* (Dublin: UCD Press, 2016), p. xvii.
2 Eithne Shortall, 'Patriot Gaze', interview with Thomas Kilroy, *Sunday Times*, 17 April 2016, p. 18.
3 Ibid., p. 18.
4 Thomas Kilroy, 'Pádraig Pearse', in *Signatories*, pp. 25, 22. All subsequent references to the play in the text are to this edition.
5 Quoted in Brian Crowley, '"The Strange Thing I Am": His Father's Son?', *History Ireland*, vol. 14, no. 2 (2006), p. 12.
6 Pearse wrote this in his short-lived newspaper *An Barr Buadh* in 1912. Quoted in Crowley, '"The Strange Thing I Am"', p. 13.
7 Ruth Dudley Edwards, 'Paving the Way to Hell', *Irish Times*, 3 July 2004, p. A10.
8 Shortall, 'Patriot Gaze', p. 18.
9 'Patrick Pearse 1879–1916', http://www.bbc.co.uk/history/british/easterrising/profiles/po11.shtml.
10 The 1916 Easter Proclamation, which was drafted by Pearse, states: 'The Republic guarantees religious and civil liberty, equal rights and equal opportunities to all its citizens, and declares its resolve to pursue the happiness and prosperity of the whole nation and of all its parts, cherishing all the children of the nation equally.' In August 2015, same-sex marriage became legal in Ireland when the Thirty-fourth Amendment of the Constitution (Marriage Equality) Act was signed into law, having previously been approved by popular referendum.
11 Queen Elizabeth I to William Shakespeare in Thomas Kilroy, 'The Trials of William Shakespeare', unpublished typescript, 2015, p. 87 of 89 pp., manuscript courtesy of Thomas Kilroy. The phrase echoes almost verbatim words spoken by the eponymous heroine of *The Madame MacAdam Travelling Theatre*.

Select Bibliography

I. BY THOMAS KILROY

1. Plays

Blake (Oldcastle: Gallery Press, 2015)
Christ, Deliver Us! (Oldcastle: Gallery Press, 2010)
The Death and Resurrection of Mr Roche (Oldcastle: Gallery Press, 2002)
Double Cross (Oldcastle: Gallery Press, 1994)
Ghosts: after Ibsen (Oldcastle: Gallery Press, 2002)
The Madame MacAdam Travelling Theatre (London: Methuen Drama, 1991)
My Scandalous Life (Oldcastle: Gallery Press, 2004)
The O'Neill (Oldcastle: Gallery Press, 1995)
'Pádraig Pearse', *Signatories* (Dublin: UCD Press, 2016), pp. 19–27
Pirandellos: Two Plays (Oldcastle: Gallery Press, 2007)
The Seagull: after Chekhov (Oldcastle: Gallery Press, 1993)
The Secret Fall of Constance Wilde (Oldcastle: Gallery Press, 1997)
The Shape of Metal (Oldcastle: Gallery Press, 2003)
Talbot's Box (Oldcastle: Gallery Press, 1997)
Tea and Sex and Shakespeare (Oldcastle: Gallery Press, 1998)

2. Fiction, Essays and Criticism

'Groundwork for an Irish Theatre', *Studies*, vol. 48, no. 190 (1959), pp. 192–98
'Her Whiteness Attracts a Blackness', *Irish Press*, 1 February 1980, p. 1
'The Irish Writer: Self and Society, 1950–1980', in Peter Connolly (ed.), *Literature and the Changing Ireland* (Gerrards Cross: Colin Smythe, 1982), pp. 175–87
'Ireland's Pseudo-Englishman', *Magill*, vol. 11, no. 5 (1988), pp. 52–54
'Secularized Ireland', in Edna Longley (ed.), *Culture in Ireland: Division or Diversity?* (Belfast: Institute of Irish Studies, QUB, 1991), pp. 135–41
'From Page to Stage', in Jacqueline Genet and Wynne Hellegouarc'h (eds), *Irish Writers and Their Creative Process* (Gerrards Cross: Colin Smythe, 1996), pp. 55–62
'The Anglo-Irish Theatrical Imagination', *Bullán*, vol. 3, no. 2 (1997–98), pp. 5–12

'The Wildean Triangle', in Bernhard Reitz and Heiko Stahl (eds), *What Revels Are in Hand? Assessments of Contemporary Drama in English in Honour of Wolfgang Lippke* (Trier: WVT, 2001), pp. 47–53

'A Personal View of Theater', *Princeton University Library Chronicle*, vol. 68, no. 1/2 (2007), pp. 599–608

'A Playwright's Festival', in Nicholas Grene and Patrick Lonergan (eds), *Interactions: Dublin Theatre Festival 1957–2007* (Dublin: Carysfort Press, 2008), pp. 9–19

'Adaptation: A Privileged Conversation with a Dead Author', *Irish Times*, 13 February 2010, p. 47

'The Intellectual on Stage', *Irish Pages*, vol. 7, no. 2 (2012), pp. 97–106

'Playing the Monster on Stage', *Irish University Review*, vol. 45, no. 1 (2015), pp. 81–89

II. ABOUT THOMAS KILROY

1. Interviews

Dawe, Gerald, 'An Interview with Thomas Kilroy', in Gerald Dawe and Jonathan Williams (eds), *Krino 1986–1996: An Anthology of Modern Irish Writing* (Dublin: Gill & Macmillan, 1996), pp. 230–35

Dukes, Gerry, 'Tom Kilroy in Conversation with Gerry Dukes', in Lilian Chambers, Ger FitzGibbon and Eamonn Jordan (eds), *Theatre Talk: Voices of Irish Theatre Practitioners* (Dublin: Carysfort Press, 2001), pp. 240–51

Gillespie, Elgy, 'Elgy Gillespie Talks to Thomas Kilroy', *Irish Times*, 26 April 1972, p. 12

'Thomas Kilroy', in Daniel Murphy (ed.), *Education and the Arts: The Educational Autobiographies of Contemporary Irish Poets, Novelists, Dramatists, Musicians, Painters and Sculptors* (Dublin: Trinity College Department of Higher Education, 1987), pp. 189–97

Kurdi, Mária, '"The Whole Idea of Writing Historical Fiction is Paradoxical": Talk with Irish Playwright Thomas Kilroy', *Hungarian Journal of English and American Studies*, vol. 8, no. 1 (2002), pp. 259–67

O'Rourke, Christopher, 'Speaking with . . . Tom Kilroy', *InCognito: An Irish Journal of Literary Culture*, no. 2 (1997), pp. 9–16

Roche, Anthony, 'An Interview with Thomas Kilroy', *Irish University Review*, vol. 32, no. 1 (2002), pp. 150–58

Walsh, Caroline, 'Caroline Walsh Talks to Thomas Kilroy', *Irish Times*, 25 November 1978, p. 8

2. Criticism and Commentary

Bertha, Csilla, 'Thomas Kilroy's *The Shape of Metal*: "Metal . . . Transformed into Grace" – Grace into Metal', *ABEI Journal*, no. 9 (2007), pp. 85–97

Dawe, Gerald, 'A Life of Our Own: *Double Cross* by Thomas Kilroy', *Theatre Ireland*, no. 15 (May/August 1988), pp. 24–26

Dubost, Thierry, *The Plays of Thomas Kilroy: A Critical Study* (Jefferson, NC and London: McFarland, 2007)

Dunne, Phil, 'An Uncluttered Window on Irish Life: The Work of Thomas Kilroy', *Studies*, vol. 89, no. 354 (2000), pp. 140–47.

Fallon, Gabriel, 'All This and the Abbey Too', *Studies*, vol. 48, no. 192 (1959), pp. 434–42

Fogarty, Anne, 'The Romance of History: Renegotiating the Past in Thomas Kilroy's *The O'Neill* and Brian Friel's *Making History*', *Irish University Review*, vol. 32, no. 1 (2002), pp. 18–32

Innes, Christopher, 'Immortal Eyes and Fearful Symmetry: Towards a Drama of Vision', *Irish University Review*, vol. 32, no. 1 (2002), pp. 164–74

Lanters, José, 'Groping towards Morality: Feminism, AIDS, and the Spectre of Article 41 in Thomas Kilroy's *Ghosts*', *Estudios Irlandeses*, vol. 13, no. 2 (2018), www.estudiosirlandeses.org

McMullan, Anna, 'Masculinity and Masquerade in Thomas Kilroy's *Double Cross* and *The Secret Fall of Constance Wilde*', *Irish University Review*, vol. 32, no. 1 (2002), pp. 126–36

Mason, Patrick, 'Acting Out', *Irish University Review*, vol. 32, no. 1 (2002), pp. 137–47

Murray, Christopher, 'Worlds Elsewhere: The Plays of Thomas Kilroy', *Eire-Ireland*, vol. 29, no. 2 (1994), pp. 123–38

——, 'Thomas Kilroy's World Elsewhere', in Jacqueline Genet and Wynne Hellegouarc'h (eds), *Irish Writers and Their Creative Process* (Gerrards Cross: Colin Smythe, 1996), pp. 63–77

O'Brien, Emmaleene, 'The Birthing Process in Thomas Kilroy's *The Shape of Metal*', in Cathy McGlynn and Paula Murphy (eds), *New Voices in Irish Literary Criticism: Ireland in Theory* (Lewiston: Edwin Mellen Press, 2007), pp. 137–49

O'Toole, Fintan, 'Double Vision: The Ambivalences of Thomas Kilroy', *Magill*, vol. 11, no. 11 (1988), pp. 57–59

Pelletier, Martine, '"Against Mindlessness": Thomas Kilroy and Field Day', *Irish University Review*, vol. 32, no. 1 (2002), pp. 110–25

Richards, Shaun, 'Subjects of "the Machinery of Citizenship": *The Death and Resurrection of Mr Roche* and *The Gentle Island* at the Dublin Theatre Festival', in Nicholas Grene and Patrick Lonergan with Lilian Chambers (eds), *Interactions: Dublin Theatre Festival 1957–2007* (Dublin: Carysfort Press, 2008), pp. 61–74

Roche, Anthony, 'Thomas Kilroy', in Martin Middeke and Peter Paul Schnierer (eds), *The Methuen Drama Guide to Contemporary Irish Playwrights* (London: Methuen Drama, 2010), pp. 145–61

Szabó, Carmen, 'Doublings: Problematic Identities in Thomas Kilroy's *Double Cross* and *The Madame MacAdam Travelling Theatre*', in

Richard Cave and Ben Levitas (eds), *Irish Theatre in England* (Dublin: Carysfort Press, 2007), pp. 169–82

Trotter, Mary, '"Double-Crossing" Irish Borders: The Field Day Production of Tom Kilroy's *Double Cross*', *New Hibernia Review*, vol. 1, no. 1 (1997), pp. 31–43

Woodward, Guy (ed.), *Across the Boundaries: Talking about Thomas Kilroy* (Dublin: Carysfort Press, 2014)

III. OTHER SOURCES

Amor, Anne Clark, *Mrs Oscar Wilde: A Woman of Importance* (London: Sidgwick & Jackson, 1983)

Arden, John, *Armstrong's Last Goodnight: An Exercise in Diplomacy* (London: Methuen, 1965)

Bair, Deirdre, *Samuel Beckett: A Biography* (1978; New York: Summit Books, 1990)

Barnes, Ben, *Plays and Controversies: Abbey Theatre Diaries 2000–2005* (Dublin: Carysfort Press, 2008)

Benjamin, Walter, *Illuminations*, ed. Hannah Arendt, trans. Harry Zohn (New York: Schocken, 1969)

Boa, Elizabeth, *The Sexual Circus: Wedekind's Theatre of Subversion* (Oxford: Blackwell, 1987)

Brook, Peter, *A Theatrical Casebook*, compiled by David Williams (London: Methuen, 1988)

Brown, Terence, *Ireland: A Social and Cultural History, 1922 to the Present* (Ithaca and London: Cornell University Press, 1981, 1985)

Bruce, Harold, *William Blake in This World* (London: Jonathan Cape, 1925)

Chambers, Colin, *Peggy: The Life of Margaret Ramsay, Play Agent* (London: Palgrave Macmillan, 1998)

Crowley, Brian, '"The Strange Thing I Am": His Father's Son?', *History Ireland*, vol. 14, no. 2 (2006), pp. 12–13

Dean, Joan FitzPatrick, *Riot and Great Anger: Stage Censorship in Twentieth-Century Ireland* (Madison: University of Wisconsin Press, 2004)

Deane, Seamus, *Celtic Revivals* (London: Faber & Faber, 1985)

Devitt, John, in conversation with Nicholas Grene and Chris Morash, *Shifting Scenes: Irish Theatre-Going, 1955–1985* (Dublin: Carysfort Press, 2008)

Dupin, Jacques, *Giacometti: Three Essays*, trans. John Ashbery and Brian Evenson (New York: Black Square Editions/Hammer Books, 2003)

Eagleton, Terry, *Heathcliff and the Great Hunger* (London: Verso, 1995)

Eaves, Morris, *William Blake's Theory of Art* (Princeton, NJ: Princeton University Press, 1982)

Ellmann, Richard, *James Joyce*, rev. ed. (Oxford: Oxford University Press, 1982)

——, *Oscar Wilde* (London: Hamish Hamilton, 1987)

Falkenstein, Len, 'Critical Remembering: Reading Nostalgia in Contemporary Irish Drama and Film', *Canadian Journal of Irish Studies*, vol. 25, no. 1/2 (July/December 1999), pp. 264–76

Fassler, Barbara, 'Theories of Homosexuality as Sources of Bloomsbury's Androgyny', *Signs*, vol. 5, no. 2 (1979), pp. 237–51.

Foucault, Michel, *Madness and Civilization: A History of Insanity in the Age of Reason*, trans. Richard Howard (New York, Toronto and London: New American Library/Plume, 1971)

Gilchrist, Alexander, *The Life of William Blake*, ed. W. Graham Robertson (London and New York: John Lane, The Bodley Head, 1907)

Girard, René, *Violence and the Sacred*, trans. Patrick Gregory (Baltimore and London: The Johns Hopkins University Press, 1977)

Gontarski, S.E., and Anthony Uhlmann (eds), *Beckett after Beckett* (Gainesville: University Press of Florida, 2006)

Hibberd, J.L., 'Imaginary Numbers and "Humor": on Wedekind's *Frühlings Erwachen*', *Modern Language Review*, 74 (1979), pp. 633–47

Hickey, Des, and Gus Smith, *A Paler Shade of Green* (London: Leslie Frewin, 1972)

Holland, Merlin, and Rupert Hart-Davis (eds), *The Complete Letters of Oscar Wilde* (New York: Henry Holt & Company, 2000)

Innes, Christopher, *Avant Garde Theatre 1892–1992* (London and New York: Routledge, 1993)

James, Philip (ed.), *Henry Moore on Sculpture* (London: MacDonald, 1966)

Kazin, Alfred (ed.), *The Portable Blake* (New York: Viking, 1946)

Kennedy, Michael, '"Plato's Cave"? Ireland's Wartime Neutrality Reassessed', *History Ireland*, vol. 19, no. 1 (2011), pp. 46–48.

Kramnick, Isaac (ed.), *The Portable Edmund Burke* (Harmondsworth: Penguin, 1999)

Larson, Donald R., 'Embodying Transcendence: Grotowski's *The Constant Prince*', *Comedia Performance*, vol. 1, no. 1 (2004), pp. 9–45

Lyons, Charles R., 'Le Compagnie Madeleine Renaud – Jean-Louis Barrault: The Idea and the Aesthetic', *Educational Theatre Journal*, vol. 19, no. 4 (1967), pp. 415–25

Lyons, F.S.L., *Ireland since the Famine* (London: Collins/Fontana, 1973)

MacLagan, E.R.D., and A.G.B. Russell (eds), *The Prophetic Books of William Blake: Jerusalem* (London: A.H. Bullen, 1904)

MacLeod, Catriona, *Embodying Ambiguity: Androgyny and Aesthetics from Winckelmann to Keller* (Detroit: Wayne State University Press, 1998)

Mason, Patrick, 'A Director's Note', in *Signatories* (Dublin: UCD Press, 2016), pp. xiii–xviii

Mathews, Timothy, 'Walking with Angels in Giacometti and Beckett', *L'Esprit Créateur*, vol. 47, no. 3 (2007), pp. 29–42

Morgan, Hiram, *Tyrone's Rebellion: The Outbreak of the Nine Years War in Tudor Ireland* (London: The Boydell Press, 1993)

O'Faolain, Seán, *The Great O'Neill: A Biography of Hugh O'Neill, Earl of Tyrone, 1550–1616* (New York: Duell, Sloan & Pearce; London: Longmans, Green, 1942)

Ohi, Kevin, *Innocence and Rapture: The Erotic Child in Pater, Wilde, James, and Nabokov* (London: Palgrave Macmillan, 2005)

Olney, James, *Memory and Narrative: The Weave of Life-Writing* (Chicago: University of Chicago Press, 1998)

O'Malley, Aidan, *Field Day and the Translation of Identities: Performing Contradictions* (London: Palgrave Macmillan, 2011)

Pacteau, Francette, 'The Impossible Referent: Representations of the Androgyne', in Victor Burgin, James Donald, and Cora Kaplan (eds), *Formations of Fantasy* (London and New York: Methuen, 1986), pp. 62–84

Pinter, Harold, *Mac* (London: Emanuel Wax for Pendragon Press, 1968)

Poulain, Alexandra, *Irish Drama, Modernity and the Passion Play* (London: Palgrave Macmillan, 2016)

Rado, Lisa, *The Modern Androgyne Imagination: A Failed Sublime* (Charlottesville and London: University Press of Virginia, 2000)

Richtarik, Marilynn J., *Acting between the Lines: The Field Day Theatre Company and Irish Cultural Politics 1980–1984* (1995; Washington, DC: The Catholic University of America Press, 2001)

Roche, Anthony, *Contemporary Irish Drama: From Beckett to McGuinness* (Dublin: Gill & Macmillan, 1994)

Rudkin, David, *Afore Night Come* (New York: Grove Press, 1963)

Rushdie, Salman, 'Is Nothing Sacred?', *Granta*, no. 31 (spring 1990), pp. 98–111

Schönborn, Sibylle, '"Die Königin ohne Kopf": Literarische Initiation und Geschlechtsidentität um die Jahrhundertwende in Frank Wedekinds Kindertragödie "Frühlings Erwachen"', *Zeitschrift für Deutsche Philologie*, vol. 118, no. 4 (1999), pp. 555–71

Sedgwick, Eve Kosofsky, *Epistemology of the Closet* (Berkeley: University of California Press, 1990)

——, 'Queer and Now', in Sedgwick, *Tendencies* (Duke University Press, 1993), pp. 1–16

Singer, Jerome L., and Michael V. Barrios, 'Writer's Block and Blocked Writers: Using Natural Imagery to Enhance Creativity', in Scott Barry Kaufman and James C. Kaufman (eds), *The Psychology of Creative Writing* (Cambridge: Cambridge University Press, 2009), pp. 225–46

Symons, Arthur, *William Blake* (New York: Dutton, 1907)

Taxidou, Olga, *Modernism and Performance: Jarry to Brecht* (London: Palgrave Macmillan, 2007)

Valente, Joseph, 'Self-Queering Ireland?' *Canadian Journal of Irish Studies*, vol. 36, no. 1 (2010), pp. 25–43

Vaněk, Joe, *Irish Theatrescapes: New Irish Plays, Adapted European Plays and Irish Classics* (Kinsale: Gandon Editions, 2015)

Walshe, Éibhear, 'Sodom and Begorrah, or Game to the Last: Inventing Micheál Mac Liammóir', in Éibhear Walshe (ed.), *Sex, Nation and Dissent in Irish Writing* (Cork: Cork University Press, 1997), pp. 150–69

Wedekind, Frank, 'Was ich mir dabei dachte', *Gesammelte Werke*, vol. 9 (München: Georg Müller Verlag, 1921), pp. 419–53

——, *The Awakening of Spring: A Tragedy of Childhood*, trans. Francis J. Ziegler (Philadelphia: Brown Brothers, 1910)

Weiss, Peter, *The Persecution and Assassination of Marat as Performed by the Inmates of the Asylum of Charenton under the Direction of the Marquis de Sade*, trans. Geoffrey Skelton and Adrian Mitchell (London: John Calder, 1965)

West, Rebecca, *The Meaning of Treason* (New York: Viking, 1947)

Wicksteed, Joseph, *William Blake's Jerusalem* (London: Trianon Press, [1953])

Wills, Clair, *That Neutral Island: A Cultural History of Ireland during the Second World War* (London: Faber & Faber, 2007)

Wilson, Laurie, *Alberto Giacometti: Myth, Magic, and the Man* (New Haven and London: Yale University Press, 2003)

Index

Illustrations are indicated by page numbers in **bold**.